CASE STUDIES IN
CULTURAL ANTHROPOLOGY

SERIES EDITORS

George and Louise Spindler

STANFORD UNIVERSITY

HIMALAYAN HERDERS

HIMALAYAN HERDERS

NAOMI H. BISHOP

California State University, Northridge

HARCOURT BRACE COLLEGE PUBLISHERS

Fort Worth   Philadelphia   San Diego   New York   Orlando   Austin   San Antonio
Toronto   Montreal   London   Sydney   Tokyo

Publisher	Earl McPeek
Acquisitions Editor	Brenda Weeks
Project Editor	Michael E. Norris
Production Manager	Kathy Ferguson
Book Designer	Carol Kincaid
Electronic Publishing Coordinator	Cathy Spitzenberger

ISBN: 0-15-505172-5

Library of Congress Catalog Card Number: 97-074701

Copyright © 1998 by Harcourt Brace & Company

Photo credits: Photographs are by John Bishop, except where noted.

Cover photo: Ibe Rike, our 85-year-old neighbor. Her earrings are gold, and she wears a turquiose and coral necklace, as well as her prayer beads (1971).

Address for Editorial Correspondence: Harcourt Brace College Publishers, 301 Commerce Street, Suite 3700, Fort Worth, TX 76102.

Address for Orders: Harcourt Brace & Company, 6277 Sea Harbor Drive, Orlando, Florida 32887; 1-800-782-4479 or 1-800-433-0001 (in Florida).

Website address: http://www.hbcollege.com

Printed in the United States of America

7 8 9 0 1 2 3 4 5 6   039   9 8 7 6 5 4 3 2 1

To my parents,

Baldwin Hawes and

Bess Lomax Hawes

Foreword

ABOUT THE SERIES

These case studies in cultural anthropology are designed for students in beginning and intermediate courses in the social sciences, to bring them insights into the richness and complexity of human life as it is lived in different ways, in different places. The authors are men and women who have lived in the societies they write about and who are professionally trained as observers and interpreters of human behavior. Also, the authors are teachers; in their writing, the needs of the student reader remain foremost. It is our belief that when an understanding of ways of life very different from one's own is gained, abstractions and generalizations about the human condition become meaningful.

The scope and character of the series have changed constantly since we published the first case studies in 1960, in keeping with our intention to represent anthropology as it is. We are concerned with the ways in which human groups and communities are coping with the massive changes wrought in their physical and sociopolitical environments in recent decades. We are also concerned with the ways in which established cultures have solved life's problems. Also, we want to include representation of the various modes of communication and emphasis that are being formed and reformed as anthropology itself changes.

We think of this series as an instructional series, intended for use in the classroom. We, the editors, have always used case studies in our teaching, whether for beginning students or advanced graduate students. We start with case studies, whether from our own series or from elsewhere, and weave our way into theory, and then turn again to cases. For us, they are the grounding of our discipline.

ABOUT THE AUTHOR

Naomi Hawes Bishop was born in Boston and grew up in Los Angeles. She did her undergraduate and graduate work at the University of California at Berkeley in anthropology. Her fieldwork was on the socioecology of high-altitude langur monkeys, work that first took her to Nepal and Melemchi in 1971. Returning to Nepal in 1984, she shifted the focus of her research to cultural ecology in Melemchi and has returned a number of times to conduct this research project. She was a member of the anthropology faculty of the University of Massachusetts/Boston from 1974 to 1990. Since 1990, she has served as chair of the Anthropology Department at California State University, Northridge. She was president of the Nepal Studies Association from 1991 to 1997 and is a member of the Executive Council of the Society of Woman Geographers. She has collaborated on several ethnographic film productions with her husband, John Bishop, including *Yoyo Man* (about one of the original Filipino yoyo demonstrators in Los Angeles), *Khmer Court Dance* (a collaboration with expert Cambodian dancers and musicians documenting classical dances from the court tradition), and *Himalayan Herders* (about culture change in Melemchi village).

ABOUT THIS CASE STUDY

This case study takes us to the Himalaya, a place that many have considered to be Shangri-la: a place of beautiful vistas, self-sufficient agropastoralists, and tolerant Tibetan Buddhists. Naomi Bishop evokes the dignity and accomplishment of this way of life, which is part of the mountain herding subsistence strategy extending from the Pyrenees to Burma. But she also sets life in this rugged village in the context of the contemporary world. In the 25 years covered by this book, there have been major changes in the Nepal government and society, and these have had an impact on the village.

This is a case study about life in Melemchi, a Himalayan village at 2,600 meters elevation exhibiting most of the features of high-altitude Himalayan villages and many of the features of transhumant pastoralism (or agropastoralism) the world over. The traditional way of life in the *gode,* a temporary shelter of bamboo mats laid over a bamboo frame sheltering a family who herd *zomo*—a hybrid cross between a cow and a yak—is described in detail. The *gode* is moved from pasture to pasture, since no large bovid can graze permanently in one place without the extra labor of having fodder provided. To the Western reader this way of life may seem mean and hard, with no luxuries and many hardships, but some of the comforts of food and life inside the *gode* can be appreciated, and a reasonably good living can be made selling butter and dried cheese, as well as other family-produced products such as liquor, wooden implements, woven jackets, and paper. Sustained by many cups of butter tea and barley flour, residents find much to look forward to in the lively ceremonial calendar that centers around the village *gomba,* or Buddhist temple.

Forces for change and adaptation are numerous and strong, and the number of family *gode* has dropped drastically in the past decade. Circular migration to India and back by men, women, and families has accelerated of late due to higher demands for cash and the possibility for more active participation in affairs outside the village. A village school supplements educational opportunities provided when families are in India. And least expected, Melemchi now finds itself in a national park, with potential restrictions on traditional subsistence activities that support *gode.*

No one would characterize life in Melemchi as easy, but still, there are satisfactions denied most of us in our high-tech urbanized world. It is worth considering this as a commentary on our way of life, seen within the comparative framework provided by the cultural "other." This is the ultimate purpose of the case studies—to allow us authentic glimpses into the conditions of life under circumstances different from our own.

Beyond this purpose there is the informative value of the descriptive analysis of a form of human adaptation that has characterized a significant portion of the human population for thousands of years. The influence of environment and ecology on cultural patterns and sociopolitical structure can be seen particularly clearly in the transhumant, high-altitude adaptation. This case study incorporates both consideration of human biology and culture in its examination of demographic aspects of cultural adaptation, as well as specific discussions of the biology of human adaptation to altitude and mountain environments. This is a case study worthy of your close attention.

George and Louise Spindler
Series Editors
Ethnographics, Box 38, Calistoga, CA 94515

Acknowledgments

This fieldwork was made possible by the active support and encouragement of several people: my mother, Bess Lomax Hawes, who provided financial, logistical, familial, and intellectual help throughout the period of this research; my colleague and friend Jane Teas, who organized the Earthwatch trip in 1984 that enabled me to return to Melemchi and consider the possibility of new fieldwork there and who has been a bulwark of support throughout my professional life as we both juggled family, academia, and our commitment to remain connected to Nepal and our friends there; my colleague and friend Katherine O'Rourke, whose selfless support made our 1986 expedition a success in every way, including substantial contributions to the research design and content; my husband, John, who has been with me every step of the way, encouraging me across every one of those terrifying log bridges in Nepal and through the chasms of despair over ever having time and freedom to work on "my Melemchi material"; and, finally, my children Noah and Amanda, who lived in Melemchi twice and still want to go again. I wouldn't have been able to do this without all of you. John especially deserves recognition for taking on the work in Melemchi as an equal partner; the photographs, films, maps, and botanical specimens are all his labor. His enthusiasm, energy, ideas, and companionship made it all possible. And thanks also to Barbara Brower, who shares my peculiar interests in Himalayan pastoralists and who has provided support of all kinds at all times while this book has been under way, not to speak of forebearance and patience.

John and I owe a great debt of gratitude to several people in Nepal who gave of their time, energy, and hospitality at various stages in this project. Upendra Shumshere Rana and his wife, Sushila; Rex Shore; Graham and Shirley Rawlings; Ilfra Lovedee; Ang Gyelzen Sherpa; and Nogabu (Prakash) Sherpa all provided hospitality and assistance while we were in Kathmandu. The term "field assistant" doesn't do justice to the extraordinary breadth and depth of assistance provided by the following individuals, who managed the logistics of our expeditions, translated for us, and made sure we were able to complete our work: Mingma Tenzing Sherpa (1971–72, 1984); Ang Gyelzen Sherpa (1986); Ang Tsering Sherpa (1986); Nogabu (Prakash) Sherpa (1989, 1992, 1993, 1995); and Panche Lama (1993). Their help was instrumental and their good humor and energy appreciated, and we are grateful for their friendship and loyalty. Assistance in the field was also provided by Ken Diemer (1986), Diane Butt (1989), and my sister Corey Denos (1993), each of whom were wonderful sports and great support and comfort.

I would like to acknowledge several colleagues who have provided criticism and support during the development of this book: Alan Harwood, Timothy Sieber, and Golamreza Fazel at the University of Massachusetts/Boston; John Metz at Northern Kentucky University; and Nanda Shrestha at South Florida University. I am especially grateful for colleagues who read this book manuscript for me, providing important comments and criticisms: Barbara Brower, Antonio Gilman, Gregory Truex, and Bess Lomax Hawes. At a number of stages, students have helped me with this material, and I am grateful to them all. Special thanks to California

State University, Northridge, students Curtis Mears, who helped set up the database; Mika Ito, who input data; and Carla Trapani, who helped me so much with the final research, in addition to teaching me the pleasure of having a graduate student as a colleague. Finally, to Antonia Peña-Hernandez and Karol Chew, departmental secretaries *extraordinaire,* I offer my gratitude for all of the extra work they did so that I could complete this project.

This research has been supported, over the years, by grants from the National Institutes of Health (1971–72: NIH Training Grant No. 1224), the National Geographic Society (1986), the Wenner-Gren Foundation for Anthropological Research (1989), the Joseph P. Healey Endowment Fund (1989), the Laura C. Bolton Foundation (1992), and California State University, Northridge, School of Social and Behavioral Sciences (1993, 1995). I am especially grateful to Dean Ralph Vicero for his support of my work while I have been a department chair at California State University, Northridge. Chapters 2 and 4 are based largely on articles by me previously published in the journals *Human Ecology* and *South Asia Bulletin.*

Ultimately, this book comes about through the unfailing cooperation, generosity, and support given to us by the people of Melemchi. Initially, they wanted me to be able to complete my work with the *praken* (monkeys), even though they couldn't conceive of why we wanted to do it. Our unexpected return in the mid-1980s redefined our relationship with the village. Now we not only had children like they did, but unlike all of the other Westerners who came to Melemchi, we came back. Overcoming our difficulties with language, we became friends. People were happy to help us and were pleased at our interest in their lives and their village. In 1995, talking with some village teenagers, I realized that they were treating me the way my teenage children treat my friends—they were polite but we didn't really connect. It dawned on me that I was their parents' friend—part of the village history and their parents' lives, but not theirs. As I have accumulated geneological records, dossiers on each family full of history, anecdotes, and interviews, thousands of photographs, and reams of correspondence, I feel I am the chronicler of an era in Melemchi. It is as close to a community as I will ever have—a place where I know everybody and to whom they are related, where I know the history of important events, and where I am greeted warmly and fed whenever I drop by. As each letter comes telling of old friends who have died, we feel fortunate to have known so many people in Melemchi and shared so much of their lives. It is a privilege for which we we will always be grateful. We thank everyone in Melemchi, and through this book, honor the memory of many old friends, including Ibe Rike, Lama Pruba, Kirkiyap, Hrenzen, Norbu, Ibe Phu Dorma, Ibe Hlak Putti, Ibe Karmu, and Chungi.

Contents

Introduction

A DAY IN THE *GODE*

The rain had been falling all night. Outside, the *zomo* shift position, occasionally brushing the stone walls of the *pathi* where the family sleeps. *Zomo* are cow-yak hybrids, large dairy animals who thrive in Himalayan pastures between 2,100 and 4,000 meters altitude. There are 16 *zomo* and one large bull in this herd, all sleeping standing up in the muck that accumulates at these high-altitude shelters from the daily traffic of hoof stock and people. Twenty-one sheep and goats are safely under a shelter of tree boughs attached to the outside wall of the *pathi,* while the chickens and *zomo* calf sleep inside with the family. A Tibetan mastiff dog chained to a stake nearby is ready to bark at the sound of any intruder; last week, he was attacked by a wild pig and barely escaped with his life. Now that Langtang National Park is here, no one can kill the pigs, and they are wreaking havoc on the fields, forest, and even the herding families in their isolated pastures.

At first light, Chenga rises from her pallet of wool blankets and, blowing through a foot-long piece of bamboo, rekindles the embers of the previous night, starting the hearth fire that burns continuously, providing warmth, food, and light for her family of five. Her husband, Tandu, is also awake. Like everyone else, he has slept in his clothes and immediately steps outside through the open doorway to check on the herd. The sun has not yet risen high enough over the mountains to reach them with its warm rays. He wears his home-woven wool jacket, which provides rain protection as well as warmth, but walks barefooted. The best forage is gone, and he is tired of the mud surrounding the *pathi;* he has laid out boards to walk on near the doorway, but the continual trampling of hooves, the frequent monsoon rain, and the ground leeches that congregate near herds and moisture have made him decide to move on. Today he will leave early with a load of supplies to check out his next pasture. He is lucky—his grandfather owned excellent pastures that are his to use. Few of his brothers still herd today, so he has a choice of pastures and can move whenever he wants.

At 5:30 a.m., Chenga and her oldest daughter Putali are already making butter from yesterday's milk. Fourteen of the *zomo* are in milk now. After only a day, the milk has begun to turn to yogurt and is churned in a large wooden barrel 3 feet high and 2 feet in diameter—the two women alternate pulls on opposite ends of a thick leather strap wound around the churn paddle. By 7:30, two large balls of butter are in the wooden bucket in the corner and the leftover buttermilk has been put into a large pan and is heating over the fire. While Chenga makes cheese from the buttermilk, Pruba Doma, their 13-year-old daughter, takes the sheep and goats out to graze away from the pasture clearing. She will stay with them, bringing them back in the evening.

No one notices the rain; life goes on regardless of the weather. Summer pastures are usually wet—from either rain or the perpetual mist and clouds that hover on the high slopes. Life inside the *pathi* is dry and warm. When the sun shines, the light filters in through the woven bamboo mats, creating a reddish glow. A thick bed of juniper boughs forms the floor. As the family moves through its daily routine, the boughs are bruised, releasing a sweet fragrance. The fireplace is against a wall, with room to sit around it on three sides. It is just a depression in the ground, deep enough to create a draft when pieces of wood are arranged over it like spokes. Cooking pots rest on an iron tripod over the fire. The family sits, eats, and sleeps around the hearth, on wool blankets or calfskins. A similar mud fireplace exists in houses in the village; in fact, except for dairying chores, domestic life in a village house isn't much different from life in a *gode,* the local term for the bamboo shelters constructed by herding families. In both places, life is lived on the floor, and the hearth is its focus. Living in a *gode* is not like "camping out"; it is where people live their lives and raise their families.

Tandu finishes his last cup of butter tea with *tsampa* (toasted barley flour) mixed in to form a dough, and sets out with a 60-pound load of household supplies in a basket on his back, held on by a tumpline or rope around his forehead. Still barefoot, he will climb for three hours up to Pangkharke pasture, deposit the supplies, and check out the pasture and his stone shelter, or *pathi*. The descent will be quick without a load, and he expects to be back within five hours. Meanwhile, it is time to milk the *zomo*. The sun has finally reached the pasture, and the *zomo* are warm and ready.

Chenga puts a leather bag of salt around her neck, grabs the leather thong and wooden milking bucket, and steps outside. The black *zomo* is waiting just outside the door. She leans down to tie its back legs together with the thong and then, tucking the back of her skirt tight against her legs, she squats down next to the udder, rubbing it with some of the milk scum left on the side of the milking bucket. With long, smooth movements, she pulls down on a teat with her thumb and forefinger, alternating hands as the milk flow begins. Five minutes later, she is finished; she unties the *zomo* and whacks it on the rump as it runs off. She returns to the *pathi,* pours out the milk, and sets out again, this time with a calfskin in her hand. Putali follows her with a pan of whey. Chenga approaches a black-and-white *zomo*. This *zomo* needs to smell the skin of her dead calf in order to let down milk. Chenga lets her smell it and then sets the skin on the ground with the pan of whey on top of it. The *zomo* drinks the whey as Chenga ties its legs and begins to milk. When she is finished, she feeds the *zomo* salt from her pouch. All *zomo* are given salt during the months of lactation, because "salt makes the food taste good in the mouth so they eat more, just like with people. The more they eat, the more milk they produce."

For the next hour and a half, Chenga milks *zomo,* each requiring a slightly different technique or special treatment. One *zomo* needs her vulva massaged to stimulate urination before she can be milked. Another *zomo* can't give milk without her live calf to stimulate milk letdown. This is the calf that lives in the *pathi* with the family. Calves are kept only if the mother needs them, since they compete for milk with the herder. Chenga brings the calf out at milking time and lets it nurse for about 45 seconds before she ties it up near the mother's head where the mother nuzzles and licks it while being milked. Chenga leaves some of the milk for the calf.

The big gray *zomo* is a "man beater," and only Tandu and Chenga can go near her. "Man beaters" are unreliable, attacking people, especially strangers, with upward strokes of their sharp curved horns. The gray *zomo* is a good milker, and besides, they paid a lot of money for her, so they keep her but handle her with caution.

Once all the milk is collected, the *zomo* are encouraged to move away from the *pathi* and graze. Putali or her sister Purba Diki chase them out and stay with them as they forage on the steep slopes and forested areas around the pasture. Chenga squeezes the morning's fresh cheese into ribbons, which are laid on a bamboo mat. The mat is placed above the fire on a rack, and within a day or two the cheese will be dried into hard, sour, smoky-tasting *chiurpi,* eaten by all Himalayan high-altitude herders whatever their ethnicity. *Chiurpi* is the quintessential trail food—light, portable, good to suck on, full of fat and protein, and it lasts forever. It can be ground into a powder and mixed with *tsampa* and water as well.

There is always a lot to do in a *gode*. Chenga walks to the nearby river and carries back water, puts the next day's supply of firewood up on the rack to dry, cleans out the animal droppings from the *pathi,* and cuts fodder for the animals that don't go out to graze. Pinzo arrives looking for butter. He has walked up from Melemchi village; this is his third stop for the day. The other two *gode* had no butter. Since so many people have given up herding and gone to work in India, it is getting hard to find butter, even in summertime when production is at its peak. It is not like it used to be; even twenty years ago, Melemchi herders had so much butter they put it in tins and carried it to Kathmandu to sell. Chenga agrees to sell Pinzo some, but first she offers him butter tea from the pot that is always on the fire. *"Shey, shey* (drink, drink)," she urges as she leans forward with the pot, waiting for him to take the customary first sip. Three refills are obligatory, so Pinzo takes a big slurp, proffering the cup for topping off.

While Pinzo fills her in on news of the village, Chenga stands and begins to churn another pot of tea, her second of what will be probably eight pots for the day. She has already boiled some new tea leaves with the old brew and strained it into the thin, cylindrical wooden tea churn. Adding butter, rock salt, and a pinch of baking powder, she braces the churn with her foot and plunges up and down repeatedly to mix the emulsion. Finally, she pours it into the teapot and, from there, into Pinzo's cup. The monsoon clouds have risen from the valley floor and, while they visit, it begins to rain. Finally, Chenga wraps a ball of butter in leaves for Pinzo, sending along a bag of *chiurpi* as a present for his wife and son, and Pinzo departs.

When Tandu arrives in a torrential downpour, Chenga is spinning wool, using a spindle-top as she turns fluffy wool fibers into a single strand. Tandu reports that several streams were running so high that he had to wait for the rain to subside in order to cross over them. However, the pasture is in good shape, and he saw Sonam Dorje, who will be moving up as well in the next day or two. Chenga is pleased to hear that they will be sharing the pasture. Sonam Dorje's wife is her sister, and it will be nice to have another family around, especially since she and Tandu will have to go down to the village in another week and begin to till and fertilize their *changda* fields. Even though the girls can manage the herd alone, having Sonam Dorje's family there will allow Chenga and Tandu to stay in the village for a few days to complete the work.

Tandu decides to go down to Melemchi and bring back their 11-year-old son, Norchung, who is living with Tandu's mother while he attends the village school.

He will be needed for three days to help move the *gode*. A *gode* move is a lot of work, requiring about eight adult loads. Even if you can get friends to help, it takes more than a single day. Men carry the rolled-up bamboo mats (one load) and the butter churn (one load). The rest of the equipment, supplies, and personal belongings are divided into basket loads to be carried by Chenga and the two older girls. The younger children carry small baskets and lead the baby animals. On the last day, the herd goes along. Bells are tied on the *zomo* so that they can hear each other and be heard as they move through the forest. Tandu takes the lead, with the family following after the *zomo,* who usually move quickly in anticipation of new forage.

Tandu leaves for Melemchi. He hurries down the trail with light steps, hampered only by the two lambs he is dragging behind to sell. When he reaches the village, he goes to the house of the government schoolteacher and asks permission for Norchung to be excused. He and Norchung leave the lambs and depart immediately, in order to get up to the pasture before dark. Normally Tandu would have picked up some *tsampa* and other supplies from his house in the village. Houses are used to cache food, enabling *gode* families to travel light. Since he is moving the *gode,* Tandu will wait on resupplying until after the move.

At the pasture, the *zomo* have returned for midafternoon milking. The mist is heavy, but there is no more rain. Chenga finishes milking and walks among the herd with a drop spindle, spinning two strands of wool into the yarn she will use to weave jackets and blankets. Putali, the oldest daughter, makes another trip to the river for water while Purba Diki scrubs pots behind the *pathi,* using ash from the fire and sandy dirt. Pruba Doma returns with the flock of sheep and goats and begins to settle them

Moving the gode. *Following one of the* zomo, *the heavily laden wife brings one of the eight loads up to the new pasture. Boys living in the* gode *in 1971 often wore only a shirt. (1971)*

for the night. Tandu and Norchung arrive from Melemchi just as it is turning dark. They have some potatoes, which Chenga boils, serving them with *marza,* a paste of freshly ground chilies, garlic, and salt. She reports on the four people who stopped in to buy butter; all but Pinzo went away empty-handed. Chenga is saving their butter for butter lamps and *torma* for a Buddhist ritual the family will sponsor when they get close to the village. Butter lamps and figures made of *tsampa* flour and butter are a crucial part of most Tibetan rituals, as is butter tea for all the participants. Tandu announces that Zangbu is back from India; it looks like he must have done good business there since he arrived with porters carrying an Indian-made airtight stove. Later he tells Chenga that Zangbu plans to bring them *toljung,* the ritual bottle of beer and visitation used to arrange a marriage, when they come down to prepare their fields. Zangbu's son Dorje wants to marry Putali, who at 18 is definitely marriageable. This would be an arranged marriage; if the parents give their permission by accepting the *toljung,* the girl is grabbed by the boy and his friends without her knowledge or consent. Chenga and Tandu think the match would be good for Putali. There would still be two daughters to help at the *gode,* and by marrying a Melemchi boy, Putali would remain attached to the village and easily available to help them.

In the darkness, a small oil lamp made from a discarded tin can provides light for the family to get ready for the night. The sheep and goats have already settled on the other side of the wall. The chickens are under their basket in the corner; the calf is lying down on the juniper branches. Outside, the Tibetan mastiff is chained to a stake. Plates and cups are set in the corner to be washed in the daylight, and bedding is laid out around the fire. As the rain begins to fall, the *zomo* stand in the darkness.

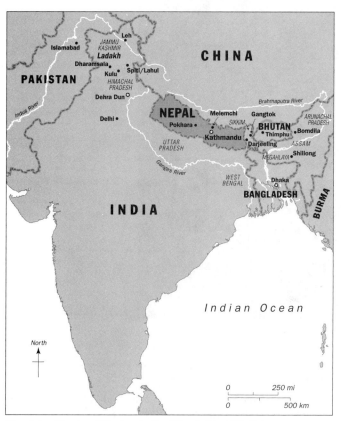

Map 1.1—Nepal and Northern India (Map by David Fuller)

1 / Melemchi:
A Village in Yolmo

BACKGROUND

In 1984, I traveled to Nepal after a 12-year absence to codirect an Earthwatch study of rhesus monkey population dynamics in Kathmandu. Before the project started, I made a quick trip up to Melemchi[1] to see the village, visit old friends, and share the

Female Himalayan langur monkey. (1972)

book that my husband and I had written about our year studying langur monkeys and living in Melemchi in 1971–72. It was a joyous reunion, tempered by the news of the death of our close friend, **Lama Pruba,** who had helped us collect all the data on human demography and history but who had just died the year before I returned. The story was that he had fallen on his gun while out hunting. The village looked remarkably similar to the one we left in 1972. The village forest boundaries were unchanged, people were still herding cow-yak hybrids called *zomo* or traveling back and forth to work in India, and the village houses (more numerous than in 1972) were surrounded by tall stands of corn ready to harvest. I had anticipated major changes, because in the 12 years since we had lived there, I had read that Nepal had experienced extensive deforestation. One source stated that as much as one-third of the forest in Nepal had disappeared over this period (Eckholm, 1975). Yet Melemchi appeared to be thriving with no apparent degradation of habitat.

This trip encouraged me to return to Melemchi and begin a study of human demography and resource use, building on the data collected from 25 families in 1971–72. My hypothesis was that Melemchi people were able to balance resources and human population more effectively than many other places in Nepal because of the particular combination of subsistence activities that were practiced there. *Zomo* herding brought income to the village without degrading the environment in and adjacent to the village. Since the herds of *zomo* never came to the village, their contribution to the subsistence base of the village came without a local cost. Circular migration to India was another source of income that brought in resources (cash) without a direct impact on the local environment. People brought back cash earned in

India to invest in land and houses and to buy food and supplies. These two sources of subsistence, combined with contraception, helped to maintain and support a growing human population while reducing its impact on the village and its surrounding environment.

This initial hypothesis quickly turned into a complex and extended topic, far beyond the scope of a single investigator with a full-time university appointment and a growing family. My strategy was to focus consistently on several topics—animal husbandry, genealogy, reproductive histories, and migration histories—in order to document changes over time at the village level. Two field seasons were devoted to collecting data on two key elements: the organization and management of *zomo* herding and patterns of circular migration. In order to evaluate the impact of these on human demography, it was also necessary to understand population dynamics in this village. How many people belonged to Melemchi? Was the village growing or shrinking? An attempt was made to identify all members of the village and establish a genealogy for each of the village clans going back as far as people could remember names and dates. I also collected reproductive histories of individual women, starting with the original 25 life stories collected in 1971 and building on this each field trip to eventually include most women of reproductive age in the village. These histories yielded basic genealogical information on each woman plus her year of birth, age at marriage, and the name, age, gender, year of birth, year of death, and cause of death of each child. Through these data, I hoped to develop hypotheses about the impact of the subsistence strategies and social organization on the population structure and through that, on the environment.

Between 1984 and 1993, we made a number of trips to Melemchi, sometimes with our children and at other times alone. A stroke of good fortune occurred when **Nogabu** joined our team. He was 10 years old, living with his family in their *gode,* when we were first in Melemchi. He remembers seeing us then at our farewell party. By 1989, he was a success in the tourist trekking business, with an Australian sponsor[2] with whom he had lived for two 6-month periods in Australia. He became our research assistant and has been committed to this project ever since, collecting data for us in our absence. Now a successful building contractor in Boudhanath, he has a home there that is a central place for Melemchi people when they are in the Kathmandu Valley, keeping him abreast of the news.

This book is about tradition, adaptation, and change. Even in a place as seemingly isolated as the northernmost village in the Yolmo Valley of Nepal, people are changing in response to global patterns, while maintaining knowledge and activities that have been part of people's lives in these mountains for generations. Nogabu is a case in point. Linked to us by fax and to the world through Star TV and Cable News Network, he faxed us when he saw news film of the 1994 Northridge, California, earthquake and recognized our hometown. Yet when he goes to Melemchi to help his aging parents, he can manage their herd, rebuild their house of stones and mud, and help organize the Tupa Sezhu rituals and altars. He represents one end of the continuum of engagement with the world outside Melemchi; in contrast, his mother, **Kali**, has lived her whole life in and around Melemchi, without telephones, televisions, or running water. Most people in Melemchi fall somewhere in between the lifestyles and life experiences of Nogabu and his mother, with everyone's life transformed in some way by the changes that have occurred in Nepal and the rest of the world during their lifetimes. This book is about that transformation.

NEPAL: A LANDLOCKED KINGDOM

Nepal is a landlocked kingdom surrounded by Tibet/China to the north and India to the south, west, and east. Although it is only 100 miles wide and 500 miles long, its location and topography result in a country that encompasses extraordinary diversity. Along its southern border, Nepal resembles North India in its tropical climate, rich alluvial soils fed by Himalayan glaciers, flora and fauna from the Oriental biogeographic region, and high human densities. Until the 1950s, much of this area was malarial jungle, isolating Nepal from the rest of the world. Once these were cleared as a part of a malaria eradication campaign, people were drawn from both India and Nepal to these areas rich in farmland. Today the Tarai holds 47% of the population of Nepal (Karan & Ishii, 1994).

But Nepal is known more for mountain peaks than for any other feature. The Himalaya resulted from the collision of the Indian continental plate with the Eurasian plate during the Mesozoic era. Obliterating the Tethys Sea, the impact produced the mountains in a series of events that continue even today, uplifting parts of the range at the rate of one centimeter per year (that is, 9,125 meters every million years; Karan & Ishii, 1994). Except in the west, the Great Himalayan Range forms the northern border of Nepal and Tibet; with peaks as high as 8,848 meters, it runs west/northwest, cut through in only a few places by high passes or major river gorges. A mecca for mountaineers and tourists alike, the Great Himalayan Range is sparsely populated; the most famous region lies around Mount Everest, where the well-known Sherpa

Map 1.2—Nepal (Map by David Fuller)

live, with summer settlements as high as 4,878 meters. The Middle Himalaya (or Middle Mountains) lies to the south, with branches running obliquely to the Great Himalaya (Karan & Ishii, 1994). Peaks in this range are no higher than 3,048 meters, the upper limit for forest in most areas. These middle mountains are inhabited by people who herd livestock and grow crops in the valleys and the slopes above, and who are highly dependent on forest resources to sustain their way of life. This region encompassed 60% of the population of Nepal in the 1960s (Karan & Ishii, 1994), a figure that has dropped precipitously since then because of outmigration. A growing population and the difficulty of intensification of agriculture in mountain regions means that people must leave in order to survive at all. In the southern part of the Middle Himalaya lie the well-known and populous valleys of Kathmandu and Pokhara, at altitudes around 1,220 meters. Farther south lies the Outer Himalaya, or Siwalik Range, with peaks between 1,000 and 2,000 meters, tapering off into the Tarai, or Gangetic Plain, shared with India.

Nepal's climate is influenced by the southwest summer monsoon, the northeasterly winter monsoon, and temperature gradients that vary according to altitude. The southwest monsoon brings warm, heavy rains to the central and eastern part of Nepal, beginning in mid-June and continuing through early September. All elevations are affected by these rains, which can cause landslides and floods in the mountains at the same time they bring life-sustaining water for the lowland rice crops. These rains don't reach the western Himalaya or the Tibetan plateau to the north, leaving these areas much drier. The winter monsoon brings brief rain to the plains and the hills, as well as winter snowfall to nourish the high mountain crops. Temperatures vary with elevation and latitude. The Tarai, in the south, is characterized by a warm tropical climate, similar to North India—warm winters; searingly hot, dry months in April through June; warm wet monsoon; and dry fall. In the Middle Mountains, the same general pattern prevails, although the temperatures are not as hot. Between 2,700 and 3,600 meters, winter minimum temperatures are not much below 2° C; summer maximums are 15–18°C, and average rainfall is 1,000 to 3,000 mm. Generally, winters are dry except for periodic snowfall, spring is hot and hazy, summer is cool and wet, and fall is dry and cooler. The snowline drops from west to east, as does the upper limit of the forest. The complex geomorphology of the mountain ranges interacts with the altitude-based temperature gradient and the west-east moisture gradient to produce each local climate. Slope, aspect, and local conditions such as shadowing of nearby peaks are just a few of the additional factors that produce the complex and diverse microclimates and microhabitats that prevail in Nepal.

Mountains and rivers form barriers to movement; along with the complexity of the Nepalese terrain, this has resulted in extensive opportunities for diversification and localization of flora, fauna, and even people. Two major language subgroups are represented, Indo-European and Tibeto-Burmese, reflecting the geographic position and historical relationships of this country. Indo-European–related languages cluster on the south and west, while Tibeto-Burmese–related groups tend to be in the northern and eastern regions. Attempts to estimate the number of different ethnic or cultural groups in Nepal are confounded by the fact that these change over time as groups interact, borrow, fuse, and fission, but it is fair to say that Nepal is a country with great ethnic and linguistic diversity. Despite the seeming obstacles to communication within the boundaries of Nepal (for example, outside of cities, telephones have been nonexistent[3]), people here are not isolated, either from other Nepalis or from the outside world. Trade, pilgrimage, military service, and migration have always contributed to culture contact, to a greater or lesser extent depending on the location within the country. Travel and communication in the mountainous regions, which make up three-quarters of the country, is by foot; goods and mail are transported by human porters or animals along footpaths, over suspension bridges, and through mountain passes. As a country, Nepal has one of the lowest densities of roads in the world (2.68 km of roads per 100 square kilometers of land; Karan & Ishii, 1994),[4] and all are in the southern portion. The first motorable road outside of Kathmandu was built in 1953. Today only two-thirds of the district centers are connected with main highways (Karan & Ishii, 1994), and villages may be several days' walk from a district center.

There are only two narrow-gauge railways in Nepal, one 47 km and the other 29 km long.[5] Air transport is now available to 42 airfields within Nepal's borders, most requiring short-takeoff-and-landing planes. Although the planes are used mostly by commercial and tourist travelers, reduced fares for Nepalis have made it possible for local people to use this transportation as well. Helicopters have emerged in recent years as another form of air transportation suited to this rough terrain. Entrepreneurs have established numerous companies, with regular service as well as charters.

The Kingdom of Nepal was unified in 1769 by Prithvi Narayan Shah of the House of Ghorka. Its present boundaries were established after the Anglo-Nepali War of 1814–16. The 100-year regime of the Rana prime ministers, which ran from 1850 until the palace coup of 1950–51, stabilized the government by setting up policies for taxation, land tenure, and the economy. These ultimately diverted much of the country's resources for the benefit of members of the Rana family. During the Rana period, the king was deprived of all power; the country existed in isolation from the rest of the world, and revenues were used to support the Rana enterprises. With the overthrow of the Ranas in 1951, King Tribhuvan reassumed the throne and Nepal began a period of transformation and modernization that continues today, heavily funded by international development money and influenced by its strategic geographic position on the Asian subcontinent, between India and China. With nearly one-third of its 147,181 square kilometers economically unfit for agriculture, forestry, or grazing, Nepal now faces a growing population, minimal experience in government management of resources, and political challenges to the monarchy and government as it has been practiced in the recent past. The democracy movement, which came to a head in 1990, resulted in a multiparty governance system, with the king remaining as a symbol of the nation, and Nepal was officially declared to be a multiethnic and multilingual nation (Karan & Ishii, 1994). Since then, it has proved difficult to actualize the potential of the recent political changes, and Nepal continues to suffer economically.

THE YOLMO VALLEY: A REGION IN EAST-CENTRAL NEPAL

The region of Yolmo lies three days' walk northeast of Kathmandu, the capital of Nepal. In Tibetan, the word *Yolmo* means "place screened by snow mountains/glaciers" (Clarke, 1980b) and refers to the wall of 5,000-meter peaks that forms the northern boundary, separating Yolmo from the Langtang Valley to the north. In its entirety, the region can be visualized as a fan, wide at the top and narrowed to a point at the bottom. Yolmo is bounded on the east by the Indrawati River and on the west by the Thare Danda, a mountain spur that drops south from the alpine lakes at Gosainkunda to the last Yolmo village of Gulphabangyang. Through the middle runs the Melemchi River, fed by streams that take glacial melt as well as moisture trapped by the mountains that form its watershed. Along the top of the fan are a series of mountain spurs that isolate Yolmo from the north; these are broken in only three places: the passes of Kanja La, Sermasalang, and Laurebina, each at about 4,900 meters in altitude. North of Yolmo lies the east-west valley of Langtang, a dry inner valley populated by Tibetans. To the north of Langtang lies Tibet.

The region surrounding the temple-villages of Yolmo is characterized by a temperate climate. Terracing for agriculture goes as high as 2,500 meters here; above that are upper temperate mixed-broadleaf forests on east- and west-facing slopes and oak forests on south-facing slopes. The rhododendron forests, for which Nepal is so famous, lie between 3,050 and 3,350 meters. The upper mountainsides provide habitat for Himalayan black bears, red pandas, gorals,[6] serows, barking deer, yellow-bellied Himalayan marmots, leopards, jungle cats, wild pigs, and rhesus and langur monkeys. While not visible to the casual trekker or visitor, nearly all of these creatures can be found around areas of human habitation at some times of year. Studies of monkeys in the Himalaya have suggested that without the opportunity to raid crops, it would be impossible for these essentially tropical species to live through the temperate winters of the mountains. This may be true for other species as well. We know of Himalayan black bears raiding cornfields in summer, leopards attacking domestic livestock and dogs in the village and *gode* year-round, and wild pigs destroying isolated potato fields.

The people of Yolmo call themselves "Yolmo people" or "Sherpa from Yolmo." Since Nepalese refer to them as Lama people, they often add this term as a surname in citizenship papers and other formal documents. Thus, a Yolmo person may tell a Westerner or government official that his name is Kami Lama, or Phu Dorje Lama. However, within Yolmo, the term "lama" is reserved for someone who can read Tibetan texts or someone who is from the village lineage lama clan.[7] In the village, it is common to add the clan name to distinguish people who have the same name. Sherpa are often named for the day of the week of their birth, such as Mingmar (Tuesday). In Melemchi, within one generation, we knew Waiba Mingmar (from the Waiba clan), Shangba Mingmar (from the Shangba clan), Mingmar Tongtong (also Waiba, so a nickname has been given), and Au Mingmar (Mingmar who is our assistant's father's brother, or *Au*). Like the celebrated mountain-climbing Sherpa of eastern Nepal, Yolmo people have their origins among Tibetans who migrated to Nepal generations ago. There are a number of these groups along the northern border of Nepal, each representing the descendants of different migrations of Tibetans from different parts of Tibet. All are Tibetan Buddhists and all speak a language derived from Tibetan; they vary in their culture and behavior depending on the time, place, and particular history of their migration.

According to anthropologist Graham Clarke (1980a), Yolmo was settled by lamas who migrated from the area of Kyirung in Tibet during the 18th century. Kyirung lies three to four days northeast of Yolmo and at various times has been

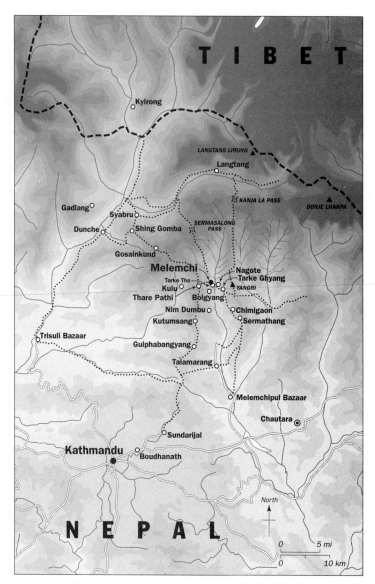

Map 1.3—Yolmo Region, plus Trisuli, Langtang, and Sindupalchowk district (Map by David Fuller)

part of Nepal. Beginning with Guru Rinpoche in the 8th century, Tibetan lamas have spent time meditating in this region, which is known for its beauty and comfort. The relationship between the rulers of Nepal in Kathmandu and Tibetan lamas or monks in Yolmo may stretch back as far as the time of the great Yogi poet Mila Repa, who meditated there in the 12th century (Clarke, 1980a). The language spoken in Yolmo is unique to this region, although it is also spoken in the village of Siran Danda, which lies in the Ghorka region to the west, between Kathmandu and Pokhara. This village was settled by people from Yolmo, who migrated there with a

Yolmo lama sometime between 1945 and 1955.[8] There is also a report of one area in east Nepal where the Yolmo language may be spoken (Clarke, 1980b). While it is possible for Eastern Sherpa from Solu-Khumbu and Yolmo people to understand each other, just as it is possible for them all to communicate with Tibetans, all three languages are distinct. It is generally agreed that Yolmo language is closer to Tibetan than is Eastern Sherpa, which may indicate that Yolmo was settled more recently.

Today, the only road into Yolmo is a dirt track that runs along the Melemchi and Indrawati Rivers. It leaves the paved road built by the Chinese to link Kathmandu with the Tibetan border and provides a very rough ride to the village of Melemchipul Bazaar, via jeep or small truck. During the dry season, it is a reliable route, but it can wash out during monsoon. It cuts about one day's walk off the trip from Kathmandu to Melemchi. Melemchipul Bazaar is a stop along the road, with stalls selling groceries, cloth, tea to drink, or meals of rice and *daal* (lentils). Travelers can find a bed at one of several hotels. Here a hotel room means a wooden frame bed with a straw mattress in a dormitory room with a single window accessible by climbing a ladder from the first floor. Washing up is done at the river. The bathroom, if one exists, is an outhouse with a hole in the ground.

A suspension bridge crosses the Indrawati at Melemchipul Bazaar. It is an improvement over the single log that we used, with zenlike concentration, in 1972. Once you are across the river, the climb begins. The trail leads slowly up the tip of the Yangri spur, first seeking and then following the spine as it climbs to 2,600 meters. The first four hours are subtropical. After carefully walking through the edges of the rice paddies along the river, you climb past houses with thatched roofs set out individually on the hillside among fields of millet and, higher up, corn. Just as in the New World, bean seeds are planted with corn, so the new corn shoots are shaded from the brutal sun by leafy green bean plants with bright red flowers, which will eventually climb the corn stalks as they grow. Small children play in front of the doors of most houses, with chickens and a goat or two for company. There is almost no shade apart from the houses. It is hard for the novice to recognize these houses and fields as a village, spread out as they are over steep hillsides. The first sign of Yolmo is a round stone pile about 4 feet tall, sprouting two tall bamboo poles strung with squares of translucent cloth. This is a *chorten,* and it is decorated with *mani* stones—flat stones inscribed with the Tibetan prayer *"om mani padme hum."* You always keep to the left side of Buddhist monuments and walk round them in a clockwise direction.

Once you get to the *chorten,* you are in Yolmo. The trail climbs a bit and then winds along the ridge between 2,300 and 2,600 meters. The vegetation is now temperate—deciduous shrubs, the odd conifer, and rhododendron—and the air becomes thin and cold. The ridge trail leads to Sermathang, one of the major temple-villages of Yolmo. In 1971 when we visited, there was one large *gomba* or temple in the village, but in 1993 there were three. Sermathang is a prosperous village that spreads out and down the mountainside. The lineage lamas of Sermathang are Sermo, and the original *gomba* here was probably established around 1910 (Clarke, 1980a). It is one of 18 temples in Yolmo founded by this lineage, which may stretch all the way back to Mila Repa. The *gomba* of neighboring Chimigaon, just slightly below Sermathang, is also a Sermo *gomba,* founded 30 to 40 years earlier by a different brother of the same lineage lamas. Residents of both villages do some agricultural work and manage household livestock; most are landlords with tenants working both rice fields and other crops.

The last temple-village on the Yangri ridge is Tarke Ghyang, a wealthy village with no fields attached except for the temple lands. Its *gomba* is centrally located, founded by a Tenyelingpa-lineage lama from Tibet between 1820 and 1830. Residents of Tarke Ghyang were herders, just like Melemchi people, having access to pasturage far up the valley and behind the village. The last *chorten* of Yolmo on the east side of the river lies at the top of Yangri peak, at 3,660 meters, a two-hour walk from Tarke Ghyang.

To get to Melemchi from Tarke Ghyang, you must descend straight down to the river, past the temple-village of Nagote. Crossing the river, you reverse the climb up a steep trail to Melemchi at 2,600 meters. The only way out of Melemchi, other than retracing your steps to the river, is to go up out of the village to Thare Pathi, a series of shelters at 3,660 meters along a north-south trail that leads farther up to the glacial lakes of Gosainkunda and then over the Sermasalang Pass into the Langtang Valley. If you are heading to the westernmost villages of Yolmo, known locally as Kulu, you go west. Those traveling back to Kathmandu turn south and follow the trail for two days, through the easternmost Yolmo villages of Kutumsang and Gulphabangyang. Neither has a *gomba* and Gulphabangyang is populated by several ethnic groups, not only Yolmo people. From there the trail winds up and down over the course of a day, taking you eventually down into the Kathmandu Valley through the Sunderijal waterworks. This high route is cool and beautiful, leading through all the

The temple-village of Sermathang at 2,600 meters looking north up the Yolmo Valley. The temple-village of Chimigaon is visible to the north. Melemchi is visible as a pale spot on the far ridge in the distance. (1993)

forest types of the Central Midlands (Stainton, 1972), with only *zomo gode* to encounter, until you leave Yolmo.

The villages of Yolmo are connected by trails. All travel is by foot, since the trails are too steep and narrow for even horses. Elsewhere in Nepal, yak or male cow-yak hybrids *(zopkio)* are used as pack animals, but in Yolmo livestock is kept for dairying and occasionally plowing, while all carrying is done by humans. Over generations, people have explored every part of the region and, as herders and farmers, know it well. They also know each other. Clans, intermarriage, and exchanges of goods and labor within this relatively small region link people together, bringing them into frequent contact. Without telephones, regular mail service, or telegraph, people remain connected through face-to-face exchanges and social networks. Word travels fast all over Yolmo, as do the local people. This is not an isolated valley, and even those families living out with their herds keep abreast of news through their frequent encounters with individuals who pass it along.

MELEMCHI VILLAGE HISTORY

At one time there were more gode than people; later the population started growing, and now there are more people than gode. Land and houses are more useful for people's future, so that's why they started living in the village. I was born in the gode and grew up in the gode. At that time there were no yak gode in the village—just zomo gode, and sheep and goat gode. People used to be very famous for being rich and having such big gode, but now they have nothing left (i.e., nothing to show for it). There is a Nepali proverb: "Chaar haat khuta, dhannai hoina; sun chandi baneko, dhannai dhann ho." It means a four-footed creature is not wealth; property is wealth. That is what the villagers found out.

Interview with **Dawa Sonam,** age 65, 1989

Some Melemchi residents today can trace their lineage back as many as seven generations, although for most it is four or five. The oldest reported birthdate belongs to **Palden,** born in 1876; we know his father's name, Meme Neya,[9] and that he had two brothers, Gyalwang and Karpu, who lived in the village of Bolongsay, a few hours' walk away. Palden settled in Melemchi, where he owned houses and fields, giving rise to a lineage of the Chiawa clan with at least 124 descendants. Not all are living and some don't live in Melemchi, but all appear on genealogical charts compiled with the help of his descendants. His brother Karpu's never-married daughter, **Kenji,** came to Melemchi to live near her cousins, and it is her funeral that is shown in the film *Himalayan Herders.*

Palden died before this study began; the earliest-born resident I met in Melemchi was his wife, **Pasang Buri,** who was born in 1886 and died in 1972. There are 18 people still alive today over the age of 70 (i.e., born before 1925); for them, time has telescoped in their memories, but they have a remarkable capacity to recall events. So, it is from the living residents of Melemchi that we can learn about the history and development of the village in the early part of the 20th century.

Melemchi's senior citizens today remember when there were very few houses in Melemchi; most informants describe Melemchi in the 1920s as a village with about

The village of Melemchi (2,600 meters). The new gomba *is visible on the lower left side of the village; houses appear as white spots amidst the fields. (1986)*

12 houses. We can't assume from this that these were the first 12 houses ever in this village, nor that there were only 12 families associated with Melemchi at that time. It is clear that the Yolmo Valley has been inhabited for at least several hundred years; while there is no historical evidence for people living in Melemchi before 1857 (see Chapter 5), it is likely to have occurred. Houses decay rapidly in this monsoon climate if they are not maintained and occupied. When houses fall down or decay, the stones are recycled, so evidence of previous houses or residence is not obvious. The anthropologist Graham Clarke neglects this factor when he claims that a document dated 1723 C.E. that refers to *Milanche* village could not be a reference to Melemchi. He argues that there couldn't "have been a village settlement at Melemchi, there being only four houses there for three generations ago." (Clarke, 1980a, p. 16). While he may be correct that the village Milanche is not Melemchi, it is quite possible for Melemchi village to have been occupied then and even earlier. The number of houses at any time are not a reliable indicator of population size for several additional reasons. Many Melemchi residents, especially in the past, didn't have houses. The traditional subsistence pattern of *zomo* herding can be maintained without a fixed residence; families live year-round with the herds out at pastures. People may be village members without village residences. Furthermore, people may have a house but occupy it seasonally. At 3,660 meters, Melemchi village is cold in winter; with only a few hours of direct sunlight each day and periodic storms that leave snow on the ground for a day or two, some people live there only in summer. In 1971, although there were 30 houses in the village, only eight were occupied in winter.

Ibe Pasang Buri, 1886–1972.
(1972)

Most families lived in their *gode* at lower altitudes or in the satellite village of Tarke Tho, about 305 meters below. At that time, few people owned shoes, and even when there was no snow, it was the same temperature inside the house or out.

All informants provided a similar list of people who owned houses in Melemchi village in the 1920s[10]—12 families. The rest lived exclusively in *gode*. Even those with houses rarely occupied them; informants said that only **Wangdi** and **Norbu** lived in their houses then. By the mid-1930s, there were 25 houses and 13 men on the *tal* (village householder) list. When we lived there in 1971–72, there were 35 houses, a three-fold increase over 50 years. It was still a very small settlement. They were clumped together in the center of the village, along a north-south line that encompasses the two sites in the village where all important events in the Melemchi annual and ritual cycle take place: the Buddhist *gomba* or temple in the village center and the Tupu cave at the top of the village at the forest edge. Only 1 or 2 houses were in the outlying area.

After 1971, Melemchi grew quickly. Between then and 1986, the number of houses had more than doubled to 78, and three years after that (1989) there were 91. In 1993 there were 100 houses. Some of the houses are additions to existing buildings, but most are new structures located throughout the bowl-shaped ledge that makes up the village.

Memories are less consistent on the introduction of agriculture to Melemchi. It is clear that throughout the lifetimes of today's oldest residents, there have been some agricultural fields in Melemchi. High-altitude wheat and barley and potatoes are the crops grown today in fields surrounding the houses, and residents talk about there being some fields present in the early years of this century: "a few *changda* (barley) fields in front of houses and a few potato fields at the *gomba*." Some herders planted potatoes out on the mountainsides near the pastures, leaving them untended for some part of their growing cycle but returning to harvest all those the pigs and monkeys hadn't taken. **Ibe Phu Dorma**, who was born in 1908, said that before people grew *changda* at Melemchi, people ate corn. Her father, **Narsung**, owned cornfields down in Nagote, which is across the river below Melemchi, as well as fields farther down the valley. Eventually, he traded the Nagote fields for fields in Tarke Tho, which was contiguous with Melemchi and more convenient. In 1971, it was still possible to clear new fields within the village boundaries, although most of the area around the houses was owned and cultivated. Today it is impossible to find new land; all fields have been purchased or subdivided.

SUMMARY

Melemchi is one of the major temple-villages in Yolmo. It is at a high altitude, has a functioning *gomba,* and is situated prominently at the end of the Yolmo Valley. For Buddhists, Melemchi contains several important sites, including the Tupu Cave at the top of the village where Guru Rinpoche meditated. It is also the temple-village with the clearest spatial integrity; the topographic features that make it possible to have houses clustered and fields adjacent make it a unique village for residents and visitors alike. Like other villages on the western side of the Melemchi River, with access to extensive high pastures, Melemchi has remained dependent on herding to a much greater extent than villages on the eastern side such as Tarke Ghyang or Sermathang. Its location, its feudal relationship with the Chini Lama of Boudhanath (discussed in Chapter 5), and its dependence on pastoralism all contribute to its marginal political and economic position relative to villages such as Tarke Ghyang or Sermathang, but its landscape and resources make it a desirable place to live.

DISCUSSION: MOUNTAIN ECOSYSTEMS—HUMAN ADAPTATION TO MOUNTAINS

Mountains cover one-third of the land surface of our planet. The people of Melemchi are among the 20 million to 30 million people in the world living above 2,500 meters in altitude (Baker, 1978), adapting to the particular challenges of mountain environments. These include extreme and unpredictable changes in temperature, precipitation, and wind. Mountain ecosystems incorporate tremendous variability, caused by local differences in slope, aspect, insolation (or exposure to the sun's rays), and climate. Their soils tend to be shallow with low productivity; surface instability, such as erosion, is common. Young mountains, like the Himalaya, experience frequent earthquakes as well. Because of these factors, life in the mountains includes a number of potential stresses for human and animal populations: cold, aridity, high ultraviolet radiation, hypoxia (decreased oxygen availability), and nutritional or energetic stress.

Biological Adaptation to Mountains   Physical anthropologists have focused on the single factor of altitude in evaluating whether and how human populations have adjusted to mountain environments. High altitudes involve hypoxic stress for animals. This means that in the "thin air," where oxygen pressure is low, tissues don't get enough oxygen unless the body can make some adjustment. Culture can't help here, as it does in combating cold stress (put on clothes) or high ultraviolet radiation (sunscreen). Physiological adaptations of the respiratory system, the cardiovascular system, and the circulatory system are required to provide adequate delivery and utilization of oxygen under conditions of low environmental oxygen pressure, such as experienced at high altitudes.

Studies indicate that living at high altitudes accelerates the growth of some body organs—the placenta, lungs, heart, and thorax—while it slows down the growth of the body itself, both before birth and during childhood and adolescence. It is hypothesized that living in a cold and oxygen-poor environment increases the demands for energy, which are met through slower growth. A smaller person requires less energy. A great deal of effort has been expended to understand whether populations at high altitudes have adapted genetically to these conditions, or whether the adaptation occurs during an individual's lifetime—what physical anthropologists call "developmental adaptation." The general observation that growth is slower at high altitudes came from the original work on high-altitude populations that was done in the Andes. Later work in the Himalaya did not confirm these results; there it was found that individuals varied greatly in height and growth rates at any altitude. Other studies of people living at high altitudes in Ethiopia, where nutrition is good, indicate no altitude-related differences in growth rates; there children at high altitudes grew as fast as those living at sea level (Pawson, 1976). So, how can this be explained?

The explanation for this confusing set of data is that hypoxic stress doesn't operate alone. Populations at high altitudes may also be subject to cold stress and to nutritional or energetic stress. At high altitudes, low oxygen pressure exists alongside climatic stresses, poor soils, short growing seasons, and isolation. Furthermore, the effects of all these factors vary depending on age, gender, and physical conditioning of the individual. And social factors also interact. A good example of this is the recent attention being given to the observation that low birth weights are common at high altitudes. Since low birth weight is associated with a greater risk of infant mortality and may also be a contributing factor in the slowed postnatal growth rates, it is important to understand its origins (Wiley, 1994). Based on her research in the western Himalayan region of Ladakh, physical anthropologist Andrea Wiley suggests that both environmental *and* social factors are important in understanding the preponderance of low birth weights there: "Sustained work, pregnancy itself, hypoxia, and iron deficiency interact to produce serious stress on the biology of reproductive women. Risk is not evenly distributed among these women; those who work less and eat more have larger, healthier babies" (p. 289, Wiley, 1997).

While it is difficult to generalize about physiological adaptation to high-altitude environments because of population differences, it is clear that the main problem for humans (and animals) under these circumstances is to get enough oxygen to their body tissues. This is done by breathing deeper, producing more red blood cells (thus having a higher concentration of hemoglobin, which binds to and carries oxygen), and, in adapted populations, having more capillaries per square millimeter of muscle. High-altitude natives, in addition, appear to have better mechanisms for the oxygen to diffuse from the blood to the body tissues; this enables them to work at peak capacity at high altitudes, something a sea-level native can never achieve. Human capacity to acclimate to environmental stress is great, especially given the assistance of culture. However, there are limitations with regard to hypoxic stress, which is expressed through the high infant mortality and small but consistent presence of chronic mountain sickness among many mountain populations.

Cultural Adaptations to Mountains   People have lived in the Himalaya for much longer than they have in the Andes or the Colorado Rockies (Moore and Regensteiner, 1983). In all of these regions, there has been very limited time for genetic adaptation to have occurred. Instead, most of these people have relied on cultural adaptations for success. One attempt to synthesize a model of cultural ecology of mountains outlined three elements for mountain adaptations: Mountain cultures all have (1) an *array of vertical production zones;* (2) an *overall strategy* for production; and (3) a *potential for change in the strategy* (Guillet, 1983, p. 567).

Mountain people face specific limitations: Vertical production zones tend to be narrow, the possibility for intensification in any mountain zone is low, the environment is unpredictable, and opportunities for large returns to capital are low, both because of the limitations just mentioned as well as the fact that they tend to be spatially and politically peripheral. As a result, mountain cultural adaptations are characterized by diversification, flexibility, and fluidity, or ease of change. Diversification involves exploiting one or more zones and managing several economic activities simultaneously. This reduces risk in an environment where there is high dependence on natural forces and maximizes access to the full range of resources available. Flexibility in response to the stresses of mountain habitats is also a key to successful human adaptation to mountains. The shifting of the household, or even individual family members, as needed in different locations over the year is an example of the flexibility required to efficiently exploit multiple zones and activities. In addition to flexibility, frequency and ease of change are also necessary to succeed in these limited environments. Long-term planning is not reliable; opportunism often leads to success.

Guillet (1983) outlines three vertical production zones available in mountain ecosystems: The lowest zone is the zone of intensive agriculture; above that is the zone of extensive agropastoralism, where herds supplement agricultural activities but intensification isn't feasible; and finally there is the pasture zone. Of course, in mountains it is possible, and indeed common, to exploit more than one of these zones, traveling up and down in elevation over the course of a day or an annual cycle.

One encounters familiar themes when reading the literature on mountain peoples, whether it is the Sherpa of the Mount Everest region of Nepal or the Swiss villagers of Törbel in the classic study by Netting (1981). The lack of possibility for intensification or expansion, and the marginality of the mountain environment itself, results in universal concern with land division and inheritance, fragmentation of the community including seasonal minimigrations, and dependence on external sources of employment, both for the cash it brings in and the release valve it provides for population growth. The conflict between the need for communal coordination of herds and the individual organization of agriculture is another theme that is worked out differently in different communities but that is common to them all. The solution lies with communal institutions, such as the ritual cycle, that coordinate and engage everyone.

Both physical and cultural anthropologists have attempted to synthesize general models for mountain adaptations. Like most models, the more data that are included, the more complex the model becomes, and the less it fits all cases. However, it is through trying to find patterns that we understand the way things may actually work, and as each model is critiqued, we gain insight into the mechanisms we are trying to study. For example, data from Ethiopian highland populations led us to understand the importance of nutritional status in mediating hypoxic stress on children's growth (Pawson, 1976). The unexpected absence of high hemoglobin counts among highland Tibetan populations caused researchers in Bolivia to consider the possibility that exposure to occupational toxins in the mines, rather than the altitude at which they lived, might account for the high hemoglobin counts of Bolivian Indians (Beall, Goldstein, and Tibetan Academy of Social Sciences, 1987). Guillet's model of cultural adaptations to mountains provoked a flurry of comment, including the criticism that his emphasis on vertical production zones emphasizes altitude over other aspects of mountain environments that may be more relevant (Federle, 1984). Netting himself has reconsidered his early depiction of the village of Törbel as an "island in the sky," an isolated ecosystem, and now views it as similar to other mountain peoples who maintain themselves by a constant flow of people and resources between themselves and the wider world (Netting, 1990). Like the Törbel villagers he studied, he viewed them as a self-sufficient and autonomous society. But his reconsideration represents the growth and change in the field of cultural ecology, as new data are incorporated into old schema.

NOTES

[1] Anthropologists always face a difficult ethical decision about using actual names for people and places when they publish the results of their research. There are good reasons both for using real names and for fictionalizing. In this instance, I decided to use the real name of the village where we lived and worked for several reasons. First, my original publications focussed on my field studies of langur monkeys, and I had not disguised the location of that work. Second, and more important, the people of Melemchi have expressed the view that I should publicize their village and their lives, and they are proud to have their village documented in books and films. Finally, Melemchi is a village that is easily accessible to people who might read this book and travel there, and accurate information would make that a much richer experience for travelers and villagers alike. I expect people in Melemchi to read my book, or have it read and shared with them. I feel it would be confusing, and perhaps insulting, to fictionalize names of people; all of the material in this book is widely known in the village so fictionalizing it would protect no one. Therefore, with only a few exceptions, I have used the actual name of everyone in the book. The main exception is in the Introduction, which is a composite of many *gode* I have visited. I chose names that would clearly indicate to Melemchi residents that the Introduction was not based on a particular Melemchi family.

[2] Sponsorship refers to a relationship between a Nepali citizen and a foreigner, in which the foreigner provides financial support. This can take a variety of forms: funds to educate or train the Nepali or his/her

children either in Nepal or in a foreign country, funds for travel outside Nepal for work or for pleasure, funds for living expenses, or funds for underwriting a local business. Opportunities for establishing sponsor relationships occur anytime a foreigner and Nepali are brought into personal contact. One of the most common contexts is tourist trekking where the tourist undergoes a physically and psychologically challenging experience, which is delivered and brokered by the Nepali guide. Friendships are forged, protection and loyalty are provided, and, in gratitude, sponsorship is offered. While not unique to Nepal, it is an extremely common phenomenon, especially for Sherpas. A recent book includes a discussion of this intriguing relationship and its effect on Sherpa communities (Adams, 1995).

[3] Recent innovations in cellular telephones and faxes have made it possible for telecommunication in the mountains without requiring the normal infrastructure of a telephone system. In 1993, we were surprised to see a cell phone available in the Yolmo village of Sermathang, associated with the National Park headquarters located there.

[4] Of the 7,330 kilometers of roads in Nepal, only 40% are paved.

[5] In 1927, the railway between Raxaul and Birganj was built to transport things from India; in the 1930s, another rail line was built between Jayanagar and Janakpur to transport timber from the Tarai to the Indian Railways. Today it takes religious pilgrims to Janakpur (Karan and Ishii, 1994).

[6] Goral and serow are two types of goat-antelope *(Tribe Rupicaprini,* which includes the chamois and the Rocky Mountain goat; Schaller, 1977).

[7] Each village *gomba,* or temple, is associated with the clan of its founding lama; members of this clan are known as the village lineage lamas, since their status as lama comes from their clan membership. This is explained in detail in Chapter 5.

[8] While in Kathmandu, I met several young men from Siran Danda who had come to work as laborers. None of them knew why their ancestors had left the villages of Sermathang, Chimigaon, and Tarke Ghyang in Yolmo. One man in his early 20s said his grandparents had migrated; they first spent a few days in Boudhanath and then went west until they found "good forest where mushrooms grew" where no one was living at the time. Today, people in Siran Danda still speak Yolmo language, but they have intermarried with Tamang and other ethnic groups in the area. The 70 households have a *gomba,* and they import painters from Sermathang village in Yolmo to maintain it. Their marriage and death customs have shifted from the Yolmo tradition to the local one, except for the Yolmo death rituals called *gewa* and *nangla* that follow cremation (see Chapter 5). They also don't celebrate the Nara festival, a defining element of Yolmo temple-village culture.

[9] *Meme* is the Yolmo honorific term for an esteemed elder, or grandfather. For some men, it becomes an automatic part of their name; for others, it is used by people when they wish to address the person. *Ibe* is the equivalent for women. There is no hard and fast rule, but, generally, someone over the age of 50 may be referred to by these terms.

[10] The first houses belonged to Norbu Danen and Kampa Kangyul. Shortly after, Ghale Purba and Palden built, followed rapidly by Ghale Wangdi, Ghale Norbu, Pasang Gyelzen, Baru Tundu, Ghale Lemba, Sing Pema, Shangba Kalden, and Kulu. By 1935, additional houses had been built by Meme Mingur, Samden Gopu, Shu Lama, Thum, Narsing, Ghale Namgyal, Topke, Tashi Pasang, Chele, and Tewong.

2 / *Zomo* Herding: Adaptation to the Local Environment

ZOMO HERDING: A DAIRYING OPERATION

Zomo herding is a domestic enterprise organized around the production of dairy products: butter and cheese. It requires the labor of at least two adults to carry out the daily dairying chores and maintain the household and the animals. The *zomo* herd must be moved from pasture to pasture in search of adequate grazing. Large bovids cannot stay in one place throughout the year unless they are given fodder, which entails substantial labor and resources. In Melemchi, herds are managed by single-family units who own their animals, own or rent their pastures, and move over the mountainsides with their herd living in temporary shelters called *gode*. This is called transhumance or transhumant pastoralism, since the animals are moved seasonally among pastures over an annual cycle. True nomadism refers to a lifestyle in which there is no fixed abode; people and their animals move continually, living in tents. Goldstein (1974) has argued that the term *agropastoralism* is best for a situation like Melemchi, where fixed village agriculture is combined with "pure" nomadism; families in Melemchi may have fields and houses in the village that they maintain, yet they live away from the village all year with their herds.

Families with *zomo* herds live in *gode,* which are huts made of bamboo mats arranged over a structure of bent bamboo poles, or they live in *pathi,* which are stone-walled huts with plank roofs. The word *gode* is used to refer both to the dwelling itself and to having a herd and the herding lifestyle. Phillipe Alirol has said: "The word *goth (gode)* has a greater meaning than that of a simple shelter. To own a *goth* is to have a herd, to be a herdsman, and thus to identify oneself with a cultural group (Sherpa, Gurung . . .), traditionally dedicated to herding" (my translation; Alirol, 1981, p. 197). Most of the pastures or *kharke* have been in families for generations, and many have at least remnants of stone walls, around which the *gode* is constructed.

Melemchi *zomo* herds average 20 *zomo*. They are rarely fed fodder; instead, they go out each day with supervision to graze the vegetation on the hillsides and forest surrounding the *gode*. Brower (1991) suggests that *zomo* may differ from yak in that they are more willing to browse. Certainly *zomo* are observed in forested areas foraging among the shrubs as well as ground vegetation.

Each family has its own set of pastures among which they move over the year; the sequence is generally the same from year to year, but the length of time at each varies with the weather, availability of forage, and other demands on the family.

Zomo gode *at Nading pasture. The structure of bamboo mats is called a* gode. *Note the Tibetan mastiff tied outside on a pile of manure that sprouts vegetation. (1986 photo by Katherine O'Rourke)*

Almost none of the pastures are more than one day's walk away from the village, although the distance can be considerable. Pastures differ in altitude, aspect, vegetation, and amenities such as access to water, shelter type, and proximity to the village. (See Map 2.1.)

The maintenance of *zomo* herds is a full-time occupation that takes place most of the year at distances that are incompatible with farming activities. In the early part of this century, residents of Melemchi had much larger *zomo* herds, and most of them did not grow crops in the village. Once agriculture was introduced, households developed ways to do both. With sufficient labor, families can bring the *zomo* down to Melemchi for a week in October, when their manure can be used to fertilize the wheat and barley fields and their owners can plow and plant before taking them to winter pasture. In spring, some family members can be spared to plant corn while others keep an eye on the herd. Since herds are low then, it is possible to prepare the cornfields while the herds are nearby. Harvesting corn and potatoes in summer presents the greatest difficulty since herds are up at 3,660 meters altitude. In reality, most households today who still herd *zomo* do not maintain fields in the village. They buy grain from relatives or others with a surplus or trade dairy products for it. It has always been feasible to barter dairy products for needed supplies of grain and forgo agricultural activities altogether.

Melemchi village, from 1,200 meters above Tarke Ghyang. Every clearing is a pasture for Melemchi herders. Below the village the cleared fields of Tarke Tho are visible. (1986)

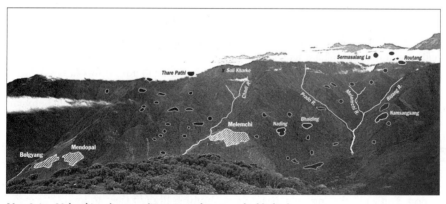

Map 2.1—Melemchi and surrounding area with pastures highlighted

DOMESTIC ORGANIZATION OF HERDING FAMILIES

When a young man separates from his family at maturity, usually to get married, he receives from his parents either a few head of livestock or one or more fields; in the case of a wealthy family or one with few sons, he may receive both fields and animals.

Along with the livestock, he inherits rights to the parental pastures, or *kharke*. It is rare that a young man has a house. Only the youngest son, who is expected to remain in his parents' house once he marries and care for them in their old age, will have a house at marriage. All other sons will build their own houses.

Shangba Mingmar is one of five brothers; each of them received 9 *zomo* from their father at marriage, except Shangba Mingmar. He received 3 buffalo and 2 corn-fields in Tarke Tho (below Melemchi) when he married at the age of 21. He sold one field to buy his first *gode*. He bought his first house when he was 32 years old; by then he had four children and had lived both in the *gode* and in Sikkim working on road crews. **Tenzing Norbu** didn't own a house in the village until he was 41 years old, and he and his wife waited another 11 years before they lived in it; even today, he spends most of the time living out with his herd, while his wife occupies their house in the village. This pattern of delayed house ownership is the common one in Melemchi and relates to the historic importance of *zomo* herding in the village and the incompatibility of this form of agropastoralism with village residence.

The number of *zomo* inherited varies, depending on the size of the parental herd, whether or not the parents themselves continue to herd, and the number of heirs. Melemchi men interviewed in 1971 indicated that most had received between 8 and 10 *zomo*, plus a bull. A few men report receiving only 5 *zomo* at marriage, which they supplemented by purchasing more. One man inherited 35 *zomo* when he married but sold them in order to go to work in India where he thought he would make more money. He later bought and sold *gode* several times, building up a sizable herd each time. He gave his three older sons 10 *zomo* and 2 sheep each when they separated from the family. Only one of them remains in a *gode* today; the others prefer life as circular migrants. The fourth son, the youngest, is a wealthy contractor in India and will inherit the parental house.

A young couple begins with a small herd of *zomo* and rights to the family *kharke*. Ownership of the *kharke* may be either shared among brothers, or they may individ-ually own them but share use. Parents assist the young couple by visiting and con-sulting on a regular basis. However, such assistance is not required. By the time they are married, children raised in a *gode* have extensive experience performing the work of a *gode* household. Between the ages of 5 and 12 years, children help with domestic tasks, such as carrying water, tending chickens and baby animals, caring for younger siblings, and assisting their mothers with chores. They also can go out with the herds. By 12 years of age, children are able to participate in adult physical labor, albeit with lighter loads. They may even provide labor within the village as a part of reciprocal labor arrangements, carrying manure to fields or carrying loads of fire-wood. Fodder gathering, which involves climbing high in trees to lop off branches and then carrying the huge bundles on their backs using tumplines, is generally the work of 15- to 18-year-old boys, as well as men. Adolescent boys also help to man-age the animals around the homestead and travel back and forth between the *gode* and the village on supply runs. They know the surrounding topography well—the loca-tion of everyone's pastures, where to find water, and the location of other *gode* fam-ilies. They whoop and shout as they move swiftly through the forest, announcing their presence to friends and predators alike. Girls begin helping their mothers with dairying chores by the time they are 12 or 13; once in their midteens, they are capable of managing the *gode* for periods without their parents present. They milk, feed, and care for the animals; they assist their mothers with churning butter and drying cheese; they fetch water and are able to cook and make tea in the absence of their mothers. Life in the *gode* is intimate and provides ample opportunity for family members to learn every role.

In a *zomo gode,* there is a division of labor among men and women, although it is possible to interchange most duties if necessary. Milking is one task that is difficult to alternate. In nearly all Melemchi *gode,* women do the milking, and some animals do not permit anyone else to milk them. Women often miss village events because they are needed at the *gode* for milking. In one case we witnessed, a woman gave birth while her *gode* was in the village en route to a high pasture and within the hour was helped outside by her husband to milk several of their *zomo.* She collapsed and was taken inside, only to be brought out again and set up to milk a few minutes later. A tourist onlooker was horrified at what she perceived to be brutal and sexist treat-ment of this woman. In fact, both the husband and wife knew that she, and she alone, was the only one who could milk those particular animals. At least five men told of selling their *gode* when their wives had either died or been injured in such a way that they could no longer milk. No doubt it was the combined effect of the particular relationship between animal and caretaker and the loss of an adult worker that prompted the sale, since maintaining a young family and herd without a wife would be virtually impossible. Women who sold *gode* when their husbands died said they couldn't manage it alone.

In a *gode,* men's duties include carrying the heavy equipment and bamboo mats between pastures (in addition to general load carrying), cutting firewood, supervising livestock breeding, making advance trips to new pastures, buying and selling live-stock, making supply runs to the village, and traveling to sell butter and cheese. Women maintain the household (cooking, cleaning, child care), milk the animals twice daily, make butter and cheese every other day, carry water, spin wool and weave cloth, care for small household livestock (chickens, calves, a few goats or sheep), and maintain the *gode* while men are away. Men and women agree: it is a hard life in the *gode*, especially for women.

> *Milking and looking after the* zomo *is women's work. We make cheese, make butter—it's all women's work. Men don't have much work to do—they look after the house, climb trees to cut fodder, and cut wood.*
>
> **Kando,** 33-year-old mother of two children (five more children were born in the following 9 years)

> *We started the* gode *eight years ago. The man works taking the* zomo *to the forest, and the women milk and clean up the* zomo *shit and make butter. It is hard work in a* zomo gode. *If the husband stays all the time in the* zomo gode, *then it isn't such hard work. If the husband doesn't stay all the time in the* gode, *then it is very, very hard work. I have to do all his work and all of mine. I have three sons. We don't want to give the* zomo gode *to our children.*
>
> **Maya,** 25-year-old mother of four, who came to the *gode* one week after she married her husband, Kami

It isn't until children are 5 or 6 years old that they are able to help with even the smallest tasks. As a woman milks each of her *zomo* twice daily (a task that can take more than an hour and involves complete concentration to maintain her own safety as well as the animals'), she cannot be distracted by watching out for her toddlers. Maya locks her small children in the *gode* itself when she goes out to milk. Older children, however, are of crucial assistance to their parents. The predominance of large family size in Melemchi, especially prior to widespread availability of contraception, has no doubt contributed to the possibility for economic diversification found in Melemchi agropastoralism, as elsewhere (Fricke, 1986). It is interesting to note that, even today, the largest families are those living in *gode,* where children are ultimately an asset and where access to contraception and medical assistance is lowest (see Chapter 6).

Life in a *zomo gode* is hard. Living quarters are cramped; whole families of up to 12 individuals live in a tiny enclosure, often sharing it with several baby bovids, sheep, goats, and chickens. In winter, temperatures drop, snowstorms can last several days, and there is the added chore of cutting fodder daily when weather precludes grazing. In monsoon summer at high pastures, the areas around the *gode* become muddy and leech infested, and family members are especially vulnerable to skin and respiratory infections. And the chore of moving the *gode* occurs from 5 to 10 times per year, depending on the family's route, placing an especially heavy burden on men. Moving a *gode* involves at least eight to nine loads, with some of the locations over a half day's climb away. The bamboo mats *(partza)* are about four loads, and the household effects, minimal as they may seem to us, are another five. That is at least 17 adult trips, 9 fully loaded, over distances and altitudes that tax even local people. Extended family and friends help out. One man with a *zomo gode* for his entire adult life of 19 years complained that he would like to sell his *zomo gode* because with so many people in India, there is no one to help him move it.

ZOMO AND OTHER LIVESTOCK

What Is a *Zomo?*

A *zomo* is a female crossbreed, the offspring of a domesticated yak *(*Bos *grunniens)* and a cow *(Bos taurus* or *Bos indicus)*—in other words, it is a hybrid. Since there are a number of ways the parents can be crossed, there are a number of different kinds of hybrids, each named accordingly. The kind of *zomo* herded in Melemchi are called *urang zomo;* their father is a domesticated yak and their mother is a *Bos indicus* cow. Males are called *urang zopkio,* since *zopkio* is the word used for a male hybrid.

In order to understand the types of crossbreeds, it is necessary to know the features of the pure stock, since the mother's features predominate in the hybrid. The domesticated yak *(Bos grunniens)* is closely related to the other members of the bovid family (cows, gaur, buffalo). It is short legged and stocky, with 14 or 15 ribs (rather than the 13 of other bovids), elongated neural spines that give the male humped shoulders, and a bushy tail with a fringe of long hair along its flanks. Yak horns are curved backward. In comparison with the wild yak, the domesticated yak is small (Bonnemaire, 1984). Female yak *(nak)* and male yak look similar, although females are smaller and lack the elongated neural spines of the male.

Zomo *(female), left; yak (male), right. (1986)*

Two species of cow are interbred with yak in the production of hybrids. The humped *zebu* cow of the lower valleys of Nepal, *Bos indicus,* is called a *lango* (male) or *palang* (female) in Melemchi. These cows are well suited for altitudes up to 1,800–2,000 meters, although in summer they can go higher if properly managed. They have short hair, only a tuft of hair at the end of their tails, and are long legged and slender in comparison with yak. The other species of cow is a dwarf Tibetan version of the *Bos taurus,* otherwise known as hilly cattle. These are humpless and, thus, distinct from the Indian *zebu. Bos taurus* are small cows; females average 92 cm at the withers and weigh 150–180 kg (Bonnemaire & Teissier, 1976). Like other cows, their horns curve forward and upward, in contrast to the yak. Locally, these cows are called *pulang* (male) and *shamu* (female) and are highly favored for their hardiness at high altitudes.

Strictly speaking, hybrids should be impossible. The biological definition of a species is the largest group within which you can interbreed. However, some species are sufficiently close, either due to recent domestication or because of insufficient time or selection pressure for differentiation, that their chromosomes will match up and produce a viable offspring, especially with human assistance in the mating process itself. Left on his own, a yak is not interested in mating with a cow. It takes active intervention on the part of the herder, as well as the absence of the appropriate mate, to produce hybrid animals. Scientifically, as long as the hybrid offspring are less vigorous than either parent species, the species distinction is retained. In the case of *zomo,* although the female is more vigorous in some respects than either parent, the male is always sterile and unable to reproduce. Therefore, yak and cow remain separate species, in spite of the fact that together they can produce viable offspring.

As a hybrid, a *zomo* shows characteristics of both parent species, although maternal characteristics predominate. Thus, the *zomo (urang* [female] or *shamdzo* [male]) whose mother is a cow tends to be larger and have less hair on the tail than the *brimdzo,* who favors its smaller, stockier *nak* mother, sharing her bushy tail and heavy coat. *Brimdzo* are unable to thrive in the lower altitudes characteristic of Melemchi winter pastures, so Melemchi herders do not herd them. All *zomo* have the 13 ribs characteristic of all bovines other than yak. As hybrids, *zomo* show heterosis, or hybrid vigor; this means that the hybrid offspring show increased fitness in certain characteristics over either of the parents. In the case of female *zomo,* heterosis is pronounced; they produce more milk than either *nak* or female cows (although the fat content is intermediate) and have the potential to calve once a year. They also lactate longer after calving than either cow or yak. These traits are the basis for a subsistence strategy built around dairying. In addition *zomo* appear to have a longer lifespan (20 years, as opposed to 15 for yak/cow; Joshi 1982). Male *zopkio* are also known for their strength and docility (Joshi, 1982).

In addition to heterosis, hybridization often produces sterile males and this is the case with *zomo.* Male *zopkio* of all types are sterile; although they produce spermatogonia, these degenerate because of poorly developed seminiferous tubules. *Zopkio* do develop secondary sex characteristics and exhibit libido, but they are always castrated (Joshi, 1982).

Types of Crossbreeds   A number of crossbreeds or hybrids can be produced by breeding yak, cows, and their offspring. Table 2.1 diagrams the local terminology for the various crosses found in Melemchi.

In scientific terms, a *zomo* is an F1 hybrid; that is, it is the first cross between two pure species, a yak and a cow. When that *zomo* is bred (F1 × bull), the resulting *pamu* is referred to as an F2 hybrid. Since hybrid females are fertile, it is possible to breed the *pamu* (F2) with a bull and have an F3 hybrid *(tolmu,* female; *tolku,* male), and so forth. Unfortunately, hybrid vigor or heterosis only exists in the first (F1) generation; *pamu* and their offspring are less vigorous in every way than either parent. Although some herders may keep and breed one or two *pamu* (see below), they almost never keep subsequent generations. The only reason to do so would be to try to ultimately produce the highly coveted pure dwarf Tibetan bulls *(Bos taurus),* which are otherwise available only in Tibet, through repeated back-crossing hybrid generations with a dwarf Tibetan bull (see Table 2.2).

Other Animals in a *Zomo Gode*

Breeding Bull   A *zomo* herd includes at least one male bovid to mate with the *zomo* so that they will calve and produce milk. The quality and type of male is a matter of great importance to the herder, who gives special treatment to his bull. Melemchi *zomo* herders prefer dwarf Tibetan bulls, but these are difficult to obtain from Tibet, so they usually have some type of dwarf Tibetan bull cross. Melemchi *zomo* herds may include *pulang* (pure *Bos taurus*), *ghilang* (cross between a *Bos taurus* × *Bos indicus*), *saba* (cross of a *ghilang* × cow), and *ronglang* (pure *Bos indicus*)[1]. The *pulang* thrives at higher altitudes; in fact **Kami** told us his *pulang* has to be treated like a yak. The *pulang* sleeps in the *gode* with the family so his hooves aren't

TABLE 2.1 LIVESTOCK TERMINOLOGY (MELEMCHI)

Breeding Within Species:

YAK	DWARF TIBETAN CATTLE	LOWLAND CATTLE
Yak ♂ × Nak ♀	*Bos taurus* ♂ × *Bos taurus* ♀	*Bos indicus* ♂ × *Bos indicus* ♀
↓	↓	↓
yakpu ♂	*pulang* ♂	*lango/ronglang* ♂
brimu ♀	*shamu* ♀	*palang* ♀

Cross-Breeding: Types of Crosses in Melemchi Herds:

Yak ♂ × *Bos indicus* ♀	Yak ♂ × *Bos taurus* ♀
(yakpu) × *(palang)*	*(yakpu)* × *(shamu)*
↓	↓
zomo	*zomo*
(also called *urang zomo* or *ushu)*	(also called *brimo)*

F1 Crosses:

Yak ♂ × Zomo ♀	*Bos taurus* ♂ × *Zomo* ♀	*Bos indicus* ♂ × *Zomo* ♀
(yakpu) *(zomo* [F1])	*(pulang)* *(zomo* [F1])	*(lango)* *(zomo* [F1])
↓	↓	↓
pamu (F2)	*pamu* (F2)	*pamu* (F2)

F2 Crosses:

Bos taurus ♂ × *Pamu* (F2) ♀
(pulang)
↓
tolku (F3) ♂
tolmu (F3) ♀

compromised by standing in the mud created by the milling herd outside the *gode* in the summer mists and rain. Kami gives his *pulang* special water (from rivers rather than springs) and feeds him the best grass as well as thick fermented grain beer *(balu)* and toasted barley flour *(tsampa)* with salt. *Bos taurus* bulls of all dilutions are favored because they produce small F2 calves; this minimizes the stress on the *zomo* mother and, it is believed, contributes to her longevity. Alirol (1979) has pointed out that the goal is to produce small sickly calves that are likely to die easily, underscoring the point that this is a dairying operation, not one devoted to calf pro-duction.

Sheep and Goats   Small animals supplement the herders' income and are easy to combine with a *zomo gode*. Half of the Melemchi *gode* had sheep along with the

TABLE 2.2 BACK-CROSSING DWARF TIBETAN BULLS *(Bos taurus)*

First Generation (F1):

Bos taurus (♂) ×	Nak (♀)	=	Zomo (♀)
100%	100%		50%/50% (50% *B. taurus*)

Second Generation (F2):

Bos taurus (♂) ×	F1 Zomo (♀)	=	F2 Pamu (♀)
100%	50/50		75/25 (75% *B. taurus*)

Third Generation (F3):

Bos taurus (♂) ×	F2 Pamu (♀)	=	F3 Pamu (♀)
100%	75/25		87.5/12.5 (87.5% *B. taurus*)

Fourth Generation:

Bos taurus (♂) ×	F3 Pamu (♀)	=	F4 Pamu (♀)
100%	87.5/12.5		97.75/3.24 (97.75% *B. taurus*)

zomo herd. Sheep like the same high places that *zomo* do. Sheep are kept for wool and meat production; with two lambs and two wool shearings per year, they provide income for the families with minimal upkeep. One-year-old sheep were being sold for 500 rupees in 1986, while younger ones went for 300–400 rupees. (Five hundred Nepalese rupees is equivalent to $22.75 U.S. In 1986, the exchange rate was 22 Nepalese rupees to $1 U.S.)With a 12-year lifespan, sheep produce their first lamb at the age of 3 years. In contrast to sheep, goats are rare in *zomo gode*. Goats tend to be kept in separate herds, for sale as meat or to rent for manure production. Both sheep and goats are important sources of manure, and *gode* that include only those species may be brought down to the village beginning in September for a couple of months to fertilize the wheat and barley fields.

Why Zomo?

Zomo are the ideal dairying "machine" for middle-altitude villages like Melemchi. Physiologically, they thrive between 2,100 and 3,660 meters in altitude; cows cannot venture much above 2,100 meters, while yak begin to suffer from heat-related distress below 3,660 meters (although individual yak have been able to winter in Melemchi at 2,600 meters). As the result of heterosis, *zomo* produce more milk and lactate longer than either cow or yak. In addition, they live up to 20 years, compared with an average lifespan of 15 years for a yak or cow. Compared with cows, *zomo* begin their reproductive careers earlier: Both *zomo* and yak give birth to their first calf at 3.7 years of age, while the age at first birth for cows averages 4.3 years (Joshi, 1982). Compared with yak which have a 2-year birth interval, *zomo* can calve every year, if their calf dies after birth (Bonnemaire & Teissier, 1976). *Zomo* milk isn't

Kami's pulang *dwarf Tibetan bull* (Bos taurus). *Note the stocky appearance and the short horns. (1986)*

the richest in butterfat, but this is compensated for by the quantities of milk produced. (Yak milk is highest in butterfat content, while cow milk is lowest.) All of these features add up to the undeniable supremacy of *zomo* as butter producers. Regardless of where they live, neither cows nor yak produce butter in the quantities that *zomo* produce, nor can they live easily at middle altitudes.

HERD MANAGEMENT

Breeding

Zomo are bred between June and August, when the herds are at their highest altitudes and grazing is best. Stockmen can tell when their *zomo* are in estrus by the color of the cervical mucous. Although bovines prefer to breed true to species, few Melemchi herders report problems breeding their bulls to their *zomo*. The *zomo* don't have to be restrained, which can be the case for cows bred to yak, but breeding is supervised by the herder in both cases. With a gestation length of about 270 days, calves tend to be born between March and May. We visited **Ghale Pemba Gyalbu's** *gode* on March 1, 1989, and saw 4 newborn *pamu* and 9 pregnant *zomo* in his herd of 18 *zomo*. **Tundu Wangdi's** 7 pregnant *zomo* were due in April, and another 5 were giving milk. With a herd of 22 *zomo,* this means that 55% of his herd would give birth that year.

The purpose of breeding *zomo* is to produce milk, not calves. F2 calves (called *pamu)* are in some sense a necessary but undesired byproduct. *Pamu* are tied up and allowed to suckle only enough in the first few days of life to start the lactation response in the mother. After this, they are neglected in a variety of ways and usually die. Buddhists don't want to take a life; furthermore, in a Hindu country such as Nepal, it is especially difficult to kill any animal that is part cow. Therefore, they allow the *pamu* to kill itself by restricting food and then permitting it to gorge on indigestible grass or even mother's milk. The resulting colic produces death.

If the calf dies soon after birth, Melemchi herders report that the mother will continue to lactate for 3 to 7 months postpartum; if the calf survives, the mother can continue for as long as 2 years, but of course the milk available to the herder is reduced. One *zomo* whose calf survived was lactating 15 months after giving birth. However, this is not desired; ideally the calf does not survive, the herder gets all the milk for the first few months postpartum, and the mothers resume estrous and are bred 4 to 6 months later. *Zomo* will continue to produce milk for the first few months of gestation, although at reduced quantities.

Although *pamu* are unwanted and herders claim to never keep them, in fact, most *gode* in Melemchi included at least 1 *pamu* over 1 year of age. A survey of 10 *zomo gode* turned up 164 *zomo* and 18 *pamu* over 1 year of age. The number of 1-year-old or more *pamu* per *gode* ranged from 1 to 4, with an average of 1.8. This is the result of the fact that some *zomo* are unable to give milk without their calves

Milking a zomo. *The* zomo *is tied and drinks whey from a pan that sits on the skin of the* zomo's *dead calf. The woman sits next to her milking bucket and salt basket. Note the abundant hair on the tail of the neighboring* zomo, *a diagnostic feature of* zomo *compared with cows, which have only a tuft at the end. (1986)*

present. In some of these cases, the mother can be stimulated by seeing the hide of her calf waved from the doorway of the *gode* or placed under the pan of whey she drinks while she is milked. Occasionally, the skin of the dead calf is stuffed with grass and brought out to stimulate the mother. But, most *gode* have one or more females who actually require the live presence of the *pamu* itself. These *gode* end up with adult *pamu,* which they sell to Tibetans for meat or draft animals or else breed to the bull to produce a *tolmu* or *tolku,* which often dies of the "hot disease," which was explained as weakness associated with living at low altitudes. Those female *tolmu* that live are the ones bred back to the dwarf Tibetan bulls in the attempt to produce pure dwarf Tibetan bulls (see Table 2.2). No one wants adult *pamu* in their herd, but in fact those who have them claim that they do produce enough milk to justify their keep.

Dairying

The ultimate purpose of a *zomo gode* is the production of butter and cheese. *Zomo* are bred to produce calves that will induce lactation in the mothers. Calves are allowed to die so that all the milk is available for dairy products. These products are primarily butter *(mar)* and dried cheese *(chiurpi).* Other products are consumed at the *gode* by the family but are not commodities for sale or barter; these include milk, yogurt, and fresh cheese.

Butter, the primary product of a *zomo gode,* is made every other day. The milk is allowed to ferment slightly and thicken into yogurt. It is mixed with hot water and put into the churn, a large wooden vat about 4 feet tall and 3 feet across. In the center is a wooden pole with a pyramidal apparatus at the bottom that will whisk the butterfat out of the milk. The pole is held in place by a wooden hook and is wrapped with a long leather strap. Churning can be done by a single strong adult, or else two people work together, each pulling one end of the large leather strap that is wound around the pole in order to make it spin. Churning is hard work; it takes about 2 hours of churning (about 300 pulls) to produce butter. Toward the end, as yellow globs begin to appear in the churning milk, cold water is added to help solidify the butter. When the butter forms, it is scooped up by hand into a large wooden ladle and then squeezed and tossed between the hands to form a ball of butter. The excess moisture (buttermilk) is squeezed out in the process, and the ball of butter is put into a container.

Once all the butterfat has been extracted, the remaining milk (now called buttermilk, or *tara*) is poured into a large metal pan and heated over the fire. As it heats, the casein protein coagulates and separates out from the whey as curds. Once this occurs, a small conical basket is floated on the surface, guided by hand. If the basket won't sink, the mixture has soured and the cheese will not be good. If the basket can be pushed down into the whey, then the cheese will be good. Liquid whey seeps into the basket, while the curds are held back. The whey is ladled from inside the basket into a pan and fed to the *zomo* and bull, sometimes mixed with salt. Eventually the curd is all that remains, and it is scooped into the basket and the basket is shaken so that all the liquid comes out of it. Some of the fresh soft curds are immediately served to the family, either plain or with chili and salt. Some of the cheese may be given to

Pamu *(calf from a* zomo *and bull) staked out with a muzzle made from woven bamboo to keep it from eating.* *(1986)*

the dog, in a bowl of whey. The remainder is squeezed out between the fingers of the hand into little irregular strips, laid on a bamboo mat high over the fire, and dried into *chiurpi,* the hard, smoky, dry cheese that is sold, bartered, and eaten by all Sherpas.

Depending on the market, butter can be melted down, stored in a tin, and sold as *ghiu* or clarified butter. This commands a higher price because it is pure butterfat and stores well. Herders who don't have time to leave the *gode* to sell their butter or who don't have enough local customers will take this extra step of melting down the butter and storing it for transport into Kathmandu or some other distant market. This was more common in the past when there were many *zomo gode* and the supply of butter exceeded the local demand. Butter sold locally is not clarified; it is sold fresh by weight in quantities that can be eaten quickly before it turns rancid.

All dairying equipment for the *gode* is made by the family—the barrels, baskets, mats, and ladles are all carved or woven from local materials. Rope is woven from plant materials as well. Purchased equipment includes metal pans for cooking, some metal utensils and dishes, plastic or metal water containers, and the bells worn by the animals when the *gode* moves.

Buying and Selling Livestock

Livestock in the Himalaya is limited by altitude; cows and water buffalo flourish in the lower altitudes, up to 2,100 meters; *zomo* are in the middle band, and yak occupy the upper levels. In order for Melemchi herders to have *zomo,* they must buy them, and, until recently, it was impossible to buy *zomo* locally. Thus Melemchi has long been part of an interdependent region of livestock production and distribution that stretches north to the Tibetan border, east into the region called Solu, and west over the Laurebina Pass into the Trisuli Valley.

North of Melemchi, running perpendicular to the Melemchi River valley, lies the Langtang Valley. Langtang is an area settled by ethnic Tibetans with a few villages scattered along the Langtang River at altitudes ranging from 2,450 to 3,660 meters. It is accessible to Melemchi people via the Sermasalang Pass and can be reached from Melemchi in two days in all seasons but winter. Because of its accessibility, the high altitudes, and its proximity to Tibet, Langtang has been a source of *zomo,* yak, and *pulang* for Melemchi villagers for many years. In return, Langtang people purchase baby *zopkio, zomo,* and *pamu* from Melemchi people for pack stock, meat, and resale in Tibet. Another source of these same high-altitude/Tibetan-originated animals is the village of Syabru, which lies northwest of Melemchi on the back side of the Gosainkund Lekh. Syabru, near the junction of the Trisuli and Langtang Valleys, lies at 2,600 meters altitude. Like Langtang, Syabru is a source of buyers for Melemchi stock.

Melemchi people also obtain livestock from the Yolmo Valley itself. Herders in 1971 told of buying *zomo* in Tarke Ghyang as well as other villages on the east side of the Yolmo Valley; however, today there is little pastoralism on that side of Yolmo. Now, the villages of Kulu (behind Melemchi to the west), Bolongsay, and others on the west side of the Melemchi River constitute the livestock market for Melemchi. *Zomo* are bought from these villages for herds in Melemchi, and, in recent years, most of the herds sold by Melemchi herders have been to people in these villages.

Especially prior to the 1980s, the regions east of Yolmo were a source of *zomo* for Melemchi people. Solu, which lies about 17 days' walk east of Melemchi, was a traditional source of *zomo.* Solu villages are comparable in altitude to Melemchi, and there is only one pass to cross at 3,567 meters. In 1961, **Dogyal** purchased 18 *zomo* in Solu and walked them back to Melemchi. In 1972, **Pasang Pruba** did the same, buying 17 *zomo* in Solu.

Recently, experiments in Melemchi with cow-yak *gode,* which produce *zomo,* have sent Melemchi herders to Langtang to buy a breeding yak and south into Yolmo and Trisuli for cows. These cow-yak herds are able to replenish Melemchi *zomo* herds, although those buying an entire new *zomo* herd still go up to villages such as Kulu to find someone who is getting out of the business.

Life with Herds

Managing a *zomo gode* requires skill, knowledge, luck, and access to good pastures. One aspect involving skill is the selection of stock. A herder must be able to select good stock to begin with and then must continually evaluate his needs to maintain the entire herd at peak productivity. Naturally, opinion varies as to what constitutes good stock. Furthermore, economics may prevent a herder from selecting the ideal animal. Age is an important factor, but it is closely linked with price. The best *zomo* is one that has had only one calf—a known producer but still young. Such a *zomo* cost

5,000 rupees ($227 U.S.) in 1986. Less-expensive *zomo* are younger, but younger *zomo* must be pastured for several years without producing any milk. Since it can be difficult to tell whether a young *zomo* will grow up into an excellent producer, one herder said he buys his stock from someone he knows and trusts. Another skill is knowing when to buy and sell stock, in terms of price and availability. And finally, it is clear that knowledge of animal husbandry varies and is linked with success in managing a herd. Protecting the animals from the elements, breeding them, and management of diet (food, water, and salt) all require knowledge, experience, and judgment.

Access to good pastures is a crucial component of success in pastoralism, just as access to good fields is essential for agriculture. Appropriate forage is necessary to the health of the herd; overgrazing can deplete key species and invite invasive and inedible species to take over the pasture. A herder must have access to pastures at altitudes varying from 2,450 meters to 3,660 meters, enough to be able to move the herd when grazing requires. In addition, water sources are crucial to the health of the animals. Over and over, herders attributed health problems to bad water sources. River water is considered to be better than ground or spring water.

Finally, luck will always be a factor in an enterprise such as pastoralism, where humans are dependent on so many factors beyond their control. While there is skill involved in avoiding outbreaks of disease, in successful breeding, or in protecting the herd from predation, there is also a chance factor that results in loss of animals or poor productivity in the herd. Nearly everyone who spent a substantial portion of his adult life herding *zomo* reported at least one catastrophic loss to predation or disease.

Herding *zomo* involves the difficulties of isolation, danger, and discomfort. Although several families may join together, as the Ghale clan does every spring at Namsangsang, a high summer pasture northeast of Melemchi, or pair up off and on over the year at a particular pasture, a herding family must be prepared for an isolated existence. Women are especially isolated, since men do most of the traveling for supplies or sales. Danger lurks in the form of wild pigs and other predators. While the herd is most vulnerable to leopards and wolves, local people have been attacked by wild pigs and Himalayan black bears. *Zomo* themselves can injure humans. Many *gode* have one or more "man-beating *zomo*" who are untrustworthy around people. And *gode* life involves activities that can be dangerous—climbing tall trees to cut leaves and branches for fodder, working with huge animals with horns, and handling the ubiquitous *khukri* knives used by males of all ages. Medical assistance is far away; serious accidents require someone to run for help, often all the way to Kathmandu. There is also physical discomfort in *gode* life, despite the cozy feeling of warmth and intimacy inside the shelter itself. The weather is unavoidable—winter snowstorms, monsoon rainstorms. High summer pastures are perpetually misty, if not raining; mud and ground leeches make the area around the shelter mucky and unpleasant, setting the stage for skin lesions and infections. Lightning storms (and damage) are common; landslides and rockfalls occur. In 1972, heavy rains produced a major landslide above Kulu, killing an entire herding family and their animals; the only surviving son, who was away from the *gode,* is **Karpu,** the shaman *(bombo)*[2] of Melemchi during the summer of 1986. The daily work of the *gode* goes on regardless of the weather, the health of family members, and the social and religious calendar.

Life in a *zomo gode* has its pleasures as well. The overwhelming sense conveyed by *zomo gode* owners who were happy with their situation was their feeling of confidence, competence, and independence. They decided what to do and when to do it. Every *gode* I have ever visited is characterized by the same sense of routine, relaxation, and warm hospitality. They know how to live this life and they enjoy it. The alternatives are less appealing—life in India is foreign; life in the village is pleasant, but how could they make a living? A *zomo gode* provides income, subsistence, and a place to live while retaining access to the benefits of a village: the social and religious life, agricultural produce, and the services available in the village such as the *bombo* are all within a day's walk.

ECONOMICS OF *ZOMO* HERDING

All dairy herders face similar economic considerations. The costs of production include the purchase of stock, pasture access (food), medicine, and labor. Their income comes from the sale of dairy products and from calves. They must have places to keep their herd and a market for selling their products.

By herding hybrids, Melemchi dairy herders face additional problems. (1) They cannot produce their own stock; they must purchase replacements. (2) They cannot kill old or unwanted offspring, both because the animals are part cow and killing cows is proscribed in this Hindu country and because Melemchi people are Buddhists, who don't take lives. (3) Their herd is made up of two species, each of which has different ecological requirements. One or the other species may be physiologically stressed at some point in the year.

And finally, Melemchi herders face economic constraints that stem not from the species they herd but from factors of geography and history. Melemchi herders are isolated from services and information. They have no access to veterinary medicine; although there are a number of veterinary resources in Nepal, no clinics or veterinarians serve the Yolmo region. Neither is there access to genetically improved stock. East Nepal, for example, does have breeding and research facilities that focus on hybrid husbandry, but those resources are not available to this village. Melemchi herders have minimal opportunity to manipulate the supply and demand for the commodities they produce. They are isolated as individual pastoralists; except for occasionally joining together to send their butter out with a shared porter, they have no cooperative ventures. The closest market or bazaar is the Kathmandu valley, two to three days' walk away, so their opportunities to respond rapidly to market factors is minimal. And finally, the incorporation of Melemchi village and its pasturelands into the Langtang National Park limited opportunities for Melemchi herders to manage their own herds and resources without external interference (see Chapter 7). Under these circumstances, the Melemchi herder has adopted several strategies for protecting his investment and thus spreading out his risk.

First, consider what Melemchi herders have not done. Since the 1970s, Melemchi herders have not maximized herd size. They tell of the huge herds of the past—

their father's or their grandfather's or those of the much-remembered *zomo* barons, such as Baru Tundu or Baru Kesang. Today, they argue, it is too risky to have most of your money invested in *zomo;* they can be wiped out by disease, there may be no one to buy them when you decide to sell off, or the prices may be too low because of the many people who have given up *zomo* herding in the past years. They point out that, in hindsight, the truly wealthy and smart men of the past were those who invested in land, not animals. Animals die, but land remains.

Another option they are not following is to sell milk to the cheese factory. There is a Swiss-built cheese factory in Laurebine, high above Melemchi near the Gosainkunda Lakes. This is one of several built with Swiss government development aid to produce a gruyere-type cheese for export or sale in Kathmandu. Only one Melemchi couple ever became involved with the cheese factory.

Bolgyang Kami and his wife, **Jemiun,** kept a *zomo gode* for 12 years around Shing Gomba, which is a 2-day walk from Melemchi but near the cheese factory. They sold about 45 kg of milk per day to the cheese factory (it could process up to 200 kg of milk per day). They were paid monthly on the basis of the butterfat content of the milk, which varied with the season. They liked it because they were childless and without extra help, so they only had to milk the animals, not make and sell butter. Eventually, it became too much work for the two of them, and they built a house in the village, where they live now as farmers and tourist lodge owners. They were able to take advantage of this opportunity because Bolgyang Kami's wife was from Kulu and had access to pastures near the cheese factory. For others in Melemchi whose pastures are nearer the village, it would be financially unfeasible to rent pasture. And one *zomo gode* owner said he didn't want to supply the cheese factory because then he wouldn't have the butter and cheese for his own household, nor the whey to feed his animals.

What Melemchi people are doing is to spread out their economic risk in a number of ways. One way is to herd sheep and *zomo* together; sheep provide an additional source of income and do not add appreciably to the workload. Another way is to produce *zomo* rather than herd them. This option became common in Melemchi beginning in the mid-1980s, when herders sold their *zomo* herds and began herding cows with a breeding yak. The resulting *zomo* calves can be sold profitably; the workload is reduced, since the milk goes to the calves, not butter; and cows can be brought to or near the village for much of the year, enabling the herder to farm. This option is discussed in detail in Chapter 7. Another way to avoid excessive risk is to continually buy and sell herds, as needed, for optimal productivity; the possibility to "start fresh" enables a herder to get rid of problem animals or recoup financially and try again. Variations of this strategy include buying and selling specific animals within the herd or trying new combinations of species, sizes, or genetic diversity for the herd. Finally, Melemchi agropastoralists use agriculture and herding together to reduce the dependence on either single source of income and subsistence. As mentioned earlier, it is possible to combine some village agriculture with herding, although it is not clear that a nuclear family can both herd *zomo* and grow wheat and barley. More commonly, either some family members farm while others herd, or they plant corn in low fields while the herds are nearby.

DISCUSSION: *ZOMO* HERDING—A FORM
OF MOUNTAIN PASTORALISM

A recent volume summarizing research into the origins of agriculture and pastoralism in Eurasia (Harris, 1996) concludes that by 6000 B.C.E. agropastoralism was established in South Asia. Wheat and goats, and probably barley and sheep, were introduced into South Asia from Southwest Asia, where they originated; the evidence on cattle suggests they may have been domesticated locally either in eastern Iran or South Asia (Meadow, 1996). So, from the beginning, pastoralism seems to have developed along with agriculture and should not be viewed as a strategy of last resort for agriculturalists pushed into marginal habitats. On the southern slopes of the Great Himalaya, pastoralism has permitted agricultural communities to extend their use of upper elevations into areas where agriculture is either marginal or impossible.

Himalayan pastoralists herd one or more of the following species: sheep, goats, cattle, water buffalo, yak, and yak-cattle hybrids. Livestock are kept by Himalayan people because they provide transportation, agricultural labor, food (milk, meat, and blood), raw materials (wool, hair, and horn), and manure. Through the labor and products of animals, humans gain access to energy sources in the environment that exist in a form indigestible to people, such as plant cellulose. The particular combination of agriculture and pastoralism found in any particular place depends on both ecological factors and historical and social factors. Altitude, availability of adequate amounts of water, availability of nutrients, competitors, and seasonality all limit the distribution of species of both plants and animals. For example, sheep and goats seem to thrive in any altitude where humans can live, while bovines are more sensitive to the differences in temperature, oxygen, and vegetation types that characterize different altitudes. Likewise, crops are limited to certain altitude zones, as well as regimens of water, sunlight, and soil nutrient content. Culturally, yak and their hybrid offspring are herded primarily by Tibetan-derived groups, while a variety of ethnic groups herd sheep. But the ultimate choice of agropastoral strategy is based on a number of factors, with environmental limitations or cultural preferences being only two of the determining elements.

Pastoralism and agriculture are combined in the Himalaya in a number of different ways, depending on the local situation. Melemchi provides an example of the *gode* system, in which family-owned herds are moved through a series of pastures over the year in a pattern determined by the climatic and nutritional needs of the animals. This is a middle-altitude strategy, using the vertical zones between 2,100 and 3,660 meters altitude. The lower elevations around the village and Tarke Tho below lie within a single agricultural zone suitable for corn, wheat, barley, and potatoes. All of these crops are rain fed; irrigation is not necessary due to the high natural rainfall in this part of Nepal. Above 3,050 meters lie subalpine pastures suitable for grazing but not year-round agriculture. By bringing the herds down for one week prior to planting the village wheat and barley fields, Melemchi herders can exploit the full range of habitats available to them through agropastoralism.

The *gode* system in Melemchi is a system of dairy herding; agriculture is secondary or alternative to herding. The herds cannot be maintained within the confines of the village; there grazing is in direct conflict with agricultural needs. Furthermore, the herds are too large to be sustained in a small space. In Melemchi, dairying is a family enterprise; families own their own herds and their own pastures, and the family moves together with the animals. One of the reasons for this is that dairying is labor intensive and requires the daily labor of several adults. Individual families operate on their own to manage the complex combination of pastoralism and other activities, giving them maximal flexibility to adjust to changing and unpredictable conditions. In Melemchi as elsewhere in the Yolmo Valley, pastoralism is not a communal activity but rather one of individual family entrepreneurship.

A different system for combining pastoralism and agriculture, called the *goth* system, has been found among some groups living lower in altitude than Melemchi. As described by several researchers (Panter-Brick, 1986; Metz, 1994), the *goth* system is a villagewide system that coordinates the movement of livestock primarily to produce manure for agricultural fields. It is a form of agricultural intensification that permits greater productivity from poor mountain soils by permitting use of fields at different altitudes, all of which are intensively fertilized by herds. Metz studied the village of Chimkhola, which is located at 1,800 meters but "controls about 70 km^3 of agricultural fields, degraded shrublands, forests, and alpine pastures, which range in elevation from 1550 to 4000 m" (Metz, 1994, p. 372). The people of Chimkhola grow three different crops on agricultural fields that are as far as several hours' walk away from the village in different directions. The maintenance of livestock herds that can be kept directly on the fields for the weeks prior to planting contributes valuable nutrients through manure and urine, which improve soil fertility.

Families work primarily in the fields; one member of each household lives with the herd in a portable *goth* structure of bamboo mats built over poles, constructed either directly on the field to be planted or adjacent to forest where the animals can graze. For example, in Chimkhola the *goths* spend 3.5 months each year at the potato fields. Metz points out that this is a tremendous drain on forest resources, since *goths* require wood for their construction, fodder for maintaining the animals, and firewood for a duplicate household. Communal control is a necessary component in this marginal environment. Village leaders coordinate the movement of herds and the agricultural cycle so that families can farm widely dispersed fields in different ecological zones in a labor saving manner. Villages using the *goth* system are primarily dependent on agriculture; the livestock is a crucial element that both makes it possible and ultimately threatens its viability. To be successful, the *goth* system requires forest resources around the fields to support the livestock, and, as population pressure increases, those resources are becoming depleted. Metz notes that the supplementary income from Ghurka army pensions, which come to more than 100 households in Chimkhola, has served as a temporary buffer against the problems of deforestation and habitat degradation that loom in the future for some *goth* families.

The *goth* system as reported in Chimkhola and Salme is an example of agropastoralism where agriculture predominates and pastoralism supports it. The main contribution of the cattle or buffalo is fertilizer. The *goth* system is found at lower altitudes, where agriculture predominates; it permits intensive use of agricultural fields at several altitude zones but is dependent on the (finite) supply of forest resources from above. Variations include Tamang villages where water buffalo are kept for manure but not moved from field to field (Hoffpauir, 1978) or villages where flocks of sheep or goats are taken to high pastures in communal sheep herds for much of the year, while large livestock remains in the village for manuring fields (e.g., Gadlang village in the upper Trisuli Valley, Alirol, 1976).

In Khumbu, the high-elevation valley that abuts Mount Everest, Sherpa people also farm and herd (Brower, 1991; Stevens, 1993). Here the partial rain shadow provided by the Great Himalaya limits summer rain, permitting agriculture at higher altitudes than in Melemchi or farther west (Metz, 1989b). Species are limited to barley, buckwheat, and potatoes, at scattered fields ranging from 3,050 to 4,880 meters altitude. The growing season is short and the agricultural land poor and in short supply. There is no possibility to subsist primarily on agricultural products grown locally; trade has been the major source of income in this region located conveniently along trade routes between India and Tibet. At these altitudes, pastoralism exists in support of trade and cattle breeding more than agriculture. While dung may be used in fields, at these altitudes it is also an important source of cooking fuel, since forests and firewood are in short supply. Here, herds of female yak are maintained to produce hybrids for sale, while male yak herds carry loads. Hair is also a valuable commodity for sale, trade, and production of blankets, rope, and other items. Yak are moved in an irregular pattern, up and down throughout the year rather than the transhumant route of the *zomo*, high in summer, low in winter (Brower, 1991). Although the female yak may be milked, they are not primarily dairy animals. Most of the milk goes to the calves that are raised for sale, while the rest supplies the family with butter. In this most marginal habitat, fodder is grown in privately owned hayfields and stored to supplement the natural forage.

These three patterns represent three different variants of agropastoralism found among Tibetan-derived peoples living above 1,800 meters in the Himalaya. Each meets the dual demands of pastoralism (mobility and adequate resources to support large herds of animals) and agriculture (lack of mobility and intensive human labor), along with the special limitations of the particular environment. In each of the three, people combine herding livestock groups with fixed agriculture, but differences in environment, culture, and history result in different systems of management. Pastoralism is a crucial component of the subsistence strategy in each locale, even as its purpose varies among them.

NOTES

[1] A proliferation of terminology denoting distinctiveness is usually an indication of an area of cultural importance. The extensive elaboration of different names for various genetic crosses confirms our observation that Melemchi herders believe that heritable factors are of great importance and are used in making management decisions about their herds.

[2] *Bombo* are shamans who mediate between humans and the spirit world, seeking the causes of illness and other problems and effecting cures (see Chapter 6).

[3] Panter-Brick (1986) describes a similar pattern in the village of Salme in the Trisuli Valley just west of Yolmo. She points out that by moving the animals closer to sources of food and to sites in need of fertilizer, the *goth* system achieves remarkable economy of energy for the people of Salme, who are themselves energetically stressed at some times of year, especially women in some periods of their reproductive cycle.

3 / Life in the Village: Adaptation to the Local Environment

Seen from above, Melemchi village is a slightly flattened oval scar two-thirds of the way down a small southern mountain spur. Surrounded by forest, the village is demarcated by a small river on the west side and the edge of the spur on the east. The northern and southern boundaries are human-made: Prayer flags and a stone *mani* mark the southern entrance to the village, while its uppermost limits are set off by prayer flags fixed to bamboo poles high in the forest above the village, at 3,050 meters altitude. This is the Melemchi *guthi,* the land designated as belonging to the *gomba* of Melemchi and signed over to the first Chini Lama in 1859. People who live on this land today still pay the descendants of the Chini Lama two *pathi* of grain for the right to live here and are responsible for maintaining the *gomba* and the land attached.

Below Melemchi, at 2,500 meters, the slope drops off rather precipitously. Scrub vegetation predominates here, no doubt the result of grazing many household animals over the years, as well as the gathering of firewood and fodder. These areas are the common lands for the village—now anyone can graze their livestock or collect fodder on these lands throughout the year, just as anyone can graze their animals in the forested areas beyond the area of habitation. When there were many *gode,* this area was off-limits to village livestock from April through September to permit grass to grow for the *gode* when they came to the village in late September. But in recent years, that rule has been suspended. Below this common land lies the village of Tarke Tho, a very old settlement that stretches down from 2,440 to 2,135 meters altitude. Most people who live in Tarke Tho also are residents of Melemchi—24 of the 30 houses in Tarke Tho in 1989 were owned by Melemchi residents. Of the remaining 6, only 1 is owned by a person with no ties (through marriage) to Melemchi people. Tarke Tho has no *gomba;* in fact, this may be the impetus for many to maintain dual residence. Several *gode* owners told us they had bought land in Melemchi early in their marriages in order to belong to the *gomba;* it was much later that they built houses and lived there, but they wanted to be members.

Another reason people own land in both Melemchi and Tarke Tho is the difference in altitude. Corn grows much better in Tarke Tho than in Melemchi; although corn can grow at Melemchi's altitude, and people have planted it there, people usually leave their Melemchi fields fallow in summer and grow their corn below. Traditionally, Melemchi people descended to Tarke Tho in winter, with their animals, including their *gode,* both for the more equable winter climate and because of the grazing there. In Melemchi, the fields are all planted with wheat or barley in early November, and livestock is banished for the winter. Winters in Tarke Tho not only provide grazing, but also the opportunity to manure and prepare the cornfields. During the winter of 1972, only eight families stayed in Melemchi—a total of 35 people. All other Melemchi residents not in India at the time lived down below in Tarke Tho, either in houses or (most) with their *zomo* herds in sheds or *gode*. Some came up as soon as their corn was planted in late March, while others waited until June. Even those who wintered in Melemchi said it was a recent change for them; they had always gone down to Tarke Tho. By winter 1989, more families were staying up in the village and stall-feeding their animals. Still, nine households followed their customary pattern and took their livestock down for the winter—27 cows, 19 buffalo, 39 sheep/ goats, and 5 *zomo*.

In contrast to the rich green surrounding Melemchi, Tarke Tho looks sparse and dry. It consists of narrow terraces, steeply pitched, leading precipitously down to the Melemchi River. As Melemchi has grown prosperous, the population of Tarke Tho has shrunk. Fewer Melemchi people are planting there, content to leave their fields fallow or rent them to others, as other sources of income make it possible to buy corn. In 1989, 6 of the 30 houses in Tarke Tho were broken down and uninhabitable. Now all but a few use it only as a place to live while they plant corn; they make the daily trek down and back to harvest the corn, but otherwise it appears to be a ghost town.

The forest above Melemchi village is off-limits to cutting; only dead wood can be culled from this area. It is a primary oak *(Quercus semicarpifolia)* forest, typical of south-facing slopes in this zone, at altitudes between 2,450 and 3,050 meters (Stainton, 1972), with *Quercus semicarpifolia* comprising the top canopy almost exclusively, interrupted by small stands of much taller *Tsuga dumosa* (hemlock), and in the understory various species of *Ilex* and *Lindera,* which dominate smaller shrubs of *Virburnum, Berberis,* and *Daphne* (the paper plant). In the upper reaches of the forest, around 2,900 to 3,050 meters, stands of bamboo, fir, and rhododendron appear. The boundaries of this forest remained identical between 1971 and 1993, although internal gaps in the canopy have appeared where large old trees have fallen or were hit by lightning. The eastern boundary, marked by the river, joins an abutting slope that faces southeast. It has a different composition: mixed scrub and upper temperate broad-leaved forest of the upper midlands type (maple, magnolia, broad-leaved oak below; up higher, hemlock, fir, and rhododendron). Here many Melemchi villagers gather fodder from the undergrowth and scrub.

HABITATIONS

The first impression of Melemchi, in contrast with other Yolmo temple villages along the ridges and upper slopes of the Melemchi River valley, is of a flat, open expanse. The village slopes downward from the forest in a broad swath of unmarked terraces dotted with houses. Although the elevation changes 150 meters from top to bottom, it might take 20 minutes to walk it and it changes very gradually. Melemchi houses are separated by terraced fields but connected by a series of paths. Nearly all houses are visible from any one, although the distances between some may be large. Most houses are built so they face south, down the valley. No matter where you stand in Melemchi, there is a panoramic view of most of the village and the valley to the south.

A Yolmo house is built from mud and stones, with wooden window and door frames, 2-foot-wide planks for the floor, and, until recently, a roof of wood shingles arranged over wooden rafters. Now, these roofs are being replaced by sheet tin, which is not nearly as aesthetic visually or aurally but more durable and economical of forest resources. The traditional roof requires a tremendous investment in wood, especially since it must be replaced every 5 years. The house has two stories, although people only live on the second floor. In many parts of Nepal, livestock live underneath the living floor, providing a furnace for the family, but in Yolmo, the household cow lives under the front porch or if there are several, in an adjacent shed. The ground level is used to store firewood and dried hay. The stairs in the front of the house lead up to the porch, a wooden platform where dishes are washed, large items are stored, and people sit out in the sunshine weaving, making bamboo mats, or just keeping an eye on the village. Off to one side of the front door is the bathroom, an area set off by a hanging cloth "door" and consisting of just a hole in the plank floor. Piles of forest floor litter are left in the corner to be swept down after use, eventually producing a rich source of compost for the fields. Every few months the compost below is shoveled out into baskets and carried to the fields. The immediate application of composted litter and the open ventilation both above and below the floor result in little problem with odor.

The family living space itself is L-shaped and consists of a single large room, lighted only by the doorway and a single window with two wooden shutters. There is no furniture; people sit and sleep on the wooden floor, although always with something between them and the floor—an animal skin, woven blanket, bamboo mat, or piece of carpet. Storage is limited—at the end of the house nearest the door, the family's clothes and bedding are stacked up against the walls, either in metal trunks or in neatly folded piles. Other items are stored up in the rafters, hidden from sight by the ceiling planks. Sherpa houses are dark—until electrification in 1993, houses were lit at night by one or two small kerosene lamps made from cans or jars. The perpetual wood fire creates soot, which darkens all the surfaces inside. The walls are lined with wooden shelves, sometimes with cabinets. The shelves hold things that are for public display—photographs in frames, special purchased items, rows of cans and bottles (some filled but others empty), dishes, teacups, and, finally as you get closer to the hearth, cooking equipment. In wealthy households these shelves may be carved; they may even have cabinet fronts with elaborately carved Buddhist motifs (lotus flowers or dragons) and, more recently, carved cabinets with glass windows in them. Food is not displayed. The most conspicuous display of wealth is one or more rows of covered copper pots, which are lined up along the side walls or on shelves behind the hearth. These pots are not used for cooking; rather they are a form of display as well as a storage system, and some households have as many as 15 or 20 while others have none.

The bare wooden floors lead to the hearth, which is a smooth, mudded square about 1 yard on all sides and framed by a narrow plank 1-inch high, at the end of the house away from the door and opposite the window. A shallow depression in the mud makes a space for air to feed the fire; split firewood is arranged in spokes over this indentation and the fire remains in the center. As it burns, the wood is pushed in. A metal ring with three legs holds the cooking pots over the flames. A fire is burning whenever anyone is home. Smoke is pulled up by a draft created in the roof shingles; despite this, most houses are often very smoky, since wind and rain keep the draft from working as designed, and the wood may not always be dry. Between the hearth and the window is the family altar, a shelf or alcove that holds photos of the Dalai Lama[1] or family members, especially if they are lamas, as well as bowls of water and flowers and a butter lamp (a metal bowl packed with butter and a wick). Incense is burned there every morning and evening. In summer, real flowers are changed daily; the rest of the year, plastic flowers bought in Kathmandu are used, as well as an electric candle that comes on each evening when the current turns on. The altar lies over the sleeping platform, which forms the window seat for the house. Raised 8–12 inches off the floor and covered with mats, quilts, or carpets, this platform is where the householder couple sleeps. During the day, it is where honored guests sit—literally above everyone in the home.

Melemchi houses are only a few degrees warmer inside than out, but they do protect residents from inclement weather. People sit around the fire, for sociability and warmth, always eating or drinking something. Those of higher status sit next to the host, in order of descending status, so when newcomers arrive, there is a shuffling of location as people adjust. The female householder sits on the left side of the fire; she is surrounded by cooking equipment and food stores and can survey the entire house from her vantage point. The male head of household sits opposite her on the

Ibe Balmu, age 43, in her house. Note the carved wooden cabinets, the rows of copper pots above the hearth covered with cloth to keep them clean, the open fire, and the bamboo drying rack above the fire. She sits in the place of the woman of the house; the male householder would sit next to the fire in front of the cabinets. (1972)

Ibe Balmu, age 64, in her house. Note the new airtight stove, which uses less fuel and makes less smoke but provides little heat. Instead of an animal skin, the floor has a woven rug. The cup on the plank is for butter tea, which she pours from the teapot in front of her. (1993)

right side of the fire; no other male displaces him from this spot. His seat does not give him the same vantage as his wife, but he is next to the areas of high status and honor—the altar and the raised platform. All guests of high status will be urged to sit on the platform and will be provided with a small wooden table for food and drink. Others will sit alongside the male host in descending order of status or age. Or, they may sit around the hearth. Food should always be off the floor, so those sitting around the hearth rest their cups on the plank that borders it, even though it is only 1 inch off the floor. Others farther away are given wooden planks or small tables for their food, if at all possible. Children sit toward the back of any group, farthest away from the fire and food, and are displaced immediately by anyone older. Women cluster on the women's side and are likely to help make tea, wash dishes, or serve, while men sit near the household head. Both men and women provide hospitality for their guests.

Houses in Melemchi stand singly or may be attached side by side in a row—in one case, a family with four sons built a long building with four houses, each with its own stair and porch. Melemchi houses have a packed-dirt courtyard in front, suitable for threshing or spreading out grain to dry; the house and yard are surrounded by a stone wall 3 feet high. Most houses now have a small walled vegetable garden adjacent to the yard; it may include a fruit tree (apple or peach), always garlic and chilis, and, in recent summers, more and more kinds of vegetables: pole beans with bright orange and white flowers, cabbages, and pumpkins interspersed with giant dahlias, small gladiolas, marigolds, and phlox. In the early 1970s, cultivated vegetables were not grown in Melemchi. People did grow garlic, mustard seed, and chilies, but the only fresh vegetables were those gathered wild in season: green herbs from the fields, bamboo shoots, tree fungi, and mushrooms. The recent popularity of these gardens of flowers and vegetables results from the establishment of a horticultural station in Yolmo at Sermathang village during the early 1980s. It provided a local source of seeds and advice. The increased exposure of villagers to life outside the Yolmo Valley has no doubt also contributed in creating new appetites and expectations for life in the village.

COMMON PROPERTY

Gomba (Temple)

Melemchi residents own their houses and fields; as residents in the *guthi,* they are also required to maintain and support the *gomba.* The Melemchi *gomba* has been rebuilt several times at least; residents told us in 1971 that the *gomba* had been in its present location for about 100 years. Prior to that, it was located on the eastern edge of the village. The most recent renovation began in 1983, following similar renovations of the *gomba* in the other main Yolmo temple-villages. Throughout the region, villages replaced their mud-and-stone one-story structures with large cement-walled, two-story *gomba* complete with tin roofs. These new *gomba* are refurbished inside as well. Professional painters painted the frescoes, new statues were built, and in most *gomba,* but not Melemchi's, the statues were encased in glass cases. In Melemchi, they kept the old statues, and there were no glass cases, so the new gomba retains more of the old look inside while the outside is modernized. All the physical labor for the renovation work in Melemchi was done by residents under the orders of the Chini Lama, who provided the cement and raw materials. During the project, the rules for taking animals down to Tarke Tho in winter were changed to permit residents to remain in the village over the winter months to be available for work on the *gomba.* Residents worked for free, and the job, which began in 1983, was finally finished in 1991, despite many disputes, slowdowns, and changes of personnel. Half the inside painting was done by Tamang painters from outside the valley, but, after a dispute over wages, the job was finished by painters from Chimigaon in Yolmo. In December 1990, the Chini Lama sent word that residents of the village should not return to India for wage-labor jobs so that they would be present for the reconsecration; those in India were called home. This caused much concern among some residents who wanted to be a part of the ceremonies but were reluctant to lose jobs awaiting them in India. The Chini Lama attempted to levy large fines on some who left for India in spite of the edicts, but these were never collected. More than 500 people attended the reconsecration ceremonies in March 1991, which were presided over by a lama from Kathmandu.

Daily rituals must be performed in the *gomba* twice a day. That duty falls to a family of Tibetan refugees who have resided in the village since 1960. (Before that, a Tibetan painter who painted some of the walls in the old *gomba* performed the job.) **Meme Gyau,** and now his grown adopted son, Pinzo, have cared for the *gomba* daily for the past 35 years, changing the water in the altar bowls, lighting the butter lamps, and saying the prayers. Each household makes an annual donation of 1 *pathi* of grain to them for this service, in addition to any gifts they receive from the Chini Lama.

Chutta (Water-Driven Flour Mill)

The Tibetan refugee family is also responsible for grinding all the grain that is paid to the Chini Lama as taxes on the *guthi* land. As a result of this assignment, they have become the millers for the entire village. As compensation, they take a small portion of each bag of grain they grind at the water-driven flour mill, or *chutta*. The mill sits alongside the small river that bounds the village on the east. To start the process, Pinzo climbs above the mill to the river, where he shifts the large stone slab out of its cradle. By shifting the slab out of its cradle, he opens the flood out into the mill channel. The flow powers the two huge flat grinding stones that lie parallel to each other. As the grain drops a few kernels at a time into the central hole, the top stone rotates against the stationary stone, producing a fine flour.

Village Water System

The water system is another kind of common property in Melemchi. No one bears official responsibility for it, but it is maintained for the benefit of everyone. There are five year-round springs in Melemchi, and, until 1983, the spring closest to the houses provided water for everyone. Water ran continuously there from the spout, and residents walked down a steep hill to a spot under two trees at 2,560 meters altitude where the spring emerged to fill their narrow-neck brass jugs. The water quality was excellent and the supply was good, but it was a struggle to carry the water back up the hill. Several times each day, every household sent someone to make the trip, returning up the steep path to the house with a full jug balanced on his or her back, the weight borne by a *naamlo* (or tumpline) around the forehead. It was inconvenient and difficult, but everyone did it and always had.

The first piped water system was brought in 1983 to run water to the Chini Lama's family's house. It was a neoprene pipe paid for by the Chini Lama family; the source wasn't high enough in altitude, and the pipe had to dip before it came back up the hill, making water pressure a problem. It never worked well and was soon supplemented by a water tank built in the village above the original spring. A large-diameter pipe was installed high up into the forest and run underground into the tank. The pipe was provided by the government water ministry at the villagers' request, but they provided the labor. Since the tank was now located more centrally within the village, it was easier to get to, although water was still carried by the jugful home on people's backs.[2]

The tank system worked well for a brief period, but the number of houses in the village had increased, and many of the new outlying houses were still far from a water source. Tapping into the big tank, several subsidiary smaller tanks were added at other locations. Then a few additional lines were spliced into the existing ones, with stopcocks attached, and spigots were set up in a few locations right next to particular houses, all in the central ("old") portion of the village. In 1986–87, the system seemed to work pretty well. People were beginning to grumble over the politics of the location of the water taps, but there were several locations in the village where water was available, and when the system broke, **Pinzo** or some of the head men were called out to fix it.

By winter 1989, major problems had developed. Several people living at the top of the village spliced into the main line above the big tank and thus diminished the flow into the tank; others spliced into the closest line to their houses and tried to bring water into their courtyards and even into their individual houses. There were no stopcocks and no systemic regulations, and finally the water dwindled to a trickle where it flowed at all. People complained that they had worked on the system and given money for pipes but didn't get a drop, while others had their own private water supply. The pipes froze and split, and the few stalwarts who had always been depended upon to fix the system when it broke began to refuse. Finally the main pipe was cut (vandalized) and the village decided not to repair it. Once again, people carried water up from the old spring.

Tupu Cave (Guru Rinpoche's Meditation Cave)

The Tupu cave is also a part of the Melemchi *guthi*.[3] Located at the northernmost edge of the village, right in the center, it is a small house built under a huge granite boulder. Stone walls demarcate a small courtyard in front, and inside, walls form two tiny rooms. Tupu is reported to have been built by Guru Rinpoche, who brought Buddhism to Tibet in the 8th century; he is said to have meditated in this cave but found it too dark, so he made indentations shaped like the sun and the moon over the door. Water is reported to drip inexplicably from the corner of the sun, although there is 8 feet of solid rock above it. The cave is occupied periodically by monks in silent retreat who arrange with villagers for food supplies to be brought to the courtyard and left there. Otherwise, villagers stay away, even when the cave is unoccupied. The annual festival of Tupa Sezhu is held at the cave every year in late summer.

LAND OWNERSHIP

At present, all land in the Melemchi *guthi* is owned; there is no unclaimed land to develop. Until recently, all a person needed was to locate a vacant area, demarcate it, and ask permission from the Chini Lama to build a house or field there. Permission was usually granted, and after a small payment to the *gomba,* the land was theirs. Alternatively, land still can be bought from someone who is willing to sell. Strictly speaking, *guthi* land is owned by a religious institution or association, not individuals; in the case of Melemchi, it is the Chini Lama who administers the *guthi,* so he is the de facto owner and it is to him that taxes are paid. But individuals have always claimed to "own" their land, both house lots and fields, which are passed on through inheritance or sold. The youngest son inherits the family home and land; other sons must buy or develop their own plots. In the case of very wealthy families, the parents may give some of their land to each married son, saving their primary parcel for their heir. Daughters never inherit land; while women can own land, they always buy it. A widow holds her husband's land until the youngest son matures; if there are no sons, the land is divided among male first cousins.

In the mid-1980s, with land reform in Nepal, government surveyors came to Melemchi to measure, demarcate, and register the land. For the first time, villagers have their land registered with the government in their own name. It didn't happen easily; some people told of intimidation by members of the Chini Lama family to make them register the land as *guthi*. But once several people stepped forward and registered the land in their own names, others followed suit. Unfortunately, even by 1993, people still had not received actual land ownership certificates; despite their walking several days to the district center in Chautara and paying for the certificates, none had been received. Villagers were beginning to speculate about foul play, but it could have easily been the result of bureacratic problems as well.

Land may be rented out to others to farm for a share of the produce. It can also stand fallow for years without affecting its ownership. A number of Melemchi residents are landlords elsewhere, of land bought with proceeds of *zomo* herding or wage labor. This extends well beyond Tarke Tho. Melemchi people own fields in a number of other villages at lower altitudes in the Yolmo Valley: for example, Chyamdo, Kuisangpal, Bolgyang, Nagote. These fields are leased to tenant farmers. The proceeds are shared according to the system called *mouy*. In this system, three crops are planted in a single year: rice, millet, and corn. The landlord takes the rice crop, and the tenant gets the other two. Each year the arrangement is renegotiated. Alternative systems for sharing profits also exist. Families also own pastures and grazing rights in villages other than Melemchi. *Zomo gode* that graze only on the Melemchi side of the Melemchi River pay 100 rupees to the Melemchi *gomba;* those with pastures on both sides of the river pay 80 rupees tax to the Nagote *gomba* and 20 rupees to Melemchi.

AGRICULTURE

Agriculture Within the Village Boundaries

The primary crops grown in the fields surrounding the houses of Melemchi are barley *(changda)*, wheat, and potatoes. Wheat and *changda* fields are the prime fields in the center of the village, while potato fields are more commonly found in outlying areas. There have been years in which corn was planted in Melemchi, but the last time this was widespread, in 1984, residents agreed that it made the village dark and caused problems with livestock, which grazes freely during summer months. Since then some families on the edges of the village plant a summer corn crop, while others grow a few corn plants in their kitchen garden plots. Most people still grow their corn down in Tarke Tho.

No one in Melemchi has ever practiced swidden agriculture, or shifting cultivation; that is, where fields are prepared, planted, harvested, and then left fallow for a period of years until they revert to their original state, only to be cultivated again years later. Although older residents know about the practice, they say it was used for lower fields near Tupkang. Fields in Melemchi are permanent, once prepared. The village terraces slope gently and are not buttressed by stone walls. Nor are there many walled fields. Farmers erect temporary fences of brush and thorns to dissuade predators such as livestock, deer, or monkeys and hang various devices to scare away birds.[4]

The herbaceous layer that grows on the terraces year-round may help to retain the soil in the face of torrential monsoon rains. In the summer of 1972, we measured over 100 inches of rain in a period of 10 weeks. Snowmelt in winter and summer rains are the only sources of water for agriculture. Melemchi has no irrigated fields.

All fields, whether planted in corn, *changda* (barley), or potatoes, require compost. Informants maintain that potatoes require the most compost, but all fields require amendments. Night soil (composted human waste) mixed with forest leaves is carried to the fields and dug in. The compost is spread on the fields as they are being plowed; we watched a child walking ahead of a pair of bulls, spreading compost from a basket just in front of the plow. Chemical fertilizers are not used in Melemchi. All summer, household livestock roam freely throughout the village fields, providing 4 to 6 months of manure, albeit randomly applied. More direct application of fertilizer is accomplished by setting up movable sheds right on the fields so families can live with their livestock staked out wherever manure is needed. If you don't have any livestock, it is possible to rent a herd. One man, **Sonam Gyelzen,** owns a flock of goats which he rents for periods of a couple of weeks; during the day, the renter takes the goats out to the field he wants manured, and at night, he brings them back to a small enclosure under or near his house where the manure falls on ferns and leaf litter, producing a rich fertilizer that can be carried to future fields. One *gode* owner kept his herd on someone else's potato fields just below the village in winter 1989; he told us in February that he would have normally moved on up to his next pasture by then, but he promised to spend a few more weeks there fertilizing the fields.

Wheat and Changda

It is believed that the first people who came to Melemchi brought *changda* with them; current residents say that both *changda* and potatoes have been planted in Melemchi for as long as they are aware. *Changda* is a type of high-altitude barley *(Hordeum vulgare)* that is used for *tsampa,* a staple food among people of Tibetan origins. *Tsampa* is prepared by stirring barley in a dry pan over a hot fire (often with some live coals in the pan) until it "pops" and then grinding it into flour. With a wonderful nutty flavor, *tsampa* is mixed with liquids such as salted butter tea into a porridgelike consistency, or it can be made into a ball of dough, from which pieces are pinched off and eaten. Since *changda* grows only at middle to high altitudes, it is also sold to those living at lower altitudes. Tibetans and Sherpa living in Kathmandu purchase *tsampa* brought in from villages such as Melemchi.

Wheat and *changda* are planted at the same time; most of the fields are planted in *changda,* but a little wheat is also grown for bread flour. Unleavened wheat flour breads are important, both for Losar (Tibetan New Year) meals and for the ceremonial bread at the summer Nara festival; otherwise, Melemchi people don't make bread of any kind. Any excess wheat is traded for lowland grains. *Changda* ripens slightly ahead of the wheat. Its heads are heavy with long hairs; they bend over when ripe and hang down, while wheat stands straight up. Early rains are less likely to cause problems for *changda,* since the water runs right off the inverted grain head and is directed away by the stiff hairs.

Wheat and *changda* are planted between October and December. The fields are plowed by a pair of bulls; there are several pair in the village that may be borrowed or rented. Manure and compost are worked into the soil while plowing; then the field is smoothed over using short-handled hoes. The seed, the best of the previous crop, is sown by hand. In 1972, **Kirkiyap** planted 40 *pathi* (104 kg) of *changda* seed and reaped 320 *pathi* (832 kg) of *changda;* he has some of the best fields, but his wife was quick to add that they work very hard. The periodic snows provide moisture for the seedlings to germinate, and by early March the fields look like a lawn with grass 4 to 6 inches high. Other than keeping the chickens and birds from eating the freshly sown seed and weeding the fields periodically during the spring, there is no other work involved in *changda* until harvest time. In late spring as the *changda* ripens, the village is a vast expanse of mostly golden fields, with blocks of green wheat mixed in.

Grain is harvested by all able-bodied family members, who work very quickly to bring in the harvest before the monsoon rains begin around mid-June. The grain

Melemchi village in harvest season. Wheat fields stand straight and are darker than the changda *(barley) fields. A temporary cow shed has been set up on a recently harvested field; the owner's household livestock are staked out on it. Our house is the house with the half-white wall on the left. (1972)*

heads are pulled off the stalks, a handful at a time, by catching them up between two bamboo sticks and pulling up sharply. In a second movement, the bits of stalk remaining on the heads are cut off by pulling the handful over a flat circular knife that is worn in the harvester's waistband. The heads are put into a basket, while the bits of stalk fall to the ground. Harvesters move through the fields, plucking a handful at a time in swift, fluid movements; they are followed by others who cut off the headless stalks left in the ground near their bases and pile them into bundles of straw, which they take home to store for winter fodder. Those without *changda* fields, or those who didn't plant that year, assist others in the harvest; otherwise, every family works simultaneously on their own fields. Finally, the fields are left with stubble which serves as summer grazing for the village livestock.

Meanwhile, the grain must be threshed and stored. The *changda* is singed to burn off the hairs and loosen the grain; then it is beaten with wooden flails by two or three people working in the courtyard of the family house. The flails fall in alternating rhythm, and when the hull is beaten off, the grain is scooped up into flat baskets for winnowing. As the basket is tipped slightly and shaken from side to side, the material inside falls to the ground. The heavier grain falls down, while the chaff, hulls, and other debris fly away on the wind. For the 3 or 4 weeks of the harvest, the village air is full of flying debris and everyone has red eyes and running noses.

Once the harvest is completed in early June, the fields are left fallow until fall. Some people occasionally plant a second crop of *changda* in August; there is no time for the seed heads to develop by the time the winter crop must be planted, but the half-grown seedlings are harvested for winter fodder.

Potatoes

Potato fields are individually owned and registered at the district center. People pay taxes on those fields to the government, not the *guthi*. Although no one knows when potatoes first came to Melemchi, elderly villagers today said their parents grew both potatoes and *changda* in the village.[5] Melemchi potatoes are small and sweet; several varieties are grown, and, in recent years, villagers have experimented with varieties introduced by the agricultural station in Sermathang, especially in response to several bouts of blight and disease. Potatoes are planted in Melemchi in February and are harvested in July and August. Large fields are plowed by bulls, while smaller fields are prepared by hand with hoes. Potatoes need a great deal of compost, but they are otherwise left alone except for weeding. Outlying fields are susceptible to predation by wild boars.

Potatoes are a dietary staple in Melemchi. In the early 1970s, potatoes were eaten both dried and fresh. Each fall, some of the potato crop and all of the radish crop were sliced and left to dry. Dried potatoes were cooked along with dried radish into curries and eaten in winter when there was no fresh food available. Now, no one dries potatoes; all potatoes are stored whole and eaten fresh. Most commonly, Melemchi potatoes are boiled in their skins and then peeled and eaten, one at a time, dipped in *martza:* a paste of hot red chilies, garlic, and salt pounded fresh in a mortar. Potato curry and mixed vegetable curry have become common as well, in recent years, now that rice is widely available. Twenty-five years ago, no one ate rice except at special occasions. Melemchi people do not cook the various types of potato pancakes or potato noodles that are common among the eastern Sherpa communities.

Corn

Corn is the fourth important crop for Melemchi people, but, as mentioned already, most of the corn crop is grown in Tarke Tho. Corn is ground into cornmeal and eaten as mush with a small amount of curried vegetables or, more often, with a dairy food such as milk, yogurt, or curried cheese. While common in 1971, especially among poorer families, cornmeal mush is rarely eaten today; its low status comes from its association as a food of Tamang or lowland people. Corn is also used to make *balu,* a fermented beer mash made from ground corn. *Balu* is often the only food carried on journeys by Melemchi men; they either eat it as is or dilute it with water.

Subsidiary Crops

Radishes have already been mentioned as an important supplement to the diet in the early 1970s in Melemchi. No one grows radish anymore. When asked, people say that they grew them originally to sell to people living below, but the supply outstripped the demand and they finally stopped growing them. It is clear that Melemchi people consider radish a low-status food and are uncomfortable even acknowledging that they ever grew and ate them. Millet is another low-status crop; grown at lower altitudes and eaten widely in Nepal, millet is used in Melemchi only to produce grain alcohol for drinking. Melemchi people either purchase millet or use that grown by their tenants on their lowland fields for liquor production. Millet is a winter crop in this region and could be grown in Tarke Tho, but live-stock graze there in winter, so Melemchi people never bother to grow it there. The only other crop in Melemchi is apples. There is an apple orchard in Melemchi, owned by the Chini Lama family. It is one of several past experiments in developing cash-producing projects in Melemchi. Apple cultivation has been successful in several areas of western Nepal; in addition to fresh fruit, dried apples and apple brandy are exported out of these regions for sale in Kathmandu. The apple orchard in Melemchi has never been successful, probably because there was no consistent attention to it by the Chini Lama family members. The trees can produce good apples, but many are misshapen, insect ridden, small, and flavorless; monkeys, deer, and livestock are a nuisance and can spoil the trees and the crops. The orchard has fallen into disarray in recent years, but various houses in the village have planted single apple or peach trees in their kitchen gardens for family consumption.

Gathered Products

Herbaceous plants growing in the *changda* fields are weeded out in early spring and eaten as a curried vegetable with rice or cornmeal mush. Bamboo shoots are available for about three weeks during January high up in the village forest; throughout the summer monsoon, mushrooms and tree fungi appear in the village forest and are collected and cooked.

Meat is generally not available in Melemchi, although, in recent years, families have begun to store dried meat for special occasions or guests. As Tibetan Buddhists, Melemchi people are proscribed from killing animals, although not from eating meat. Some villages get around this problem by inviting non-Buddhists up from lower areas to slaughter for them. Melemchi is too isolated and, until recently, too poor to be able to do this. Therefore, meat is generally not available unless an animal dies of natural causes or is ritually sacrificed (usually a chicken) by the *bombo,* or shaman. At Losar in 1989, we were surprised to be served dried meat at a number of houses. It seems that in the previous fall, several families joined together and paid for the slaughter of several water buffalo so that everyone could have meat for Losar. This was quite different from our experience 25 years before. Then we lived in the village for over a year and ate meat only once, when we bought a wild pheasant that had been killed.

Some Melemchi men, despite their religion, have always been willing to hunt animals; most households own a gun, if only to salute the New Year, and periodically men in the village were provided with bullets and directed by the Chini Lama to shoot wild animals, both for meat and for musk. People also shot predators of their live-stock—wolves and leopards—and even monkeys or deer that raided their fields. No one viewed this as in deep conflict with Buddhist teachings. It seems the absence of meat in the diet of Melemchi people may be more pragmatic than moral. In 1971, no one had cash to pay for bullets, the guns were unreliable and thus wasteful of ammunition, and an animal killed and eaten was an animal that couldn't produce eggs or milk or manure. With their recent increase in wealth, more villagers are willing to pay for animals just to eat them, and dried meat is becoming more widely avail-able, although still not a regular part of the diet.

DIET

The traditional Melemchi diet, as we experienced it in 1971, was based on dairy products and grain. People with herds had seasonal access to butter and its byproducts: fresh cheese, dried cheese, and yogurt. Even those family members living in the vil-lage got frequent infusions of these products from their relatives. Corn and barley were supplemented with potatoes and radish; fresh vegetables were rare and available only seasonally. Fruit was not eaten. Everyone kept chickens, although eggs were treats and usually served to guests or sold to tourists. Butter tea (strong boiled Tibetan tea churned with butter and salt) was the staple beverage and every household had a pot ready throughout the day. Since cash was scarce, it was only used for items like tea, salt, mustard oil, cigarettes, and matches. No one had white sugar; it was a once-a-year treat at Losar to eat the molasses-like brown sugar, called *gur,* sprinkled over pounded rice. Rice was primarily served at festival meals when each member of the village was given a share of the rice.[6] No one ate meat—livestock and chickens were too valu-able as producers to use them for meat, and, as Buddhists, Melemchi people were unlikely to kill their own animals anyway. People did take the opportunity to eat their *zomo's* unwanted calves once they had died, or any other dead animal.

Twenty-five years later, the Melemchi diet has changed substantially. An infusion of cash from wage labor has enabled people to purchase coffee, tea, sugar, white flour, salad oil, dried noodles, and many other consumer items. A villager has opened a store selling these commodities, as well as mantles for kerosene lanterns, candles, and the occasional bottle of Fanta soda or beer. There are still many families who cannot afford such items, but many others can. Most people now eat rice every day; corn-meal or millet mush is forgotten and used only to make distilled liquor. Potatoes are still highly valued, but no one dries them anymore, and radishes are no longer planted. Most families have kitchen gardens, so in summer the vegetables eaten with rice are likely to be beans, squash, or cauliflower. Butter tea, or *pe cha,* is still the staple beverage, but special visitors are now offered cups of instant coffee with sugar and milk. Even some people in *gode* have a small can of milk powder to use in the months when the *zomo* aren't producing. Chickens are regularly killed for picnics; young people will get together and chip in to buy a chicken or two. Occasionally, groups of families join to purchase a buffalo for slaughter (by an outsider), dividing up the meat and drying it for later.

VILLAGE LIVESTOCK

At 2,600 meters, Melemchi is near the upper altitude limit for cows, is as high as water buffalo are comfortable, and is near the lower limit for *zomo*. In fact, the only livestock kept year-round in the village are water buffalo and cows; hybrids and yaks are brought down at certain times of year but spend very limited time, if any, in the village. The village livestock population is largest in summer months when most people come up from Tarke Tho, and smallest in winter when all but stall-fed animals are banished from the village to protect the wheat and *changda* crops.

People keep household livestock primarily for milk; in addition, these animals produce manure and calves, which can be sold. Bulls are kept for plowing. No one uses bovines for carrying loads in Yolmo; all carrying is done by people.

The village livestock constitute a fairly sizable biomass. In summer 1986, there were 120 cows, 53 buffalo, 5 sheep/goats, and 3 *zomo/pamu* in the village—a total of 181 animals. In winter 1989, the population dropped to 59 cows, 36 buffalo, 7 sheep/goats, and 4 *zomo/pamu*—a total of 106. However, since so many people take their livestock down to Tarke Tho in winter, it is more consistent to add in the 80 animals housed in Tarke Tho, and then the numbers are very close to summer 1986 figures—the winter total is 186. Feeding and caring for these animals requires work; buying them requires capital. Who undertakes these obligations and on what basis is a particular animal selected?

Cows

Cows have advantages over buffalo and zomo, especially for the elderly. Cows are smaller and therefore have smaller appetites. They eat less fodder when they are tied up and will graze on their own. They are less expensive to purchase, and they can live at lower altitudes than zomo or yak, so owners may stay year-round in the village, in their houses and near their fields. The drawback to cows is that they produce much less milk than either zomo or buffalo. Typical yields from a lowland cow after giving birth is only one or two *pullu*[7] per day, and this diminishes as the calf gets older. No one makes butter from cow's milk; it all goes to the calves or for daily consumption in tea. Cows are kept to produce household milk and especially calves for sale. They are the animal of choice of the elderly and the poor, as well as others who just prefer to manage cows.

Most of the cows in Melemchi were inexpensive, common lowland cattle— *palang,* as the villagers called them. However, several people in Melemchi had bought hybrid cows that cost much more money, were much larger, and were expected to produce high-quality calves. These cows, *zarshie palang* or Kathmandu cows, are the result of foreign development projects for improved productivity which crossed local cows with Jerseys and other European varieties. They are purchased south of Melemchi, nearer to Kathmandu. They are highly productive but cost a great deal. **(Mingmar TongTong** spent 3,000 rupees [$136] on his *zarshie palang* in Kulu in 1986. At the same time, he bought a local lowland cow for 800 rupees, or $36.) Unfortunately the improved cows did not thrive in Melemchi; they had huge appetites, and, despite being fed more fodder and expensive grain, most were wasting away in the high altitude. This is a good example of the difficulty in improving productivity through introducing new genotypes; domesticated livestock has been under long-term selection for fitness in local environmental conditions. Furthermore, even if there were an improved variety that could tolerate the local altitude and climate, these cows need extraordinary amounts and quality of food for optimal maintenance.

Water Buffalo

Water buffalo present a different set of advantages. They have higher milk production than cows, permitting the limited production of butter for household consumption. Their milk has a high fat content, and buffalo produce much greater quantities of milk than do cows. They also produce milk for over a year following the birth of their calf, much longer than cows. Villagers reported a range of 3–7 *pullu* per day, with most buffalo falling in the higher end of the range, even 1 year after the birth of their calf. Although buffalo butter is white rather than yellow and considered less tasty than *zomo* butter, it is fine for family consumption (which is primarily butter for making butter tea and heating *arak* liquor). Buffalo are much larger than cows and generally don't graze on their own. People reported that buffalo like to be stall-fed, which make them much more work for their owners. However, their larger body size yields more manure, and, because they are usually kept tied up, the manure is easily recovered. Water buffalo do cost more, and, notably, everyone who owned buffalo in Melemchi had access to money from India. Not only are they more expensive than a cow to buy, but also the stud fees are higher and the grass tax paid for buffalo is higher than for cows. However, buffalo calves are sold at a higher price. Male buffalo are kept until they are 3 years old, and then they are bred and sold for meat. People claim they are dangerous after this age, and no one had a fully adult male buffalo.

Buffalo seem to be preferred over cows if a person has the money and the labor to keep them in fodder. **Ibe Putti,** a woman in her 70s, told us she keeps two cows and their calves because "buffalo are too lazy to graze; they just stand in one spot and wait to be fed." When asked how much fodder his buffalo ate, one man answered: "As much as I can cut, that's how much they will eat." Fodder gathering is usually done by older children, especially boys, as well as women, who often go out in groups. One March afternoon, we encountered a group at the village edge on their way to get fodder: **Bibi,** 40 years old, and her teenage niece and nephew; two boys in their early 20s; **Ibe Kuisang Doma,** who is at least 50; and **Hrenzen,** a man in his 40s. Except for the trio, each person was from a different household with his or her own animals to feed. If boys are available, they can climb high in the oak trees to lop off sprigs, which are gathered up by their compatriots on the ground. When women or girls go out alone, they gather leaves from lower branches or shrubs or collect bundles of vines. Once collected, the fodder is arranged into a bundle, as much as 5 feet across, and tied together with rope. The rope is slipped over the gatherer's forehead and the bundle is worn home—a "walking bush."

In winter 1989, **Ibe Balmu's** two buffalo and one calf ate two huge loads of fodder every 3 days. **Hlakta** feeds two large basketfuls of fodder every day to his three buffalo, plus midday grazing when the fields are available. **Kuisang's** nine cows need only five or six baskets per day; cows need much less, both because they are smaller and because they often graze on their own. Still, Kuisang lives with her elderly sister, and if it weren't for her nephew **Kami,** who lives with them, she would be unable to keep the cows. Active though she is, she can't consistently cut and carry that much fodder. Village livestock is also fed dried hay, especially during winter. Cows in milk are fed salt to make them eat more food; it is believed salt makes their food taste better so they eat more and give more milk. And household livestock are also fed the mash left over from liquor distillation.

Most households have either cows or buffalo; those that have both usually have buffalo for milking and a pair of bulls for plowing. In summer 1986, more village households had cows than had buffalo or a combination: 17 households had cows only, 10 households had buffalo only, and 6 households had buffalo and a pair of bulls. The rest of the population had livestock in *gode* or no livestock.

Sheep and Goats

It was relatively uncommon for sheep and goats to be kept in the village, because they need to wander and cannot be herded easily. The few that are in the village are kept penned up for manure. They are sheared twice a year, and the wool is either sold or used by the household for weaving jackets. Goat hair is not processed, and neither sheep nor goat milk are consumed. Male goats and sheep are sold for slaughter in the fall. A few families send small numbers of sheep or goats out with *gode,* paying for their care.

Zomo/Yak

The only *zomo* living in the village are those few 1- or 2-year-olds born to household cows bred to yak. This is a recent cash-producing strategy of elderly householders who find the care of a young *zomo* no more demanding than a calf, while the sale price is much greater. It is difficult to arrange, since the cow must be brought to the yak for breeding, but a few families have had some small success. Occasionally, a *gode* herder brings a few adult *zomo* to the village for convenience, but none live year-round at this altitude. Yak come to Melemchi in the wintertime when the cow-yak herd is brought down to lower altitudes[8]; the cows are kept even lower for several months, while the yak may be tied and stall-fed in the village. This has been only moderately success-ful; many people believe that Melemchi village is too low for a yak to be healthy.

OTHER SUBSISTENCE ACTIVITIES

Household Maintenance

Melemchi households are neolocal; young couples traditionally live on their own in their *gode*. Only the youngest sons remain in the parental house when they marry, unless they have a *gode*. A number of elderly residents live alone because their chil-dren are in India or have died. All remain active; most have at least one head of household livestock that requires daily care and fodder, and all cook for themselves. In some cases, grandchildren stay with them for periods of time to assist with fetch-ing water and other chores, not to mention providing company.

In addition to agricultural tasks and care of livestock, a number of maintenance activities occupy all but the youngest members of a family. Daily tasks include food preparation and consumption, fetching water, gathering leaf litter in the forest, altar maintenance, and housecleaning. These primarily fall to women and children, although elderly bachelors take care of all of these themselves as well. Men tend to focus on more long-term maintenance tasks, such as maintaining a supply of fire-wood, building repair, and animal care and breeding. Woodcutting takes place during particular times of year when other work is slack, unless there is a big tree fall in the forest. An individual may stake a claim to any dead or fallen tree, so any loud crash in the forest produces a flurry of activity as people try to locate and claim the wood. The trees are cut inside the forest and brought down by basket loads. Girls and boys are engaged to bring the firewood from the forest edge to the houses, where it is stored underneath the second story to dry.

House building and repair also require wood. For this, men climb high onto adja-cent slopes, since the village forest is off-limits by edict of the Chini Lama. Once appropriate trees are located, the timbers are prepared on the spot so as to reduce the amount of weight transported back to the village. Because axes and *khukris* are used, there is a substantial waste of wood in preparing the floorboards, roof timbers, and shingles. Often several men are involved in carrying the timbers back to the village. In the dampness of summer, wooden parts of the houses rot and need replacement. Even under the best of circumstances, with wood fires burning in the house year-round, wooden shingles must be replaced frequently, and houses left empty for a year or two while the family is in India can literally fall down. Most houses need work every year, and the work is heavy so men share these tasks. This means men spend time not only on their own houses but also on other families' houses to repay the help they received for their own.

Other Activities

Liquor Production   In 1972, there was one distilling device in the village, which was borrowed whenever anyone had enough extra grain to make *arak*. It mostly saw use in preparing the liquor for village celebrations and rituals. People drink two kinds of alcoholic beverages in Melemchi: fermented grain beer called *balu* (made from corn or millet) and *arak,* which is the distilled form. Although Sherpa in Khumbu make rice beer, until very recently in Melemchi rice has been too expensive to eat regularly, let alone use for alcohol, so rice beer is never made in Melemchi.

Making *balu* is a fairly simple process. Grain is soaked and mixed with special yeast and sugar, then left in a large container in a warm spot in the dark to ferment for several weeks. We wrapped our New Year's *balu* in blankets to keep it warm in winter; once ready, it is diluted with water to taste and drunk cold. Distilled liquor, or *arak,* starts with *balu.* The *balu* is distilled in a pot–still composed of a large copper pot covered with a clay cylinder in which an earthenware jug is placed to catch the liquor. Above the jug, inside the cylinder, is a conical copper pot. The vapor from the heated mash cannot escape the cylinder; it rises until it hits the conical copper pot, which is filled with cold water. The cold surface causes the *arak* vapor to condense on it and drip into the jug below. *Arak* is generally drunk warm, although it is a matter of individual taste. Most households have a small metal frying pan that is used to heat *arak;* a large pat of butter is first melted, then the *arak* poured in and gently warmed. Unless you drink it quickly, the butter congeals around the top of your cup as it cools.

By the late 1980s, many residents owned a distillation apparatus and made liquor, some for sale and others just for their own consumption. Grain was plentiful, since so many people were away in India. Money from children or savings made it possible to buy large quantities of grain, and there was time and space (in the empty houses) to make the liquor. People seemed to be drinking much more; in fact, many elderly people with time on their hands consumed liquor daily.

Craft Production

Bamboo　In December, a number of the village men, along with men from villages much lower then Melemchi, head up into the higher part of the village forest to cut bamboo. The bamboo has firmed up after the summer growing season but is still supple and easy to handle. However, it is heavy and awkward to manage the pieces, which may be 8 to 10 feet long, so the men set up something like a slalom course in the forest, grab a bundle of cut green bamboo, and run downhill dragging it behind them, guided by the stakes set up to keep it on the trail. The weight of the bamboo and the steep slopes propel them quickly down the 620 meters to the village below. Once home, they immediately split it into strips, peel it, and leave it to dry. This will be used throughout the year to weave baskets for carrying items and mats to form the roofs of *gode* or sheds. Other things made of bamboo include household containers of all sorts and sizes, and even tiny muzzles for the *zomo* calves so they can't eat anything. Some men make items for sale, within the village and beyond, while others make just what they need for themselves as they need it.

Wood Carving　Traditionally, men carved much of the wood that appears in their houses: from cabinet work to furniture to implements. Wooden spoons, ladles, boxes, instruments—all are carved by Melemchi men using their *khukri* knives or wood-working tools. *Khukris* are also used to cut floorboards to size. Several men were known for making *damian,* the small, lutelike four-stringed instrument used for solo

Ghale Sherap Zangbu, age 60, weaves a doko *or carrying basket from bamboo collected high above Melem-chi. People carry loads as heavy as 45 to 50 kg in baskets on their backs, secured by a head strap. Ghale Sherap Zangbu has just returned to live permanently in his Melemchi house after spending his adult life working in India with frequent visits home. (1993)*

playing and singing. Carved from a single piece of wood, with a dragon head on the top or scroll, and decorations ranging from the zodiac to lotus blossoms on the back of the belly, *damian* have a skin head, strings made of gut, and a pick made from a sliver of bamboo. These instruments are sold both in the village and to tourists.

Weaving and Spinning   Sheep wool is spun by women using either a drop spindle or a hand spindle. Once the wool is cleaned, carded, and spun, it is used to weave the traditional jacket worn by Yolmo men and children. The wool is undyed; most jackets are the pale gray-brown color most common in Yolmo sheep, while the more coveted jackets are those made from dark brown wool. Women weave wool cloth using backstrap looms. The fabric is woven to be about 2 feet wide, and it has a dark brown wool selvage on both sides. Once woven, it is washed in boiling water and kneaded, usually by foot, until it thickens and felts up. The resulting fabric is only about 12 inches wide and is sewed together in strips along a central back seam up to the nape of the neck; sleeves are added along with an underarm seam and the jacket is finished—warm, waterproof, and even sheds dirt. Most women weave these for their own family, although they will also sell them to others. Although elderly residents in 1971 told us of wearing cloth made from stinging nettles (and such cloth is being made elsewhere today in Nepal, especially as part of development efforts in women's crafts), these jackets are the only fabric being produced in Melemchi. All other clothing is made outside the village.

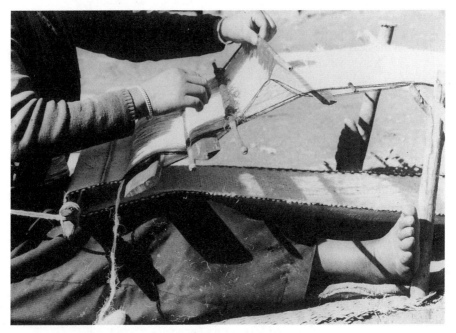

Woman weaving wool jacket fabric with a backstrap loom. (1986)

Nettle cloth is made by boiling nettle fiber (not the small species used for food, but the larger one, which produces good fiber) with ashes for about three hours. (The nettles are harvested after they grow and begin to turn dry. The fiber is peeled off the woody core and bundled; Melemchi people can trade the fiber today with Tamang down valley who will trade 3 *pathi* of corn or rice for 2 kg of nettle fiber.) The resulting material is kneaded with rice husks to make it soft and to separate out the dark flecks of bark. It is then dried for three days and spun into thread using a drop spindle. In Melemchi it was woven into cloth rather like burlap or used as the warp thread with wool as the woof. Nettle fibers can also be used to make rope. All of the rope in Melemchi today is made by twisting nettle fibers tightly together in a several-stage process. It is used for tying animals, carrying loads, and tying together parts of houses. Even with daily use, nettle rope lasts for at least a year.

Paper Production   One family in Melemchi has always made paper, both at the request of the Chini Lama for use in the *gomba* and for sale within the village. Paper is made from the bark of the daphne plant, a shrub with purple flowers that grows thickly along the edge of the village forest. (A different type of daphne, also at the village edge, with yellow flowers, is used to make rope.) Huge numbers of daphne shrubs must be cut down and stripped of their bark. The bark is cooked in large pots with ashes for many hours. A device similar to a butter churn is used to separate the fibers. A screen made of coarse nettle fibers is floated on the surface of a vat of water, and the pulp is spread out on the screen. The screen is then lifted and laid on a rack near the fire to dry. Once it is dry, the paper peels right off. Paper production requires tremendous amounts of wood, both for the long cooking process and to speed the drying process. In addition, it generates huge amounts of barkless daphne shrub wood, which is useless. Once Melemchi was incorporated within the national park, paper making ceased because it was illegal to cut flowering plants in the park.

DISCUSSION: MIDDLE MOUNTAIN AGRICULTURE—PRECIPITATING A CRISIS?

Hill farmers are highly dependent on forest products. Forests support hill agriculture directly by providing fodder and browse for livestock needed to plow fields or produce manure. Forests also provide leaves for composting, another form of fertilizer for fields that may support more than one crop per year. The firewood necessary for daily life and for the preparation of products for barter and sale (paper, butter, and cheese) also comes from forests, as does the timber for buildings, implements, and equipment in hill regions. A less obvious role played by mountain forests is serving as reservoirs of future agricultural land. Although it is possible to clear-cut a forest for a field, it is more common for forested areas to be slowly degraded in quality through use until they are finally transformed into fields. Forests also have a role in the maintenance of mountain slopes; there is some evidence that forested slopes are less likely to suffer mass wasting, as well as surface erosion. All in all, agropastoral subsistence in the Himalaya is predicated on access to forest.

During the early 1970s, several published reports suggested that population pressure on mountain environments in the Himalaya was resulting in unprecedented levels of deforestation and subsequent erosion (Eckholm, 1975; Sterling, 1976). Forest loss in Nepal was estimated at one-third of the total forest over 15 years (Eckholm, 1975). This concern became generalized and extended into a broad scenario of environmental disaster that encompassed the entire Himalaya, referred to as the Theory of Himalayan Environmental Degradation. As described in Ives and Messerli's book, *The Himalayan Dilemma* (1989), the scenario links environmental problems in the hills (population increase, deforestation, erosion, and landslides) to problems downslope in North India, where rivers carrying high sediment loads from the hills seasonally flood agricultural regions. Ultimate blame is placed on the hill farmer, who, in trying to eke out a subsistence for an ever-growing population, is believed to contribute to problems downstream by cutting down the forests at an unprecedented rate for firewood, fodder, and agricultural land. This results in local shortages of firewood, which then necessitates burning dung and so robs the mountain fields of their primary source of fertilizer. As the fields become less fertile, more forest is cut down for increasingly lower quality fields, and eventually the entire process results in slope instability and soil loss. Mountain soils carried in runoff silt up reservoirs, which shortens their lives; flooding increases on the Gangetic Plain; and islands form in the Bay of Bengal.

It is easy to see how this scenario developed such popularity. Anyone visiting the middle hills in Nepal can see that human population has outstripped the capacity of the local subsistence system, leaving most villages with several months of food shortage. Not only is food in short supply, but so is fuel. In many villages, people talk of traveling long distances to obtain daily firewood. Even in Melemchi, where population pressure has been alleviated by activities that keep people out of the village, the village boundaries are surrounded with oak trees so frequently lopped for fodder that they resemble leafy telephone poles. There is a crisis in the middle hills of the Himalaya.

However, it may be that the scenario is incorrect when it attributes the cause of the problem to burgeoning hill population. One argument against the model focuses on just when the deforestation occurred—was it the result of recent population explosions or did it precede it? Several researchers have pointed out that deforestation in the Himalaya has a long history, and in most instances it is due to state exploitation of forest resources, not local overuse. Evidence has been presented that in Nepal, the primary areas of forest loss since the 1950s were in the Tarai and the Siwaliks, not the Middle Mountains. Between 1964 and 1977, the Tarai lost 27.5% of its forest cover and the Siwaliks, 10.2%, while the forested area in the Middle Mountains was reduced by only 1.5% (Ives & Messerli, 1989). And deforestation goes much further back in history than the 1950s. Research focused in the Sindu Palchowk district of Nepal (Mahat et al., 1986),[9] shows that beginning with the regime of Prithvi Narayan Shah in 1769, forest was converted to agricultural fields at increasingly rapid rates due to the possibility for taxing agricultural land. The state could reap tax benefits from land used for agriculture; since the Tarai forests were being protected to keep out the British Raj, hill forest tracts provided good prospects for forest conversion. The forests of Sindu Palchowk were also under heavy pressure from the national government's iron ore smelting operations, which required charcoal for the smelting process. Iron ores were brought to Kathmandu for smelting, and forests of two nearby districts, including Sindu Palchowk, were sources of charcoal. Finally, in the 1930s, the Rana regime began to build palaces at an unprecedented rate, and timbers were taken from the regions outlying the Kathmandu Valley, which include the Sindu Palchowk district. By the mid-1900s, forest resources in this district were so depleted that the growing human population began to migrate to Sikkim, Darjeeling, and Assam (Mahat et al., 1986). Those forests lower in altitude and closer to Kathmandu were the more vulnerable; hence the area around Melemchi was spared. Similar scenarios have been documented elsewhere in the Himalaya—in India, timbers were taken in great numbers to build the Indian Railway system, the summer hill stations for the Raj, and for road construction (Tucker, 1987). It is clear that throughout recent history, at least, the demands of the state for forest resources to support itself have had great impact compared with the daily demands of hill populations for their subsistence needs.

Other aspects of the Theory of Himalayan Environmental Degradation are also being called into question. Data on the role of forest vegetation in reducing soil erosion or mass wasting are conflicting and far from clear. Some studies indicate that deforested areas are more prone to mass wasting, while others show that mass wasting results from geomorphological aspects of the mountains themselves (see Metz, 1989a). It is clear that more attention must be paid to the roles of human versus natural processes in slope problems; as young mountains, the Himalaya are subject to natural processes quite independent of human activity. The causal linkage between the obvious problems in the hills and the seasonal flooding and destruction on the Gangetic Plain is also far from established (Hamilton, 1987).

Some researchers are looking at the hill farmer as part of the solution, rather than the problem. Studies of indigenous systems for maintaining the landscape point to the positive role of local human intervention. Through active maintenance of terraces, traditional systems of protecting forests (Brower, 1991), and pursuit of a mixed and continually adjustable subsistence strategy, hill farmers have attempted to address local manifestations of environmental crises (in some cases successfully; for example, reclaiming major landslides [Ives, 1987]). We cannot, however, assume that all indigenous practices are beneficial. Systems of regulation that work well on a small scale may not be the appropriate response when new external pressures are introduced.

Middle hill villages are not "islands in the sky"; rather, they are linked in regional networks of environment, population, and resources. In the case of Melemchi, the region extends as far as North India, where wages earned by Melemchi villagers in construction projects (see Chapter 4) return to the village in the form of airtight stoves or metal roofs. On the ground level, there is a linkage between the management of upland forest catchments and the hydrology of the region, ultimately experienced by the farmers of the Gangetic Plain. But there are many other levels of cause and effect involved. Each hill farmer, no matter how isolated he or she may seem, makes choices that affect and are affected by choices and decisions being made far away from them. Hill villages are affected by state policies and local politics, as well as by their own decision-making processes. Poverty is at the root of the environmental crisis, but that must be addressed at levels above the village. Discussions of resource scarcity in the hills must be conducted in the context of a political-economic perspective that examines differential access to resources available in a country such as Nepal (see, for instance, Zurick, 1988; Metz, 1989a). Villages like Melemchi, which today still have access to forested zones above agricultural land, permit us to study the symbiotic relationships among agriculture, livestock, and forest in mountain subsistence systems at the local level. This is baseline information, helpful in understanding the interdependence of the Himalayan environmental region, but it is only part of the picture, which includes international politics and the world monetary system as well.

NOTES

[1] Even though they are Buddhists of the Nyingmapa sect and not the Gelugpa branch like the Dalai Lama, the image of His Holiness the Dalai Lama is found in many Melemchi households.

[2] In 1989, villagers asked us to make a sign in English forbidding bathing or washing clothes in the water tank. Apparently, European tourist trekkers had been bathing nude in the middle of the village in broad daylight in the rather small (and, one would have thought, obvious) village water supply. Village people were horrified and embarrassed, but no one wanted to risk losing their business by offending the tourists directly.

[3] A *guthi* is land donated by the king to a priest, in support of a temple. Melemchi is a *guthi* controlled by the Chini Lama of Boudhanath. This is discussed in detail in Chapter 5.

[4] The most ingenious one we saw was set up by a young boy during monsoon. He built a tiny waterwheel that hit against a string made of bamboo strips that stretched 100 meters through the fields to a yak bell. As the water in the little stream turned the wheel, it pulled on the string and the yak bell sounded.

[5] Potatoes are relatively recent in Nepal. Scholars estimate potatoes, originally from the New World, were introduced into Kathmandu, southern Tibet, and India by the mid-1800s (Stevens, 1993).

[6] It was customary for women to collect the share for each member of her household, except her husband, in a towel. She would than dole out handfuls of rice to her children (who put it in their hats to eat as they ran around with their friends) and take the rest home. Her husband would eat his rice on a plate with curry at the festival. I finally seized on this as a way to avoid the inevitable respiratory infections that plagued us after eating at festivals. I began bringing a towel to gatherings and collected our share of rice to take home to give to our elderly neighbor, Ibe Rike (cover photo).

[7] A *pullu* is a local liquid measurement corresponding to 1.5 pints.

[8] Chapter 7 discusses the new form of *gode* composed of cows and a yak, which was an experiment for some Melemchi herders beginning in the mid-1980s.

[9] Melemchi village is in the far northwestern corner of this district.

4 / External Migration

CIRCULAR MIGRATION IN MELEMCHI: WHO, WHAT, AND WHERE?

History of Circular Migration in Melemchi   In interviews in 1971, people referred to external migration as "going to Burma." Clearly some people had actually gone to Burma, but, in fact, their destinations included Gangtok, Sikkim, Assam, Bhutan, and a number of places in the eastern Indian state of Arunachal Pradesh, including the Buddhist pilgrimage site Bomdila (see Map 1.1). Jobs for Melemchi men and women included road building—mostly portering, or breaking up and carrying rocks and mud—and limited building construction; women with young children worked providing food, tea, home-distilled liquor, and ran tea shops or hotels where workers could sleep, socialize, and gamble. A few Melemchi sons or daughters found work with Westerners, either as an *ayah* (child caretaker) or in some other service job; none of these ever returned to Melemchi to live. And three Melemchi men enlisted in the Indian army Ghurka regiments; the first two villagers to go out of Nepal were two men who heard from other Yolmo villagers about army jobs shortly after World War II. Their stint was short; both fell ill, and neither stayed long enough to earn a pension. The third villager who had enlisted was killed in combat. Although he received death benefits, they were "eaten" on the way back to the village, and his young son received nothing. In our 1971 interviews, people agreed that work in the higher altitude areas was more difficult and harder to find, given the competition from Khumbu Sherpa as well as other Nepalese, but that the climate was more agreeable than the tropical climate of Assam, where Melemchi people became sick easily.

By 1986, more of the circular migrants were working in western India than in Arunachal Pradesh. While members of certain families continued to work and live in Bomdila or Darjeeling in the east, most families shifted to Kashmir (Ladakh) or the Himachal Pradesh valleys of Lahul, Spiti, and Kulu. The two most common locations were Ladakh and Riwalsar, which is a pilgrimage site at a lake where Guru Rinpoche meditated before he brought Buddhism to Tibet. All of these are high-altitude locales where road building and other types of construction are under way, either for tourists or the Indian army. Although jobs still revolve around construction and support services, fewer people are porters or carry and break rocks, while more supervise crews and provide skilled carpentry. Women with small children still provide food, drink, and lodging; unencumbered women do manual labor. And a number of families report that wives can also be put on the army payroll, even though they do not do any work for the army.

Who Migrates?   A few of the trips out of Nepal are unrelated to work—some people go on religious pilgrimages, while others visit relatives who have settled in India. There are also some people, mostly the very young or the very old, who have never left Melemchi. Those adults who have never gone explain that they don't want to go; they can't speak the language, they like the hard life in the village, and they don't want to do the kinds of labor required in India. However, by 1993, nearly everyone in Melemchi had some experience outside of Nepal.

Men, women, and children separate from their families in the village and go to India, or whole families go together. Men travel alone, escort groups of young relatives, or take their families. When women go, they travel with others. Women have been known to remain in their *gode* with the help of their older children, while husbands leave for periods of up to 2 years. Alternatively, one woman stayed in Ladakh, living in an army tent with two older children, while her husband returned to the village for 6 months to take care of maintenance tasks and look after younger children left in the care of grandparents. Children as young as 12 years old are sent by their parents, or beg to go, or run away and join up with villagers en route. Several families with relatives working in the east put their children in boarding school in Darjeeling, India, near their relatives. Other children are enrolled in school wherever their parents are working in India, or they may be left in the village to go to school there while their parents and siblings leave to work in India.

While men predominate in external migration, women are well represented: In a 28-month sample of all travel by Melemchi residents in and out of the village between May 1989 and September 1991,[1] men account for 65% and women for 35% of the people going to and returning from outside Nepal. However, women are much less likely than men to make the shorter trips to Kathmandu for shopping, building supplies, or visits. For trips between the village and Kathmandu during this period, men accounted for 82% and women for 18%.

Why Do They Migrate?   It is difficult to generalize about the temporal patterning of circular migration in this village, because it is a flexible strategy which responds to individual needs. This is demonstrated by the reasons people give for returning to the village. During the sample period of 28 months, people offered a variety of reasons for returning to Melemchi from India:

- To attend or perform funerary rites for a family member who died either in India or in the village.
- To visit family members—children who had been left behind, elderly parents, or wife and children.
- To accompany someone else back to the village. These cases involved trips to fetch and return elderly villagers who made brief trips to India to visit their children.
- To attend to business. This included making payments on house purchases, purchasing land or houses both in the village and in Kathmandu, or getting citizenship papers. By 1989, it had become important to have citizenship documents, as well as land-ownership documents. Getting citizenship papers requires a journey to the district headquarters in Chautara, two days' walk from Melemchi.
- To attend the reconsecration of the village *gomba* (temple) in April 1991.

- To escape problems in India. In fall 1989, 10 people returned from Ladakh due to the escalating violence between Buddhists and Moslems there, and 2 villagers who set out for India were turned back. Yolmo people were not directly involved in the trouble, but the curfews and curtailment of activity had an effect on their lives and livelihoods. Several of those who came home in fall 1989 returned to Ladakh after 3 months, but others waited in Melemchi until March before returning. The only 2 who didn't return were 2 18-year-old boys who remained in the village, 1 to help his family and the other to look for work in the trekking industry.
- To resume their village lives—build a house, farm, purchase a herd, and so forth. This might be a permanent stay or only a year or two while they maintain their property and participate in village affairs.

Patterns of Migration   Given the variety of reasons for returning to the village, and the different circumstances involved in each, it is obvious that the timing of arrivals and departures and the length of stay in the village depends on why they returned. Those who return to conduct funerary rites come throughout the year, and their stay tends to be short. Likewise, those coming for a special event will time their visit accordingly. Business trips also tend to be brief, perhaps because they usually include men who have the greatest earning potential and some job security in India. Others of Melemchi's circular migrants follow a seasonal pattern. They schedule their visits home around work seasons, which are related to climate. In the high-altitude locales where Melemchi villagers seek employment, work shuts down in the winter when it is too cold and inclement. Therefore, those who want to spend part of a year in the village and have no other limitations return home in November or December and leave again for India in March or May. (Those working in Ladakh tend to return to India around March, while those going to Spiti, where high passes close off the valleys until late spring, leave in May.) This schedule brings them home for Losar, or New Year, which is a time for family visiting and celebration. Another important festival in the Yolmo region is Nara, which is held each July. Every village member must contribute money and labor to this weeklong festival (or arrange for family members to contribute their share). Yet the migration sample indicates that people do not generally travel home for Nara. In the 28-month migration sample, there is no record of external migration in June, July, and August. In fact, during these months, the village population is at its lowest—both because large numbers are in India taking advantage of peak availability of high-altitude work and because the herds are highest and farthest from the village. Anyone returning from India and present at Nara has come well in advance of the summer months. This has nothing to do with the difficulty of travel during these wet monsoon months; in fact, people travel frequently between the village and Kathmandu during this period.

Obviously, for some in this village, the pattern of circular migration is related to the seasonal availability of work. Workers planning to visit Melemchi during the year will tend to return home for the winter and go back to India in late spring. But a substantial number of migrants do not come home every year. And for many others, their trips home are in response to a variety of other considerations, so they come and go in all months except summer. There is only one generalization that can be made about the amount of time spent in and out of the village: Those who traveled in or out of the village to India during the 28-month sample period spent shorter periods of time in the village than they did away. But a longer range view is necessary to see how this fits into a lifetime pattern.

ALTERNATIVES TO MIGRATION

In order to understand the particular form migration takes in this village, it is necessary to consider the historical context of migration and just what options are available to residents. People have been leaving Melemchi to spend time in India and nearby countries since the early 1950s. Earlier migrations were more likely to be permanent; since 1971, few people have left Melemchi for good. However, in the 1970s and 1980s, circular migration over short- and long-term cycles became increasingly common. What other options exist for these people to obtain both a subsistence and cash income, and how and why is this important?

Since the 1950s, people farmed in this village, producing grain for food and for barter. In addition, they practiced transhumant pastoralism with herds of *zomo* and sheep, which produce cash, through butter sales, as well as commodities for subsistence and barter. Today, those who herd may herd *zomo* or cows with a yak—an exclusively cash-producing strategy in which the hybrid offspring *(zomo)* are sold and all dairy products go into their production (see Chapter 7). Another economic option is to buy fields and rent them to tenant farmers; many householders in this village own rice fields down in the lower valley and receive both rice and cash in return. A fourth option is trade; Sherpas elsewhere are well known as traders between Tibet and Nepal and India, but such activity has been limited in Yolmo. Before 1950, some men from Yolmo engaged in sheep trading with Tibet. They traveled to Tibet, accompanied by a large entourage of friends and porters loaded with copper or silver coins, bought 400 to 500 sheep, and brought them back down the Trisuli Valley to Kathmandu for the Dassai festival. These trips, and this option, were limited to the wealthiest men of the Yolmo Valley, and only one or two Melemchi men participated before the border was closed. Now there are no real opportunities for trade for these villagers.

A fifth option, which is important in the Solu-Khumbu region, is employment as a trekking guide or within the tourist industry. It is odd that despite Yolmo's proximity and ties to Kathmandu, this has never developed in Yolmo. Today there are only a handful of young men from Yolmo who work in the trekking business. In Melemchi, it is explained that although they are novices, they don't want to start at the bottom—as porters—yet they lack the skills in English to get jobs as guides. Going to India is viewed as more desirable and more lucrative.

BENEFITS AND COSTS OF MIGRATION

Considering the options, it appears that migration to India for wage labor, especially some form of circular migration, can provide cash income, which otherwise is only available to those wealthy enough to be absentee landlords of rice fields or those with a *gode*. Not all young men inherit *gode,* and today *gode* life is increasingly viewed as extremely hard and isolated; those with *gode* are interested in selling them. Circular migration can be the source of funds to purchase rice fields or herds, which will then provide cash for the future. Over a lifetime, families use circulation to provide income as well as investment.

But migration has costs. Many families have at least one member who has died in India from diseases such as measles, malaria, tuberculosis, or skin infections or from alcoholism or from injuries suffered while working. There are terrible stories of injuries and deaths of Melemchi people from rock slides, blasting accidents, and industrial accidents. The work is backbreaking in many cases—especially for those poorest and least skilled. Some never return to India, claiming the work was too hard. Others, while acknowledging that the workday of 6 to 8 hours is an improvement over the village work schedule, point out that leisure time has its downside: gambling, excessive alcohol consumption, and fighting are endemic in the work camps. An additional cost borne by these circular migrants is separation of families. Depending on circumstances in the work setting, families may leave one or more children with their paternal grandparents in the village—sometimes leaving the youngest and taking those who can work and sometimes leaving the oldest so that they can help their grandparents and taking the baby. The children left behind do not appear to thrive—in a number of cases, these children are exceptionally small in stature and appear to be several years younger than their chronological age. They wait to be retrieved by their parents. In some cases they suffer additional trauma through the death of a parent away in India. Two preadolescent brothers were left in the village with aged grandparents while their mother and father worked in India. The return of their father brought tremendous relief and joy to the boys, only to be shattered by the news that their mother had died in India. Only a few weeks after he had returned to Melemchi, their father left again for India without them. As a single parent, he couldn't manage the boys in India until they are grown. Marriages also suffer, as spouses are separated for long periods of time, and women are left with the complete burden for subsistence and child care. Many of these women wait long periods for husbands who return empty-handed; this can result in permanent disruption of families.

Not everyone makes money in India; some men and women are better able to capitalize on opportunities in India than are others, which has become increasingly a source of disparity in wealth in the village. One man said that he comes home periodically because if he stays away too long, people will say he couldn't make any money there and is afraid to come home. This is because these jobs are not secure, there is ample opportunity to gamble away earnings, and living costs are high. The rule of thumb is that it requires two people to work in order to have any money to bring home—a man alone cannot do any more than maintain himself there. Even those with skills are not guaranteed an adequate living. A skilled carpenter returned to Melemchi in the winter of 1989 with his wife and four small children. It was clear that they brought no money home with them. They were too late to have planted their fields, and, although they owned a house, they were totally dependent on relatives for food and assistance. He earned good money in India because of his skills, but he had been the sole support for his family there because his wife had to look after the children, so there was no savings to bring home.

Since circular migration has both costs and benefits, how do people maximize the benefits? It appears that they do this by maintaining flexibility in their options, just as they do in adapting to the middle-altitude zone in which they live. By moving back and forth, in differing combinations, maintaining households and attachments in the village while taking advantage of opportunities in India, these families are able to adapt to a rapidly changing political and economic situation. One of the difficulties in this analysis was that few patterns emerge—it is impossible to generate predictable relationships among family size, situation, and migration patterns. This is supported by my experiences in Melemchi over the years. In interview after interview, people would predict when they would next go to India, or who in their family would go or not go, and, in fact, it would turn out quite differently. In 1986, one 40-year-old man who had a *zomo gode* for 20 years said that, despite the fact that all his siblings had gone to India, he had no interest in going—that people who went to India were soft. In 1989, he said that he would like to sell the *gode* and have his family live in the village. On April 4, 1990, he and his wife did sell their *gode,* but instead of living in the village, they left for Bomdila with their two daughters and a son, staying for 6.5 months before returning to their house in Melemchi.

WHY CIRCULAR MIGRATION? WHY COME BACK?

One of the most notable things about this group of circular migrants is the importance of maintaining ties with the village—despite its reputation amongst even its residents as something of a "backwater." Very few Melemchi people who marry in India marry people from outside Yolmo, and most of the marriages are either within the village or with members of Yolmo villages that traditionally provide marriage partners. Marriages between Yolmo people are arranged and transacted in India, with elder brothers or male relatives making arrangements and standing in for the parents who are home in Melemchi. All householders retain and fulfill their tax and labor obligations to the village and the *gomba,* even while they are in India for several years. They pay up when they return, they make good on their labor commitments, or they arrange with relatives to do it for them. One of the incentives for maintaining these obligations is the strong sentiment expressed for having death rituals performed in the village *gomba.* Only those who are members can have this done, and although these people go to places in India where they are near Buddhist ritual centers and among people who share their Tibetan Buddhist culture, they want to be cremated in the village.

DISCUSSION: CIRCULAR MIGRATION—ONE OPTION
FOR HIMALAYAN HILL PEOPLE

Migration, or population movement, can take several forms. It can be permanent, in the sense that people intentionally leave to change their place of residence; it can be long term, in which migrants may stay away for long periods of time (2 or 3 years or more); or it can be temporary or circular, in which migrants move back and forth between their residence and their work site in a seasonal or nonseasonal pattern, remaining away for shorter periods of time. Circular migrants move with no intention of long-term or permanent change in residence. It is "a lifecourse strategy which both recognizes the long-term nature of some mobility strategies, and which provides a framework for understanding unfolding sequences of migration" (Bailey & Hane, 1995, p. 173). In Melemchi, migration is generally a temporary or circular phenomenon—people leave for wage labor in India and return to their residences in Melemchi. This is *external* migration, or migration beyond national boundaries. In a country where *internal* migration is increasingly common, and in some cases encouraged (e.g., government resettlement efforts to resettle hill people in the Nepal Tarai), the villagers of Melemchi are focused on opportunities outside Nepal. Since 1971, only a few Melemchi residents have resettled within Nepal—all moved to an urban life in the Kathmandu Valley. More common, individuals leave the village to seek wage labor in India, Assam, Sikkim, Bhutan, Burma, and most recently Taiwan with the intention of returning to Melemchi or, in the past 5 years, the Kathmandu Valley. They pay their Nepalese taxes and take care of their local obligations in Melemchi while they are away. Money earned in India comes back to Nepal to be used to buy land, build houses, or sustain lives in Nepal—usually in the village or in the Yolmo Valley, although, as noted above, sometimes in Kathmandu. These circular migrants do not, as a rule, purchase property in India.

Population movement within Nepal and between Nepal and India is not a recent phenomenon. Historically, the major migration of Nepalese citizens to India began with British and Indian army recruitment as early as 1816 (Elahi & Sultana, 1985). As soldiers remained in India and brought their families, Nepalese enclaves arose in such places as Bakloh, Dharamsala, Dhera Dun, Darjeeling, and Shillong (Elahi & Sultana, 1985). Later incentives for Nepalese migration came from tea plantations, railway yards, and mines in Assam and West Bengal (Elahi & Sultana, 1985) and the reclamation of land for rice fields in Assam (Shrestha, 1985). By 1961, an estimated 498,000 Nepalese lived in India (Shrestha, 1985). There were also periodic migrations of Nepalese back to Nepal. Events such as the discharge of soldiers after World Wars I and II, the enactment of the Burmese Citizenship Act of 1964, and recurring unrest involving local indigenous populations in Assam, Burma, and Sikkim have all precipitated the return of Nepalese citizens to Nepal (Kansaker, 1985). These returned migrants added to the strain of rising population in the hills and land tenure systems that favor the wealthy over the poor. The eradication of malaria in the Nepal Tarai in 1958 (Kansaker, 1985) made it possible for resettlement efforts to focus there; prior to this, emigration to India was the only option for hill people to escape the economic conditions in the hills (Shrestha, 1985). Beginning in 1956, a series of land resettlement programs designed to shift the population from the hills to areas of the Tarai were initiated by the government of Nepal (Kansaker, 1985). These government-sponsored programs for internal migration were ultimately of limited effectiveness (Kansaker, 1985; Shrestha, 1990), but they highlight the emphasis on internal migration rather than external migration as a response to economic and ecological problems in the hills. In the mid-1950s, 90% (195,300) of the absentee population of Nepal were external migrants to India, while by 1981 that percentage dropped to 68% (Shrestha, 1993); the increase in internal migrants no doubt reflected the government efforts to resettle people in the Tarai.

For hill people, circular migration outside the country for wage labor is an alternative to resettlement or migration. It is not unique to Melemchi. R. English, writing about the formation of the Himalayan state, says, "Since the land reforms of the 1960's, hill-men continue to supplement family incomes by taking work for years at a time as road builders and timber cutters in Sikkim, Bhutan and in India's western Himalayan districts" (1985, p. 76). Circulation is not a search for land, such as the internal migration from the hills to the Tarai. Rather it provides an infusion of capital that can sustain households in the hills without requiring the upheaval of permanent relocation. This can be the case even if the family is landless. For example, pastoralism does not require fields, so people leave Melemchi and return with cash for a herd. Although all land in the village is now owned, land continues to be bought and sold. Those without agricultural land can also lease it from villagers, who receive half of the harvest. With the number of residents away in India increasing, there does not seem to be a shortage of land to farm for those wishing to remain in the village and grow crops.

Circular migration has been viewed as a response to economic factors, in particular as a response to modernization and capitalist penetration into market societies. In the case of internal migration in Nepal, Nanda Shrestha, in his book *Landlessness and Migration in Nepal* (1990), attributes the rise in migration to internal and external governmental policies that maintain and propagate the cycle of underdevelopment that spawns migration in the first place. For Melemchi migrants, economic factors are certainly salient; the need for cash and the desire to participate in a market economy have been growing. However, there are cultural and behavioral norms as well that predispose Melemchi and other Yolmo residents to circular external migration, as opposed to other types. For residents of Melemchi, periodic absences from home have long been a part of their lifestyle. As transhumant agropastoralists, their families pursue simultaneous multiple subsistence activities in different locales, shifting family members and jobs over an annual cycle between pastures and village residences and fields. Yolmo pastoralists also take periodic trips north, south, and east of the region to buy and sell animals and products. Usually, these trips are undertaken by men, with women left to maintain the herd and care for the children. Additionally, some residents own property outside of the village and spend time away from the village tending to affairs elsewhere. Wealthy pastoralists have traditionally invested profits from butter sales in rice fields down valley that are farmed by tenant farmers; periodically, landlords must check on the crops and harvest. The sheep trade with Tibet prior to 1950 involved being away for up to 4 weeks at a time once a year; young men and women traveled with the traders, for the adventure as well as the possibilities for small business, just as they now accompany adults going to India. Therefore, for Melemchi residents, the absence of individuals within the family that comes from circulation for wage labor in India is accommodated just as these other activities have always been accommodated. It is a Himalayan example of what has been referred to elsewhere as "livelihood mobility," or the idea that "human mobility is fundamental to livelihood" (Richardson, 1982, p. 35).

Circular migration is not a simple seasonal deployment of men who move back and forth between their village and a work site. Rather, it encompasses complex arrangements of family members through time and space between two countries, in

Ghale Pemba Gyalbu, age 53, and his family in front of their zomo gode *in 1989. Later that year, he sold his* gode, *and by 1992 his six oldest children were in Ladakh, India, and he bought a village house, where he lived with his wife and three youngest children.*

response to a variety of needs and opportunities that shift all the time.[2] It involves individual and household information networks; people go where others already are or have been, and they use social networks to obtain work. Finally, there are cultural and environmental determinants to Melemchi circulation. They seek work in high-altitude regions where there are Tibetan Buddhist populations present. Aside from Ladakh in Kashmir (a culturally homogenous Tibetan Buddhist region), the other two most common locales for Melemchi migrants are the Buddhist pilgrimage site of Riwalsar in the western Himalaya and the eastern Himalayan pilgrimage site of Bomdila. Culturally comfortable, they are also physiologically adjusted to the high thin air at these places and are used to physical labor.

The recent increase in numbers of Melemchi people in India is only an exaggeration of a pattern that has time depth in this region. Since the 1950s at least, migration has been interdigitated with pastoralism in Melemchi and other villages in Yolmo. In interviews in 1971, people described their lives as periods spent in India alternating with periods of transhumant herding. Family after family explained how they sold their herd (or lost it to disease or predators), went to India, returned with cash, bought another *gode,* and so on. Decisions about the timing of these cycles depends on age and number of children, age and health of livestock, personal interest by both husband and wife in each subsistence choice, and opportunity. These decisions are highly idiosyncratic and represent choices based on numerous factors that differ from family to family and within a family over time. Interestingly, one of the common factors precipitating a move, either to go or return from India, is the death of a family member. Both men and women told of selling herds when their spouses died; a single adult cannot manage a transhumant large animal herd. In these cases, the herd was sold and the remaining family set off for India. Likewise, the death of a spouse or, more common, a child brought families back to the village, sometimes permanently.

What we see today in Melemchi is the same pattern as seen in 1971, differing only in scale. Herding still provides an excellent opportunity for cash income, albeit in a difficult and isolated context. At present, young people perceive that migration produces cash more easily than herding. Furthermore, they believe there are additional tangible and intangible benefits from contact with the world beyond the Yolmo region. However, as a strategy, migration depends on political events and situations that are beyond their control and that change rapidly. As their travels take them beyond the Buddhist pilgrimage sites and relatively familiar Hindi language into Taiwan and South Korea (see Chapter 7), they will leave the more familiar role of high-altitude laborers embedded in a similar cultural context and enter the world of the guest laborer and factory worker. It remains to be seen whether the close ties to the village that have sustained the circular migrations in the 20th century will remain in the 21st as new labor opportunities and longer distances take Melemchi residents farther and further from home.

NOTES

[1] The data on migration in Melemchi comes from two sources: (a) interviews with village residents in 1971, 1986, and 1989, in which they recalled their migration histories over their lifetimes, and (b) a 28-month sample in which all trips between the village and the Kathmandu Valley or India were recorded. The latter sample was collected with the assistance of a village member, **Nogabu**, who lives in Bhoudanath and who, as our trained research assistant, recorded these events daily between May 1989 and September 1991. Both types of data have their limitations, but together they give a fairly representative picture of patterns of movement in and out of the village over the past 20-plus years.

[2] The following is an example of a single family's migration history; while no single history is typical, it exemplifies the complexity of circular migration. **Tashi** and **Maya** married at the age of 17; he was not given a *gode,* although, as the youngest son, he received his parent's house in the village. During the first 18 years of their marriage they were circular migrants, first in Assam and later in Ladakh, which they preferred because of the climate and the fact that in Ladakh they were living among Tibetan speakers. In 1986, they had been in Melemchi for the previous 6 years, farming but not herding; Tashi had been back and forth to Ladakh a few times. In May 1986, Tashi and their 17-year-old son and 15-year-old daughter left for Ladakh, leaving Maya with their two boys, ages 11 and 9 years. In November 1986, the family was reunited in Melemchi. In March 1987, both parents and the two oldest children went to Ladakh, while the two boys stayed with their maternal grandmother (the paternal grandparents are deceased). In November 1988, father, mother, and older daughter returned, leaving the 19-year-old boy to watch over the family's possessions and tent in Ladakh. In May 1989, the parents and older daughter went back to Ladakh. The parents came back to Melemchi in December 1989 to see their younger sons and took them back to Ladakh in March 1990. In the fall of 1990, the older daughter and the middle son (now 15) were left behind in Ladakh, while Tashi, Maya, and their oldest and youngest sons returned, in part to arrange a marriage for the oldest son. A previous attempt had been made on his behalf while he was away in India. By the summer of 1992, the parents were in Ladakh with their daughter and their youngest son; the eldest son, following three failed attempts at marriage, was working in Taiwan in a garment factory; and the middle son had run away from his family and was working in northern India—whereabouts unknown. Tashi and Maya say that within 2 years they will return permanently to Melemchi and live off the proceeds of their investments and savings.

This truncated family history omits many details—in particular, why they moved each time and what each member was doing in each place—but it does illustrate the complex coordination of family members over a relatively brief period and the interrelationship of these individuals' movements and activities.

5 / Social, Political, and Religious Organization

MELEMCHI: A *GUTHI* OF THE CHINI LAMA

One of the most puzzling aspects of life in Melemchi for us in 1971 was its relationship to the Chini Lama of Boudhanath. We experienced a situation that seemed to us akin to the feudalism of medieval Europe or even in Tibet of the previous century. The Chini Lama never came to Melemchi while we lived there; we saw him only in his home at the Boudhanath stupa in the Kathmandu Valley. However, in the village we were very much aware of his existence, both through stories that people told us and through the ways in which people behaved. People were both fearful and resentful of his power and authority while simultaneously concerned with carrying out their obligations and duties as citizens within his Melemchi *guthi*.

The earliest known record of Melemchi village is in 1859, when the Melemchi *guthi* was transferred by the Rana prime minister, Jang Bahadur Rana, to a Chinese lama, Dai Fo Ching (Clarke, 1980a). A *guthi* is a tax-exempt, inheritable endowment of land for religious purposes. It is a form of *birta* land grant, used in Nepal as early as the 5th century as a form of patronage from the king or ruler. In a *birta* endowment, the recipient gains certain rights over the land he is given: "the right to share in the produce of the land; the right to the proceeds of miscellaneous taxes and levies collected from the inhabitants of the lands ... ; the right to exact unpaid labour on a compulsory basis from those inhabitants, and the right to dispense justice" in areas of civil and criminal law (Regmi, 1978, 36). In the case of a *guthi,* the land is given in support of a temple; for example, the land in the village of Melemchi was given to Dai Fo Ching (and his descendants) for support of the Melemchi temple and himself. Because *guthi* are associated with holy places, merit accrues both to the ruler who gives the *guthi* and to the *guthiyar,* the receiver.

There are several stories about how the first Chini Lama (Dai Fo Ching) came to receive the temple lands for Melemchi. According to his descendants, the village was given for service to the king during the Nepal-Tibet War of 1855–56. Their story describes the Chini Lama as living in a cave at the Hindu pilgrimage site of Pashupatinath, in the Kathmandu Valley. The king[1] heard that there was a Tibetan lama living nearby and sent for him. The king asked him to spy for Nepal in Tibet, where he went twice in this capacity. When Nepal won the war, the king offered him the position as head lama for the stupa at Boudhanath, one of Buddhism's most sacred pilgrimage sites, which is in the Kathmandu Valley, as well as its surrounding land as a *guthi*. He also gave him the village and temple at Melemchi as a second *guthi,* to serve as a mountain retreat from the summer heat of Kathmandu. The fact that Melemchi is surrounded by important sacred Buddhist places and shrines no doubt enhanced the value of the gift.

Villagers tell a different version. Their versions emphasize the original lowly status of Dai Fo Ching, some element of trickery in his being named *guthiyar,* and acknowledgment of the true founding hereditary lama lineage for Melemchi, the Hlalungba clan. In one version, Dai Fo Ching was actually the king's horse servant who accompanied the king to the village on a tax collection mission. When the hereditary Hlalungba lama couldn't pay the 1-rupee tax, Dai Fo Ching stepped forward with 1 rupee and was given the village. Since that time, all taxes have been paid to him and his descendants. Another version holds that two Hlalungba brothers fought over who would succeed to power, took their case before the king, and so irritated the king that he gave it instead to Dai Fo Ching. (Arguments over succession have a long and healthy history in Nepal.) A third version has the village available to whoever could pay the 1-rupee tax.[2] The Hlalungba lamas who were the incumbents had no money, while a lama (Lama Nakpu) in Kathmandu paid the rupee and then gave the village to his penniless and propertyless cousin, Dai Fo Ching. (One informant said that Dai Fo Ching was actually very wealthy but masqueraded as a poor man; he wore rags but had sewed gold coins into their lining.)

However it happened, from the middle 1800s to the present day, Melemchi village and Boudhanath stupa have both been *guthi* under the control of the Chini Lama and his descendants. They do not have a local clan affiliation, since they are not from Yolmo. The local Hlalungba lama clan is acknowledged by everyone to be the lineage lamas of the village. In the absence of the Chini Lama or his representative, they preside over rituals in Melemchi. However, they have no power or authority over other matters and either live as farmers in the village or else have migrated to India. Men and boys of the Hlalungba clan use the title "Lama" with their given names and all learn to read Tibetan and receive some training from their lama relatives.

There have been five Chini Lamas, including Dai Fo Ching,[3] and they have always lived in Boudhanath and governed Melemchi from afar. When we first lived in Melemchi in 1971, we dealt with Purna Badzura Lama, the third Chini Lama. (Unless specified otherwise, reference in this chapter to the Chini Lama refers to him.) The Chini Lama and members of his family have spent time in Melemchi, more so in the past than in recent years. At least three houses in Melemchi have been built by members of the third Chini Lama's family for their use when visiting in summer when the annual taxes are collected. One 70-year-old woman remembers that when she was a little girl, the third Chini Lama grew potatoes and *changda* in the village. He also had a *zomo gode,* appropriating a village girl to live with him in the *gode*. She later married a Melemchi man and had her own family. The last time the third Chini Lama stayed in the village was in 1973, when he arrived by helicopter and stayed 4 or 5 months. In his younger days, villagers recount his arrival on horseback or being carried on a palanquin. He was an excellent walker who would walk except near villages, where he would be carried for appearance's sake. Since his death in 1982, family representatives have come to the village only sporadically.

The *guthiyar* has the obligation to maintain the temple, or *gomba,* and the land that supports it and its activities. This is a trust in perpetuity, handed down within the lineage to the oldest son upon the death of the father (principle of primogeniture). He also has certain rights attached to this land. The Chini Lama gives permission for people to live in Melemchi and to be on the taxpayer *(tal)* list. He also allocates the land for house lots and wheat or *changda* fields. (Potato fields may be dug anywhere someone wants to dig them.) In the past, it was not difficult to obtain land in Melemchi. Anyone could clear an unused piece of village land, demarcate the boundaries with stones, and go down to Boudhanath to ask the Chini Lama for it. The Chini Lama would issue a piece of paper stating that the land belonged to the person. Once planted on, it became that person's land, even to sell if desired, although the Chini Lama retained ultimate rights of approval.

The Chini Lama also adjudicates disputes and dispenses justice. Petitions are brought before him or his family representative during the annual visit to collect taxes in the first month of the year (in July). All sides present their arguments, and he makes his dispensation. At other times of the year, messages are taken back and forth between Melemchi and Boudhanath, and his decisions are conveyed by village messengers. Occasionally, he sends a family member up to work out a solution or deliver a decision. One older man complained in 1993 that in the old days, Chini Lama maintained order in the village by coming up each year to handle small cases and disputes. Now members of the family don't come, and there isn't any mechanism for control except the police or the village headmen *(goba),* who have little experience in independent decision making.

The obligations of the *guthiyar* are matched by a reciprocal set of obligations for Melemchi residents. They must pay annual taxes for their fields in the form of grain—4 *pathi*[4] of barley for large fields and less for smaller fields. Each *zomo gode* must pay the Chini Lama 1 *dharni*[5] of butter. Those with village livestock must pay 5 rupees[6] winter grass tax for each buffalo, 3 rupees for each cow, and 2 rupees for each goat or sheep; if livestock aren't moved out of the village in summer, there is a 25 rupee summer grass tax levied as well. In addition, services are required of each household. Each family must carry loads to Boudhanath twice per year for free or pay a porter to do it for them. When any member of the Chini Lama family is in residence, the villagers must provide services, food, wood, and water without compensation. Any maintenance and renovation to the *gomba* is done with free village labor; the Chini Lama family provides the materials and specialized labor (e.g., muralists). When the Chini Lama family builds or rebuilds its houses in Melemchi, each village household must contribute labor as well as local materials. In 1972, a 67-year-old widow complained that she had to produce four floorboards, carry rocks for the walls, and help to build the Chini Lama's house; in addition, each four houses were also responsible for one ceiling board. Since she was too old, she had to pay someone to do everything for her. It was the third time in her lifetime that his house had been rebuilt; in the old days, she resented the fact that his girlfriends were allowed to get away with no work, while she carried her baby on her front and a load of rocks on her back.

These are the formal obligations of residents toward their *guthiyar;* informally, they are expected to do whatever is asked; there is no recourse short of appealing directly to the king, and if they incur the disfavor of the Chini Lama, he can banish them from the village.

Over the years, men from the Chini Lama family have taken Melemchi women as wives, mistresses, and servants for themselves as well as others. Those women who married into his family are viewed as having gone up in status; they are able to assist their families in the village from their position of relative power in Boudhanath. Even those who were appropriated only for a temporary period, to be a servant, to maintain a *gode,* or to be a mistress, use it as a source of status, although there are exceptions. In one instance we witnessed in 1972, a Melemchi girl of 20 was pro-cured for an American man involved in business deals with the third Chini Lama. A message came to the village calling her to Boudhanath; unable to refuse, she went to be his "servant." Two weeks later, she was sent back.

Given the centrality of the *gomba* in defining village membership, in setting the ritual calendar of the village, and in the political and social life of the village, the Chini Lama is in a powerful position with regard to village resources. In Boudhanath, he controls extremely valuable real estate in the Kathmandu Valley, not to speak of the benefits accruing to the head lama of such an important Buddhist pilgrimage site. The possibility for abuse of power is great under such circumstances, and it seems that especially the third Chini Lama was given great latitude in his activities by the government. In 1971, we experienced a feudal landlord with a virtual free hand in running the affairs of Melemchi. Villagers had no recourse against his control— over land, over residence, and over taxes—except to leave. People described life under him, and his predecessor, as so difficult that many villagers ran away. They were asked to build his houses, work for him all summer when he was in the vil-lage, endanger their lives climbing in high places to find crystals for him to sell, and provide all his household needs. Debts to the Chini Lama family, both from borrow-ing and from gambling, were cited as another reason for people running away from Melemchi to live permanently in India.

When the third Chini Lama died in 1982, the eldest of his three sons, Meme Babu, succeeded him. Meme Babu was not well at the time and had little interest in continuing the family tradition of strong involvement in village affairs. His tenure coincided with many of the changes to be described in this book, which left the vil-lagers more capable of and interested in self-governance. With the death of Meme Babu in 1989, his son Andare took charge, but at the same time democracy and rep-resentative government was established within the kingdom of Nepal. As the fifth Chini Lama, Andare Lama had no stomach for the "iron hand" of his grandfather; nor does the present government recognize the *guthi* status of Melemchi in the traditional sense. Andare and his brothers see the role of the Chini Lama family in the village as enabling and assisting villagers to govern themselves, as well as bringing devel-opment and improvements to the village, and have abandoned the feudal posture that characterized their family for over 100 years.

Mahesh Regmi, in his history of the relationship between peasants and landlords in 19th-century Nepal (Regmi, 1978), points out that the idea that the state exercises "full sovereign authority over all areas and all classes of people" didn't apply to 19th-century Nepal; in fact, the state granted those powers to the landowning elite, through *birta* and *guthi* grants, among others. Tenants on such lands had no contact with the central government at all; they were totally under the control of their landlords. These landlords combined political control with economic exploitation. They took the proceeds from their peasants with no obligation to provide compensation or benefits. Most were absentee landlords who did not cultivate the land themselves. In addition to the rights specified above, they also were entitled to collect gifts from their tenants; in other words, the peasants constituted a "blank check" for the landlords. Ultimately, the Ranas realized that this system did not serve the needs of the state, which had ceded most rights of revenue to the landlords. Bit by bit, laws were changed and land grants were altered. However, many *guthi* were overlooked, producing such late-20th-century anachronisms as the Chini Lama and his relationship with the people of Melemchi. The Chini Lama is not a unique figure, when viewed from a historical perspective; but the fact that this relationship survived so late into the 20th century helps us understand the magnitude of the changes that occurred in Melemchi village, as opposed to other Yolmo villages, over the past 30 years.

THE *GOMBA:* CENTER OF A YOLMO TEMPLE-VILLAGE

The *gomba,* or temple, is central to the civic and religious life of Yolmo villages. Now that it is a large cement structure, it can be seen even from across the valley, but its role has not changed at all from the time when it was a small wood-shingled building with crumbling mud walls. Members of the *gomba* are the citizens of the village. The political, social, and religious life of the village is intertwined as men hold simultaneously the positions of priest, taxpayer, and landlord.

Political System

Tal (Member of the Guthi Trust)   Male household heads who own land are members of the *guthi* trust, which maintains the village temple. They are *tal*[7] and, as such, are obligated to support the *gomba* and the ceremonial life it sponsors. *Tal* pay tax to the *gomba* proportional to the size of their land holdings. In addition, *tal* incur an obligation for the four major village festivals each year: to contribute labor and grain, and on a rotating basis, serve as *chiba* or principle donor for a single year's ritual cycle. Finally, the village headmen, or *goba,* are chosen from among the *tal* list. In 1993, there were 84 *tal* in Melemchi.

Anyone may live in Melemchi, participate in the ritual cycle, and even have their funeral rites performed at the *gomba*. However, *tal* membership is reserved for those who own land. In theory, this includes women, who may buy land in Melemchi, but since women don't inherit land, they are not viewed as owners.[8] Widows appear on the *tal* list but are only holding onto the membership for their son. Once a son has inherited his father's land or buys land, he can pay the fees and become *tal*. Sons who have not formally separated from their parents, regardless of their age, are represented by their father's membership. If a son builds on his father's land while his father is alive, he may request to be on the *tal* list by offering 100 rupees and *shalgar* (a bottle of liquor anointed with dabs of butter). This puts him on the list, but since he doesn't actually own land, he is an auxiliary *tal* member and won't be responsible for serving as principle donor.

Each new *tal* puts up a prayer flag and pole in front of his house or in front of the *gomba* if he doesn't own a house. These poles are at least 6 meters high, made from a hemlock tree trunk, with a long white strip of fabric inked with Tibetan prayers from a wooden prayer block attached along its length. As the wind blows the flag, the prayers on it accumulate merit for the household. The flags are taken down and replaced every New Year, accompanied by blessings of butter daubed on the pole, *shalgar* offerings, and a celebratory blank gunshot.

The *tal* list has grown along with the population in Melemchi. In 1971, there were 48 *tal;* by 1986, there were 72; and by 1993 there were 84 men on the real *tal* list. An additional 22 householders were signed up but did not own land and were thus spared the taxation. In Melemchi, any man who owns land or wants to buy land goes first to the village *goba,* pays the fee, and then asks the Chini Lama for approval. No one, in living memory, has been refused. Village membership, then, is open; even as recently as 1993, new *tal* were being added from outside the village. Almost 14% of the *tal* list in 1993 were men who came from other villages to Melemchi and bought land, often brothers and sons or fathers following relatives.

Guthi taxes and contributions are based on the size of one's fields. There are four categories of *tal* corresponding to the four sizes of landholdings: *ghima,* the largest fields; *dagar,* whose fields are half the size; *tsaudi ni,* whose fields are a quarter of the size; and *tsaudi chi,* an eighth. Annual grain tax for *ghima* is 4 *pathi* of grain; for *dagar,* 2 *pathi;* for *tsaudi ni,* 1 *pathi;* and for *tsaudi chi,* 1/2 *pathi.* Grain tax is collected once a year in mid-July.[9] Now that the Chini Lama doesn't come up to Melemchi anymore, it is collected by the village *goba.* Those who do not pay in a particular year, or who are not able to be present or represented in the village on tax day (perhaps because they are at high pasture or in India), are permitted to pay at a later date. However, those who refuse to pay are reported to the Chini Lama, and it is believed he will take away their land.

This belief is not unfounded. We, ourselves, experienced his attempts to banish us from the village in 1972. Near the end of our stay, we paid a social call on him in Boudhanath and were asked for gifts: bullets and money, to be specific. Having neither, we thought we had skillfully extricated ourselves from the situation, but after we returned to Melemchi, a messenger from the Chini Lama arrived to tell us that we were banished from the village and were to leave immediately. He also said that anyone in the village who worked for us after this announcement would be treated similarly. We decided to remain and complete our work, secure in the knowledge that we were protected by our research permits and we had done nothing wrong. Unlike the villagers, we knew that it would be very difficult for him to follow through on his threats to us; for them, however, it was a different matter. The very poor family who had been supplying us with wood stopped helping us, but our other friends helped us finish up our work. So far as we know, no sanctions were actually invoked

Bringing grain to pay the guthi *tax. Ibe Balmu is getting ready to measure her* changda *into the copper* pathi *measure in the foreground; Ibe Pema stands behind her with her grain sack on her back. Ibe Karmu, whose* changda *was a matter of dispute, turns to speak to someone behind her as she sips* arak *(liquor).*

against anyone in Melemchi following our visit, but, in fact, it is impossible for us to be aware of subtle repercussions. In some ways, we were accorded privilege and status just as the Chini Lama was by Melemchi villagers. They had little understanding and no experience of who we were, and thus we were treated like privileged guests most of the time.[10]

Goba *(Village Men Who Govern)*   The village is governed by *goba,* who act on the authority and approval of the Chini Lama. The *goba* have local autonomy but are answerable to the Chini Lama; thus, there is frequent traffic between Melemchi and Boudhanath for consultations and messages. The Chini Lama designates six or seven men as *goba* so that if one or two are in India, there will be enough to make decisions. Once he has been named a *goba,* that person remains in the position until he quits. **Urgen** was the youngest son and only 13 years old when his powerful father died; 1 year later the Chini Lama told him he must replace his father as *goba,* and he has been one for the past 43 years. The *goba* are responsible for supervising the rituals in the *gomba,* including funerals and all ritual cycle events, collecting land tax and conveying it to the Chini Lama, looking after visitors at the Nara festival, adjudicating arguments locally and representing cases before the Chini Lama, collecting wood and grass tax, and regulating forest use. The *goba* act as a unit; all are called when their services are needed. However, they don't all think alike, and there is considerable tension among the group and within the village concerning the decisions and the behavior of the *goba.* Accusations, counter–accusations, and private complaints of favoritism, graft, and manipulation of the Chini Lama abound. In recent years, with the death of the powerful third Chini Lama and the shift in Nepal to a democratic form of government, the role of the *goba* has become even more contested (see Chapter 7).

Lamas (Lay Priests)   *Tal* signifies membership and citizenship in the *guthi;* since the *guthi* exists to support the *gomba,* religious and civic responsibilities of *tal* are united in these Yolmo temple-villages. Without monasteries and monastically trained lamas, the village men themselves are the priests of the temple, or lamas; hence, people living in Yolmo villages are called Lama people. *Tal* are responsible for maintaining the temple and for seeing that the annual ritual cycle is carried out. Each Yolmo temple-village varies in the form this takes depending on its particular history and circumstance. In Melemchi, the existence of two lama lineages—the founding Hlalungba lineage and the Chini Lama lineage—one present and one absentee, one poor and one powerful—complicates the articulation of ritual and civil authority and participation. Furthermore, recent social change involving the intrusion of the central government and the diminishment of the power of Chini Lama has made the situation even more complex over the period represented by this research. Regardless, every *tal* is considered a lama, although only those Melemchi men and boys who read Tibetan books ever use that as a surname (e.g., Kami Lama and Dorje Lama). As a title, "lama" is reserved in Melemchi for male members of the village lama lineage, the Hlalungba clan; they are always referred to as "Lama"—Lama Pruba, Lama Tenzing, Lama Partop.

It is the obligation of each *tal* to donate to and participate in the ritual cycle, which includes four annual festivals, three of which take place at the *gomba.* Based on the size of their landholdings, *tal* provide grain, butter, and money for each of the festivals. For example, the four *ghima* landholders provide 25 *pathi* of *changda* each year for the Nara festival alone. In addition, *tal* are on a rotating list to serve as principle donor and host, or *chiba,* for one year's cycle. Now that the *tal* list has grown so large, this should be a once-in-a-lifetime experience for each householder. However, close relatives also help the *chiba chikla* ("one man does all"), so most people are involved several times during their lifetimes. Regardless how often one does it, it is a huge responsibility which is anticipated well in advance and dominates life decisions in the preceding years. *Chiba* plan to return from India for at least the year in which it is their turn. **Mingmar,** the *chiba* in 1972, built an addition onto his house for cooking all the food and liquor; in later years, he transformed this into a lodge for trekkers. **Dogyal,** the 1986 *chiba,* sold his *zomo gode* so he could spend time in the village preparing all the liquor, as well as doing the other duties. Once his duty was completed, he resumed herding, although he never went back to *zomo* herding. He herded cows instead.

Tal are also responsible for the performance of all Buddhist rituals associated with the *gomba;* these include funerals and death rites, the Yum ritual, as well as the annual religious cycle events. In this sense, *tal* are all priests (or lamas). Their participation is according to their abilities and knowledge. Members of the founding lama lineage (the Hlalungba clan) are the ritual leaders, unless the Chini Lama or a monastery-trained lama is available. Hlalungba men were all trained as children to read Tibetan and later receive additional religious tutelage from their relatives or from periods spent in a monastery. At present, there are two Hlalungba lineages in Melemchi. One descends from the Hlalungba lama who lost Melemchi to the Chini Lama; the other is a recently arrived family from another village.

The great grandson of the Hlalungba founders of the village, **Lama Pruba,** was the only male member of his family in residence in Melemchi in 1972. As the youngest son, he would inherit his father's land and house; his older brothers, who

Lama Pruba, age 20, prepares the colored butter decorations (karken) *that decorate the Nara* torma. *The butter is worked underwater so it will keep its shape. Lama Pruba was the oldest representative of the Hlalungba lama lineage living in Melemchi in 1972. (1972)*

stood above him in the lama lineage hierarchy, were in India.[11] In 1973, Lama Pruba married and had two sons and a daughter. Despite his age, he was respected for his knowledge of Tibetan texts and rituals and was an authoritative voice in the village concerning the performance of rituals. Sacred funerary items, such as the hat *(kiawa ringa),* the ladle, and the funeral *thanka* (sacred painting) of the god Chenrezi were kept at his house. He sat just below the Chini Lama family member at rituals. However, his accidental death at the age of 24 left the village without a Hlalungba lama resident. Since then, the village has brought in his uncles, who are also Hlalungba clan from Nagote, a nearby village, when a Tibetan lama is needed and no one from Boudhanath could come. Lama Pruba's young sons, meanwhile, have been tutored in Nagote as well as in Boudhanath. At the Nara festival in 1989, Lama Pruba's 14-year-old son, **Lama Tenzing,** sat just below his uncle from Nagote as the rituals were performed for 3 days in the *gomba,* although he was able to perform only minor roles. Finally, in 1993, Lama Pruba's older brother, **Lama Tsering,** returned from India to visit, and the villagers implored him to remain in the village and be the presiding lama. They promised him the revenue from the tourist campsite behind the *gomba,* since Hlalungba lamas don't have *gode;* as lamas, they don't want to kill *zomo,* even passively. He agreed, allowing young Lama Tenzing to leave for India with his wife and new baby.

Those village men who are not Hlalungba provide the manpower and assistance at village Buddhist rituals. Those who can read Tibetan read the texts, sitting in rank order based on the amount of religious training they have had. Those who can't read Tibetan help prepare the ritual *torma* (figures made of barley dough) and food, care for the ritual objects, play instruments at appropriate points in the ritual, and serve as hosts for all ritual events. Without resident lamas, it is the village men, or *tal,* who hold and transmit the knowledge necessary to keep the ritual cycle going. They begin participating as young boys and by the time they reach manhood have the ability to organize and run the events themselves, although not the religious authority to preside. Buddhist rituals in Melemchi are marked by argument, discussion, participation, and involvement by everyone. People wander in and out, holding and sharing opinions on how well things are going throughout the celebration. The proper performance of the rituals does not necessarily require solemnity or quiet, as we in the West expect. There are crucial elements, however, and efficacy of the ritual requires observance of those elements. At Nara in 1972, there was a thunderstorm on the second night and several of the large *torma* fell down; although they were patched up, it was considered very inauspicious. Ibe Rike fell the next day and was badly bruised; it was considered a fulfillment of the bad luck. Tupa Tsezhu was performed twice in the summer of 1986 because there wasn't enough food the first time; everyone was unhappy about it, so it was done again.

Religious Cycle

The Melemchi religious calendar is organized around six major events: Losar (Tibetan New Year in January or February), Dabla Pangdi (March), Yum (Buddha's birthday in April), Nara (early to mid-July), Tupa Tsezhu (August), Dassai (September/October), and Nyungne (October). Losar, a family celebration, is conducted strictly in the home or *gode*. Dabla Pangdi, Tupa Tsezhu, Nara, and Dassai are the four festivals assigned each year as the responsibility of a single householder, the *chiba chickla;* this household head, aided by his family, performs as principal donor and host for all four events. Different *chiba* are assigned for the Yum and Nyungne rituals.

Households and clans may sponsor rituals for themselves at other times during the year. For example, a householder may sponsor a Yum in his house. Unlike the annual Yum in which the Tibetan texts from the *gomba* are carried around the village boundaries by men and women of the village, in the case of a private Yum, villagers gather to bring the texts from the *gomba* to the house of the sponsor. As the texts are carried, drums and horns accompany them along with incense and prayers. Once inside, the books are read by literate villagers—simultaneously—for four days. The sight and sound are remarkable—individuals sit wrapped in blankets, slumped over the wide rectangular pages, murmuring the text aloud while pots of tea are carried around to keep everyone going. Participation of any kind in Buddhist rituals involves the accumulation of merit *(sonam)*. In this case, those who carry the books and those who read the books receive merit; as sponsor, the householder and family who pay for the reading (food, drink, and donations) earn the most merit from the event.

Losar   Losar is the celebration of Tibetan New Year in late January and early February by families in their homes or *gode*. There is a special meal for the family on the first day, when a new prayer flag is erected and blessed. The house is decorated with auspicious designs of flour and water. The following days involve a series of visits among a subset of families for two special meals each day: first, a plate of potato curry with fried wheat-dough twists, rice-flour flat bread, and *chiura* (pounded rice) sprinkled with *gur* (molasses sugar). This ritual food must be eaten in each of the households with whom Losar is being celebrated. Children and relatives will travel to the *gode* of a family for one day of Losar to receive and eat the special food. A second meal of curry and rice follows late in the day.

Losar can last from 5 to 9 days. In 1972, only six households lived in Melemchi during winter, so everyone shared Losar together and it lasted 7 days (we held the last party). As the village grew, it became difficult for everyone to attend everyone else's party; the food, which is prepared on the first day, was often spoiled by the time everyone had circulated. Now, families decide ahead of time and join together, either with neighbors or clan members, for celebrations that tend to last about a week. As special guests and friends of many in the village, John and I found ourselves on a never-ending circuit of Losar meals. No matter how long after Losar it was, any visit to a household with whom we hadn't spent Losar produced the ceremonial blessing of rice-flour flat breads and wheat twists, carefully saved from previous parties. Fortunately, the weather is cold at that time of year, so things spoil slowly, and we could always follow the custom of "freshening up" the bread by throwing it on the embers of the fire to soften and recook it. In 1989, in a weak and very cold moment, I wondered aloud why we had come to the field in January; why hadn't we waited until March when it was warmer? John responded, "Imagine how old the Losar food would have been by March!"

Losar (Tibetan New Year), 1972. A Tibetan lama on meditation retreat in Melemchi blesses the plates of food offerings by dipping a hemlock twig into the liquor offerings (shalgar) *brought by each family and praying as he shakes a few drops in each of the four directions. Dabs of butter bless the pots of liquor as well as the plates containing fried rice-flour flat bread, pounded rice, and molasses sugar.*

Yum   Yum is a village festival held in April in honor of Buddha's birthday. All the Tibetan Buddhist texts are taken out of the *gomba* and carried around the village boundaries.

Dabla Pangdi (or Dal Pangdi)   This is a festival held in early spring to ensure the material prosperity of each household. After reading a Buddhist text in the *gomba,* the village men march around an effigy made of straw from the previous year's harvest and branches from the incense plant, brandishing *khukris* anointed with dabs of butter, and throwing *tsampa* flour on themselves and the effigy. Eventually it is set on fire, and people take bundles of the burning figure to their own houses to purify and protect them with the burning incense. Dabla Pangdi in Melemchi is a ritual to protect the new harvest from hail; the figure holds sprigs of the new barley crop and is said to represent the demon who brings hail.[12] Regardless of its function, Dabla Pangdi ends, as most religious rites do in Melemchi, with a communal meal and dancing and singing in the *gomba.*

Nara   Nara is a 5-day festival in midsummer honoring the founders of the *gomba.* It is the most important festival in the region, and every temple-village in Yolmo celebrates Nara, although not all at the same time or for the same duration. In Melemchi:

Dabla Pangdi ritual, 1972. Dawa Sonam and other Melemchi men march around an effigy stuffed with straw and incense, throwing tsampa *flour and brandishing* khukri *knives.*

- On day 1, the *torma* are made in the *gomba* by the men and boys who will read the books;[13] the ceremonial braided, fried wheat breads *(zhero* and *pai)* are made by the rest of the men and boys in a vacant house. Once the *torma* are made and placed on the altar, there is a 1-hour ceremony in which texts are read. The entire village is fed a rice meal.
- On days 2 and 3, Nara texts are read in the *gomba,* while *zhero* and *pai* continue to be made. Everyone is fed two meals in the *gomba* annex. If there are many people around, there will be dancing on the 2nd night. There is always dancing on night 3 when relatives from other villages come to participate in Nara.
- On day 4, the bread is distributed. Everyone dresses in their nicest clothes and goes to the *gomba* to be blessed and to receive their share of the Nara bread. Names are called out, and people go forward to receive a set number of small *(pai)* and large *(zhero)* breads, according to their status in the village. Everyone stays at the *gomba* for a meal and dancing late into the night.
- On day 5, the lama gives people a blessing called *wang,* made from barley flour, sugar, and butter, for good health and a long life. Then the *torma* are broken up and given to specific people to take home. One *torma* goes to the household of the lineage lama; another goes to the *chiba,* and so forth. Everyone eats a small piece of *torma (chilap)* for its ritual benefits, while the rest of the *torma,* by now covered in mold, are fed to the livestock.

Tupa Tsezhu   This is a 1-day festival held at the Guru Rinpoche cave (Tupu) at the top of the village on the 4th day *(tsezhu)* of the 6th lunar month *(tupa)* and is a

The Nara altar, 1972. In the front is an offering of liquor (shalgar), *bowls of water, and piles of* changda *with incense sticks and flowers. Behind are the* torma, *many small conical dough statues in front with uncolored butter decorations and five large* torma *behind decorated with colored butter. In the far back are the statues that are in the* gomba *all year.*

Tibetan Buddhist celebration that occurs throughout the Himalayan region. Local belief is that it commemorates the end of Guru Rinpoche's meditation there. Offerings are brought to the cave, where a lama presides over the reading of a single text. Supplicants perform grand prostrations and receive a blessing, which is eaten. Outside, the villagers socialize, drink, and dance; a meal follows late in the day.

Dassai   Dassai is a Hindu festival celebrated throughout Nepal in October. It commemorates the triumph of the goddess Durga over the evil demons and is celebrated with masked dances and animal sacrifices that take place over many days. In Melemchi, Dassai is celebrated as a Buddhist counterbalance to the killing and blood sacrifices. For 5 days, prayers are read in the *gomba,* people avoid eating meat, and there is no celebration. On the 1st day, the lamas make the *torma* just as they do for Nara. On the days following, they read the books. People come from Nagote and Kangyul villages; everyone is fed twice a day, once at noon and once at 9 p.m. No one dances or sings secular songs; the elderly spend the evenings in the *gomba* in prayer. On the last day, the head lama gives everyone *natchha,* which is a blessing in the form of a paste made from milk, raw rice, egg, and red powder daubed onto the forehead.

Nyungne   Nyungne lasts for 4 days and is another ritual of atonement observed by lamas and elderly men and women. For the first 3 days, they meditate and pray in

*Men take a break to eat rice during the preparation of the braided breads for Nara.
Both* zhero *(square braided bread) and* pai *(individual twists) are shaped from
wheat flour dough which is then fried in butter and kept for distribution when Nara
is over. (1972)*

the small sanctuary upstairs in the *gomba*. On the 4th day, which has a full moon,
everyone from the village gathers in the *gomba* for prayers, grand prostrations, and
then a feast with dancing.

Functions of Ritual

In certain respects, these religious celebrations are similar: They involve the
reading of Buddhist texts and the performance of Buddhist rituals, literate village
men conduct the rites, the village gathers once and sometimes twice per day for a

meal of rice and dancing, and, with the exception of Tupa Tsezhu, they center at the *gomba*. Participation is expected of everyone. Membership in the village requires donations of raw materials (food or money to buy it) and labor commensurate with ability to provide, and it results in benefits that accrue to both the village as a whole and individuals *(sonam* or merit). It is considered unlucky if these rituals are not performed. Melemchi villagers take pride in pointing out that Melemchi has always celebrated Nara, while Tarke Ghyang missed several years when there were big fights among the priests. The ritual cycle makes explicit the obligations and status of each member of the village. Every *tal* is responsible for providing his share, regardless whether he is in residence or not. Each *tal* share is based on the size of landholdings. People with larger fields are expected to contribute more than people with small fields. When a household head is *chiba,* he must collect all the donations from the village *tal,* seek donations from relatives and friends throughout the region, prepare all the food and drink served at the festivals, and arrange for the materials for the *torma* and the ritual breads. This can be substantial, as figures from Nara in 1972 show: Frying the breads requires 60 kg of butter, with an additional 12 kg needed for the butter decorations *(karken)* for the *torma*. Additional butter must be provided to keep all the butter lamps lit for 5 days, including one huge lamp that burns at Nara. The Nara *torma* use 25 *pathi* of barley flour. Each day as many as 100 people will be fed two rice meals, which include two heaping plates of rice, plus yogurt, potato curry, and *daal* (stewed lentils) or other vegetable. Hundreds of kilograms of grain are needed to prepare the liquor, which is made months in advance by the *chiba* and his family. The extraordinary output required of a *chiba* in the year of his turn is balanced by the cumulative contributions of everyone else. When asked how much being the *chiba* had cost him, one man replied he could not say since he gives so much in donations each year and as *chiba* received so much in donations from everyone else. Melemchi people who attend other Nara celebrations in Yolmo will donate to them, just as others assist with Melemchi's.

The ritual cycle in Melemchi provides links between this community and others, even beyond Yolmo. Several of the celebrations are pan-Tibetan Buddhist—Tupa Tsezhu is celebrated in Solu Khumbu, in Langtang, and by Tibetans in exile in many parts of the world, while Yum and Nyungne are also found elsewhere. Melemchi sends baskets of the ceremonial Nara bread down to the Kathmandu Valley to the king of Nepal as well as the Chini Lama and his family. And *tal* in India may return home or at least send money to ensure their share of the merit gained by the performance of these Buddhist rituals each year in Melemchi.

Funerary Rites

The rituals surrounding death are Buddhist. When someone dies, drums are beaten and incense is burned, permitting villages throughout the valley to learn the news and see where it occurred. On more than one occasion, we awoke to hear funeral drums; standing on our porch, we scanned the valley for smoke and joined in the speculation over who had died. In Melemchi, a lama always comes up from Nagote to perform the rites, which may follow just one day after the death. However, there is

Ibe Kenji's funeral. Inside her house, her body sits wrapped in white cloth, wearing a five-sided cardboard hat and red shawl. Above her left shoulder hangs the thanka *(painting) of Chenrezi; in front are butter lamps brought by neighbors. The body remains in the house for one or two days while friends, neighbors, and the lamas pray before it is cremated. (1986)*

some sentiment for prolonging the start of the rites, since it is believed that the more people who come to eat and drink, the easier it is for the dead soul to leave the village. The prayer flag of the deceased is taken down and cut into pieces; it becomes the poles for the litter *(Tom)* in which the body is carried to the cremation ground. The body is placed in a seated position, knees bent and bound tightly to the chest; a rupee is placed in the mouth; and then the body is wrapped tightly in a white sheet. Adorned in red robes and a pasteboard hat of five sides *(kyowa ringa)*,[14] the body is placed in a large copper pot, or *sang,* next to the house altar. Butter lamps are lit and prayers read.

Before cremation, the body is taken outside and placed in the litter, copper pan and all. The litter is decorated with four scarves or *kata,* one on each corner for the four directions: white for east, red for south, black for west, and blue for north. The procession begins with men carrying drums, cymbals, and the *thanka* painting of the god Chenrezi, followed by the lama, who holds a bell and one end of a long white cloth *(lamna)* about a meter wide and 20 meters long that is held by men in the procession. The litter, suspended on poles and carried on the shoulders of four men, follows the white cloth, with the villagers walking alongside and behind, singing death prayers *(mani)*. The procession circumnambulates[15] the *gomba* and then stops for a few minutes while more *mani* are sung by the crowd of mourners. Finally, the procession leaves for the burning site, where they circumnambulate the *Tursa,* or stone crematorium, and then begin to disassemble the litter, whose wood will fuel the fire. The body is lifted out of the copper pan and placed on top of the *Tursa,* which is lined with fresh fir boughs. A special ladle *(narchyang)* is filled with items referred to as *chinse* (including rice, butter, millet, wheat with the bran left on [*dzau*], and a broom). These items are ladled into the *Tursa* as the body is cremated to provide for the afterlife. Women and children leave before the pyre is lit and go to the *gomba,* where they continue to sing; the men stay behind to tend the fire and chant the prayers.

There are two ceremonies held after the initial funerary rites. A *nebar* is held at the *gomba* within 7 weeks of the death. An effigy of the dead person is made, and a sign is placed on the effigy telling the name and date of death. As part of the ceremony, the lama reads the paper and burns it. The second ceremony, called *gewa,* is held later. A *gewa* lasts 2 days and may or may not involve a second *nebar* at the family's discretion. On day 1, *torma* are made and village people gather to eat an evening meal. On day 2, everyone comes from the village to the *gomba* during the day, eats lunch there, and sings funeral songs. At night, they continue to sing and dance, with a break for an evening meal. After midnight, the singing and dancing becomes secular. The following day the *torma* are broken up and given to the person who sponsored the *gewa,* usually a close relative. Most Melemchi people who die in India have a *gewa* performed in the village. In part, this is reciprocity for the hospitality extended in life. As one informant put it, "Because I ate many people's *gewa,* I must pay back at my own." In the case of someone who dies and is cremated in India, some piece of bone from their cremation, or some personal item of clothing, is put into the effigy for their *gewa* held in Melemchi.

CLANS AND MARRIAGE

Melemchi Clans

The temple-villages of Yolmo were founded by nonmonastic lamas who emigrated from Tibet, most likely the region around Kyirong just to the northwest of Yolmo. These founders intermarried with the Tibeto-Burmese-speaking Tamang from the lower elevations, so today Yolmo culture bears a resemblance both to the Tibetan and Tamang cultures. Like the Tamang, Melemchi people are a patrilineal, patrilocal society organized around clans. Clans are exogamous groups based on stipulated descent, as opposed to lineages in which descent can be demonstrated. For example, approximately 30% of Melemchi villagers in 1993 were Shangba; each individual can trace his or her lineage back several generations, but no single lineage can account for every Shangba. At some point, we just don't know how they are all related. Therefore, they are a clan rather than a lineage.

Clarke (1980c) reports that there are 14 Yolmo clans, 5 of which are found in Melemchi:

> **Shangba:** The largest clan, Shangba, represents 32% of the 1971 census and 29% of the 1993 census. Shangba believe they came as a clan from Kyirong, Tibet. Most living

Shangba in Melemchi can trace their lineage back to Meme Gokapu, who had 10 sons and 2 daughters. One son moved to Tarke Ghyang and another was sterile; the 8 others are responsible for most of the Shangba who live in Melemchi today.

Ghale: The next largest clan, Ghale, represents 30% of the 1971 census and 26% of the 1993 census. The Ghale clan claims to be from Barpa in the east; its members say they are related to the Ghale kings in west Nepal, and a few even maintain some dietary prohibitions shared with the western Ghale. The Ghale lineage in Melemchi can be traced back to Meme Tole, whose son, Zamgyal, had two sons: Pasang and Namgyal. Pasang had eight children, four of whom were sons: Lemba, Purba, Mingur, and Tewong (the youngest born in 1904). Namgyal had six children, three of whom were sons: Norbu, Wangdi, and Pema.

Chiawa: The Chiawa represent 23% of the 1971 census and 20% of the 1993 census. There are four Chiawa lineages in Melemchi today; it is not clear how they intersect with one another in the past.

Waiba: This clan represents 9% of the 1971 census and 13.5% of the 1993 census. Two Waiba brothers, Pambar and Tarpu, link most of the village Waiba together. Pambar's eldest son, Tsongdu, was born in 1905.

Hlalungba: One percent of the 1971 census and 3% of the 1993 census are Hlalungba. Hlalungba in Melemchi trace their ancestry back to Lama Pruba's great-grandfather, the man who lost the village to the Chini Lama.[16]

In Melemchi, clans are dispersed throughout the village. While there is a tendency for sons to live adjacent to fathers, this is a recent phenomenon and probably reflects the lack of open space in the village, which has grown in recent years. The Ghale clan joins together for one period in the year at Namsangsang pasture, a large high pasture north of Melemchi. Although other pastures may be shared by clan members, in these cases it results from brothers who inherit shared access to family pastures over generations. While there are no clan deities, there are some rituals that are clan specific.

Like the Tamang with whom they share clans (although with different names),[17] Yolmo clans are exogamous patriclans, and this is probably their primary function. Women marry out of their clan, and the children belong to the clan of their fathers. Kinship terminology is "two-line symmetrical or Dravidian" (Clarke, 1980b, p. 80), with parallel cousins referred to as brother *(nho)* and sister *(nhumo)*. Kinship terminology distinguishes agnatic kin (those related by blood) from potential affines (marriageable). Like the Tamang, Yolmo people prefer cross-cousin marriage, a form of marriage that has the potential to produce "intensive alliances among a small set of patriclans residing in neighboring villages" (Holmberg, 1989, p. 30–31). Both fa/sis/husb and mo/bro are called "ashang," while fa/sis and mo/bro/wife are called "ani." In this way, matrilineal and patrilineal distinctions are obliterated, producing the ideal of repeated bilateral exchange. Holmberg also points out that this pattern of marriage contributes to the absence of hierarchical relationships among clans, since they are frequently reversing their roles as wife giver/wife receiver. Hindus, Tibetans, and the more familiar eastern Sherpa of the Khumbu look upon cross-cousin marriage as incestuous and highly undesirable. Aware of this, some Yolmo villages are abandoning this preference, although in Melemchi it remains common.

Marriage

The most common form of marriage in Melemchi through the mid-1980s was capture marriage, in which the unsuspecting bride is captured by friends of the groom and weds under protest. The marriage is often arranged by the parents, and, until recently, the girl was uninformed.

Melemchi marriages occur in three stages. The first event is *nama langdwang,* or "going to ask for the bride." The parents of the groom visit the parents of the prospective bride to ask for permission for the marriage to take place. The groom's parents bring a *shalgar* offering, and, if permission is received, then the wedding is planned. Normally, the bride is unaware of this visit. In some capture marriages, the *nama langdwang* is omitted and everyone is surprised by the capture.

The marriage ceremony, itself, usually takes place early in the morning so that the bride will be caught unaware. Friends of the groom come to her house and take her to the house of the groom's father, where they are seated on a mat and a meal is served. Brides customarily fight with the captors, protesting loudly and actively, especially if they don't want to be married. The witnesses include the friends of the groom and his family. After the meal, the senior man present blesses the couple, daubing *milam* (butter blessings) on their heads. First the father, then his male relatives, wrap white cloths around the head of the groom, forming a *to* or turbanlike covering. The bride is attended to by a young woman, either a friend or a relative of the groom. At some point, the heads of the bride and groom are banged together three times *(khoibansa)* and they are considered married. Later her family may come and join the party; the presence of her father depends on circumstances including the relationship between his family and that of the groom's.[18] After these ceremonies, the village gathers for liquor and later, food, followed by singing and dancing outside the groom's father's house. Before everyone eats, white scarves of blessing called *kata* and gifts of money are given to the couple, along with brief speeches of blessing.[19] All the money given at the wedding is kept by the groom, even if the wedding is never consummated. Since the groom's family has given the village the party, the money is his, and he may or may not share it with his parents. The bride usually returns to her father's house following the wedding ceremony. She won't be expected to sleep with the groom until the third ritual has been performed: the *toljung.*

Toljung occurs in Melemchi after the wedding. The parents of the groom take gifts to the parents of the bride (4 bottles of distilled liquor, 5 bottles of beer, 2 *shalgar, 2 kata,* 4 *paisa* [pennies], and 1 special *shalgar),* saying, "Please take this *toljung."* It is viewed as payment for nursing her when she was a baby. Once *toljung* has been accepted, it is assumed that the bride will sleep with her husband in his parents' house. In cases in which the parents of either the bride or groom are wealthy, gifts may be given to the girl as well. In the event of a divorce, such gifts may or may not be kept by the girl if they came from her own parents, but they must be returned if they came from the groom's family.

The young couple usually lives with the boy's parents for at least a year. At some point, a *pashi* ceremony signifies the formal separation of a boy from his parents. *Pashi* usually occurs after marriage and is only given to boys. This is when a boy gets his *zomo* and other animals and household supplies. There is no specific stipulation

Themba and Lhakpa Diki's wedding, 1989. Before the village party, the bride sits facing away from the groom, tended by a friend. The table is arranged with a plate of rice and a plate of changda *into which the money gifts will be placed, as well as* shalgar *offerings—bottles with liquor (clear), milk (opaque), and beer (wooden pot).*

of what he will receive; it depends on the circumstances of the family. Relatives are invited to the *pashi,* and they come bringing *shalgar.*

As might be expected, marriages by capture don't always proceed smoothly. In fact, in most cases, the marriage requires "fixing." This is because the girls are often unwilling. They refuse to go with the boy and return to their parents' house to stay. The parents and friends must "fix" the marriage by persuading the girl that she should go. In the past, girls were given 3 years to fix the marriage; at that point, the couple would either live together or divorce. More recently, the waiting period has shortened to 1 year, while in a few cases (see **Kendo** later) the boy waits longer. If forced to go by their parents, girls often try to run away. Women from several generations tell of being beaten, threatened, and sent back to their husbands by their own parents, or of attempts to run away over mountain passes, only to be recaptured again and again by their husband and his friends and relatives.

Ibe Balmu, now 64 years old, tells of being captured from Tarke Ghyang: Her husband, **Kirkiyap,** was the eldest son of a large Melemchi family. His wealthy and powerful father[20] decided he should marry a girl from Kirkiyap's mother's clan; since there were no Melemchi girls of that clan, Kirkiyap was given *pashi* and received his *gode* which he maintained alone for 3 years. Finally, he grabbed Balmu who had never been to Melemchi, knew nothing about the people there, and didn't want to come. For 3 years, she ran away repeatedly, but no matter how she tried she was brought back. The men dispatched by her father-in-law were beaten if they didn't return with her, so they always found her within 1 day. Her wrists were swollen and bruised from being dragged back by her arms. Finally she reconciled herself to the marriage; in 1972, when she related this story in the presence of her husband and children (she had had 11), she seemed quite content with her life.

Kendo, now 30 years old, was grabbed in India by a Melemchi boy with the help of her older brother. She refused to go and tells about running hard through the snow, almost making it over a mountain pass, before the grabbers caught her and brought her back. She stayed with her parents for 6 years; finally, her husband asked for a final answer, and, although she never answered, she went with him and they now have two children.

Pemba Gyalmu was grabbed by a man from Kulu, her father's sister's son, when she was 19. Melemchi women don't like Kulu; it is isolated and lacks the beautiful open vistas of Melemchi. One girl told us of running away from her husband in Kulu because it was so desolate and windy there—the wind blew through Kulu making the sound "Ku-lu-lu-lu-lu." Pemba Gyalmu's father threatened to beat her if she didn't go, so she went. Her father reasoned that the boy was from a good family and since she couldn't stay with her parents forever, she would have to be married sometime. She was very unhappy with the marriage; in the midst of arguments, the boy told her that she could go anytime she wanted, since she was from a poor family and hadn't brought any wealth to the marriage. A few months later, she met her father at the Gosainkund *puja* and told him how unhappy she was in her *gode* in Kulu and what the boy said about her and her family. Her father went to her husband's *gode* in a rage, threatening to kill him, but he ran away and hid. The father and daughter returned to Melemchi. Although his sister (the boy's mother) came to Melemchi to plead for the marriage, the father was immovable and the marriage was dissolved by agreement between the parents. The girl reproached her father for ruining her life by forcing her into a marriage she didn't want, and they argued for several months. The boy remarried, and, 6 months later, so did Pemba Gyalmu. Her new husband is a Melemchi man 24 years older than she is. His wife had died 7 years before, and he had three children, one only five years younger than Pemba Gyalmu. Now, he and Pemba Gyalmu have two babies of their own and live and work with all five children in India. In both marriages, Pemba Gyalmu followed the preferred cross-cousin marriage: Her first husband was her father's sister's son, and her second husband is her mother's father's brother's son's son.

Marriages can be dissolved through a ritual known as *takpa checken* (break the string). The bride and groom tie a string around their fingers and break the string. With that, their union is dissolved. They also file a paper with the village *goba*. Until they break the string, both are held in limbo, unable to marry. If a woman remarries before the string is broken, her new husband must pay reparation to the current husband for his wedding expenses. A woman receives nothing after *takpa checken;* she returns to her parents' household and remains until she remarries, although she may keep anything she brought to the marriage. The groom keeps all of the wedding money, even if the bride never comes to stay with him. If there are children, they belong to the husband. In the case of infants, they stay with the mother until they are about 3 years old, during which time their father pays child support. Many children of divorce live for periods of time with their paternal grandparents if their father has not remarried or is working in India. This is always preferable to staying with their mother or her family, especially if she has remarried, as it is believed that children might be ill–treated by a man who is not their father or his kin.

Why Capture Marriage in Melemchi?

Capture marriage exists elsewhere in the world, usually as a way to circumvent either the costs of marriage (bride price or dowry) or restrictions on suitable marriage part- ners (cases in which two people want to marry against their families' or societies' wishes). Neither situation pertains to Melemchi, especially since in Melemchi capture marriage is the standard form of marriage whereas elsewhere it is an acceptable but infrequent alternative to other marriage arrangements. The neighboring Tamang, studied by Holmberg (1989), appear to view capture marriage as a form of elopement that avoids either parental objections to the match or an expensive village feast.

An alternative theory is that capture marriage provides an option for men who are socially handicapped (e.g., poor or ugly) and otherwise unattractive to mates (Stross, 1974). Here we may be closer to the situation in Melemchi. It is possible to consider capture marriage in Yolmo as stemming from the isolation and dispersion of *gode* life, making the problem of obtaining a wife difficult for many men. Not all Yolmo villages practice capture marriage. The villages in Yolmo who have tradition- ally practiced capture marriage (e.g., Melemchi, Nagote, Kulu, Bolgyang, and Nim Dumbu—most on the west side of the Melemchi River) are villages closely tied to *zomo gode* herding as the primary source of wealth. Even today, as *gode* disappear from Yolmo, men from these villages are still more likely to live in *gode* than are men from Tarke Ghyang or Sermathang, where religious marriages are common. *Gode* life is isolated and difficult; a man needs a wife and children to make the enter- prise succeed, and opportunities to meet potential wives are limited. Unlike Tamang villages, where young men and women meet in song contests or in agricultural pur- suits (Holmberg, 1989), opportunities for socialization and socializing are limited for children raised in *gode*. At village festivals, they are easily distinguishable from children raised in the village, as they hide behind their mother's skirts and more often are silent observers than participants. It was suggested to us that grabbing a wife solved a practical problem: There was little opportunity for courtship; there was no dowry or bride price involved, so negotiations weren't necessary; and, as a society, both Melemchi men and women were shy about being married or wanting to be mar- ried. No matter what age they are, men and women giggle uncomfortably when dis- cussing marriage with us. No one admits to wanting to be married or liking to be married. More than one woman answered our question about whether she was happy in her marriage, after protesting so vehemently when she was grabbed, by respond- ing with a shy smile and saying, "Well, what can I do now after all these children?"

It must be acknowledged that Melemchi people do not have an explanation for their tradition of capture marriage; it is their custom and goes back as far as anyone can remember. They view it today as a stigmatized custom and claim that they never knew about other systems or that grabbing marriages were illegal in Nepal. Ibe Balmu tells of seeing Yolmo women in Tibet who had been grabbed and taken far away from their homes and families. One person suggested it came from the initial settlers from Tibet who were nomads and grabbed girls from the low regions taking them up to villages in Yolmo. We witnessed one capture marriage in 1971 in which an unsuspecting woman from Tarke Ghyang was grabbed at a music recording session we were holding. She was wrestled to the floor and dragged screaming to the mat to sit next to her husband-to-be. The villagers all argued on behalf of the groom. She argued back that she was already married; her husband had been away in India but they hadn't broken the string. This was the 31-year-old groom's eighth attempt at grabbing a wife, and it was ultimately unsuccessful. The woman was allowed to slip away in the night, and no one made an effort to retrieve her. This example confirmed other statements made by women that they feared going places without their friends and relatives, since they were vulnerable to being grabbed.

The phenomenon of "fixing" marriages essentially provides a period during which the young couple can mature, prospects can be evaluated, and childbearing can be postponed. In a society in which early marriages are common, the prospective field of partners is broad, and choice depends on economic factors, a girl who is not consulted about her marriage in advance may require time to consider her options. Since children complicate divorce, it is beneficial to postpone cohabitation until the marriage is certain.

Until the mid-1980s, nearly all marriages in Melemchi involved grabbing the bride, often arranged by the parents, with only the groom consulted. A boy may be pushed into marriage by his parents anytime after age 15. In the case of a younger son, it often happens because the parents need some extra help, which a young wife could provide. In one exceptional case, a Ghale family arranged their sons' marriages when the boys were young, contracting with families of the mother's clan in her natal village. One of the sons told us he first met his wife when they actually married at age 22, although they had been betrothed most of their lives. There are several cases historically of very young marriages in Melemchi, both boys and girls, at 12 years of age. People told of young girls being grabbed by rich men who "figured that even if she doesn't like him, she will stay for the money." In such cases, the girls live with their parents for at least 2 years before they join their husbands. This is reminiscent of the way in which the Chini Lama family treated Melemchi girls, appropriating them as wives and mistresses. The girls were initially recruited as young servants, and their relationship with the Chini Lama brought benefits to their entire extended families.[21] They were usually servants to the family and then remained as mistresses. Two women in their 50s, recruited as young girls by the old Chini Lama, today remain loyal and contented members of the Chini Lama household; they gave up their chance for children of their own in exchange for a comfortable life, access to gifts and power, and the possibility of brokering for their Melemchi relatives in the process.[22]

Today, most marriages are arranged with the consultation of the bride and groom, even though the capture is still carried out and the girl protests vigorously. For many young people, their parents still arrange the match, especially in families without much experience in India. Adults interviewed today favor "love marriages," viewing them as an improvement for everyone concerned. Under the old system, capture marriages created problems between girls and their families. Now, if a young couple doesn't remain happily married, they have only themselves to blame. Parents favor marriages within Yolmo, although they also seem to accept the few marriages that involve others, such as the Tamang, Indians, and Tibetans. In India, relatives take the role of Melemchi parents in arranging the marriages that are held there. The only totally unacceptable marriage would be one within one's clan, and no example of this has ever been mentioned.

Marriage is definitely the norm in this community, regardless how it comes about. There are fewer than 15 adults who have been residents of Melemchi during the past 25 years who have never lived as husband or wife. Some Melemchi residents remain unmarried, although very few are never married. Some women were grabbed but never stayed, or in the case of several men, no woman would ever stay with them. But divorce and remarriage are easy and common.

Inheritance

Melemchi is a patrilineal society; children belong to the clan of their father. As already mentioned, boys receive animals, household goods, and occasionally fields from their parents when they have the separation *(pashi)* ceremony. Families vary in what they give to sons, depending on their wealth and the number of sons. Yolmo people practice ultimogeniture; that is, the youngest son inherits the parent's house and land. In exchange, he takes care of his parents until their death. Girls do not inherit anything from their parents, except in the cases of wealthy families in which they give their daughters gifts of money or land when they marry. Families without sons set up a formal relationship with one of their sons-in-law, giving him the rights and obligations of the youngest son. There are two such written agreements in place in Melemchi today; in one case, there were only two daughters born, and in the other case, all the sons died before the parents did.

Clarke has noted the paradox in Yolmo villages between the principle of ultimogeniture in the household and primogeniture in the priesthood. The former custom is Tamang; the latter, Tibetan. In villages like Tarke Ghyang, where wealth is based on trade and absentee landholdings, sons did not need village land and hence did not disperse. They remained in the village and at the temple, resulting in heightened competition for rank and prestige over control of the temple. In Melemchi, where the Chini Lama controlled the *gomba,* there were just a few lineage lamas (Hlalungba) present and none could control the *gomba.* Thus, the principle of ultimogeniture predominates. Ultimogeniture encourages older sons to leave and seek their own fortunes, since they won't inherit. Thus there is in Melemchi, in contrast to Tarke Ghyang, much less emphasis on hierarchy and rank, since the only access to rank and privilege is through marriage into the Chini Lama family.

HOUSEHOLDS

The smallest social unit in Melemchi is the household, usually composed of a married couple and their children. Especially prior to access to contraception, families were usually large. Children assist their parents, first with the care and supervision of younger siblings and household tasks such as carrying water and later in substantial ways, such as gathering fodder and leaf litter, washing dishes, and supervising household animals. By the time Melemchi children reach their midteens, they are capable of handling most daily adult tasks in either the *gode* or the village. In India, they work for wages, first dishwashing or chores for small restaurants and hotels or as a servant for families who will feed them in exchange for work and then, as they are physically stronger, physical labor. The parents remain in the family house, finally sharing it with the last son and his wife and children. Unmarried daughters may remain with their parents into adulthood, although most go off on their own to India. In cases of an elderly widow, a daughter may remain with her for periods of time if not permanently. A common alternative is a grandchild who lives with his or her elderly grandparents, helping with the heavy work.

Melemchi residents may live year-round in their *gode* without a house; this is most common for young couples who stay with either set of in-laws in the village when they are there. Later in life, they may build a house for themselves but use it primarily for storage as they remain out with their herd. Those living in houses year-round in the village tend to be older than 40. Most have spent their lives living in *gode* but finally pass on their herds to their sons and retire from herding to live full-time in the village, farming and raising a few household livestock. These householders most often have children or grandchildren living with them for periods of time, either their youngest children who aren't yet married or older children home from India for a while. There are six to eight elderly men and women who live alone, taking care of themselves.

A few families in 1993 still continued the pattern of living 6 months in their house in Melemchi and 6 months in Tarke Tho, either in a house or in a bamboo shed on their fields. This was the most common pattern for families in 1971, but relatively few do it today. A variant of this, seen as recently as 1993, is the Melemchi residents with houses who live out on their fields in a *gode* structure during the summer months. Several elderly women moved out for 4 to 6 months every year and lived on their village fields, tending to their cows, who grazed and manured the fields in preparation for planting. These women had houses where they stored things, but they liked living in *gode,* as they had for so much of their lives. It saved them from having to take their livestock out to graze every day. One summer when we arrived in Melemchi, we rented the house of friends who moved their entire family plus livestock out into a *gode* shelter adjacent to the house. We ate several meals with them in their warm, dry shelter as the monsoon rains beat down.[23]

The distribution of Melemchi residents through time and space has changed over the period of this study. In 1971–72, of the 308 people censused, 30% lived in the village, 39% lived in *gode,* and 32% lived in India. By 1989, that had changed: fifty percent were living in the village, 17% lived in *gode,* and 33% were in India. By 1993, overall population numbers were up, and fewer people lived in *gode* (only 5%), with the proportion of people in India growing to 63%. In order to understand the factors underlying that shift, it is necessary to examine the factors promoting change in the Yolmo valley and Melemchi in particular in the last 25 years, the subject of Chapter 7.

DISCUSSION: YOLMO TEMPLE-VILLAGES— THEMES AND VARIATION[24]

Yolmo is a geographic and cultural region defined by the presence of temple-villages.[25] These villages lie at the northern end of the Melemchi and Indrawati River valleys, on the upper slopes of the ridges descending southward from the Great Himalaya. The villages themselves are the remains of land grants (but not *guthi*) given by the Nepalese kings beginning in the early 19th century to Tibetan lamas who were living in the region on pilgrimage. These land grants may have been payment for assistance in the politically sensitive region bordering Tibet, but they also conferred religious merit on the donor king. The land grants gave the rights in perpetuity to the lama and his descendants. By custom, the position of head lama is inherited by the eldest son; as the population grew, sons within the founding lineages who would not inherit began to disperse and start new temples elsewhere in Yolmo. In one case, Clarke (1980a) documented the movement of lineage members from a single family who eventually founded 19 *gomba* and 18 villages.[26]

The lamas who founded the villages were from nonmonastic orders (Nyingma and Karmapa), so they and their descendants were free to marry. They married daughters of the local elites from the lower agricultural villages in the valley who moved up in both the geographic and hierarchical senses. Through these marriages, the local elites exchanged wealth and power for the prestige associated with membership in a temple-village. Eventually, through preferential cross-cousin marriage, these high villages became a series of villages unified through shared cultural practices, language, and kinship. Today, Yolmo temple-villages constitute a married priesthood, where a man is both a priest (lama) and a landholder, connected to a kin group but, more important, to the temple. Householders in temple-villages are simultaneously priests, farmers, pastoralists, landlords, and sponsors of the annual religious cycle. While the descendants of the founding lama lineage are considered "above" the other lineages in each village, all residents of the temple-villages (the landlords) are considered "above" those people living in the farming villages below (the tenants). Those living in temple-villages are called "Lama people," while those living below are called "Tamang." Clarke has discussed in some detail this distinction, which is complex and far from clear-cut.

> Lama and Tamang are an aspect of a total hierarchy, namely a natural, social and moral order in which altitude, wealth and virtue are linked together. The people "above" are said to have ample food, wood, and water, to be fully clothed, to have Buddhist temples and to keep their word. The people "below" are said (by those "above") not to have enough food, wood or water, to walk around without trousers, to slaughter animals for sacrifice and to be untrustworthy. . . . The culture above is usually seen from the outside as a unitary whole, an amalgam of authority, wealth and religion. (Clarke, 1985, p. 195)

In Yolmo, the wealth that is generated belongs to individuals, not the *gomba*. Unlike the monastic system in Tibet, where wealth is both created and controlled by the monastery, the wealth in Yolmo has always been ultimately under the control of the Nepalese state. This has led Clarke to note that Yolmo villages combine "secular authority from the south with sacred authority from the north"(Clarke, 1983, p.25). The secular authority alludes to the long association between Yolmo and the Royal Court, which included the appropriation of women. The proximity of Yolmo to the Kathmandu Valley and the close relationship between several villages and the royal court have been influential in local power struggles within the region, leaving some villages with an especially close relationship to the national government. The *guthi* of Melemchi remains an exception; in a *guthi,* taxes are paid to the *guthiyar,* not the government.

Tarke Ghyang is the most wealthy and influential temple-village in the region. With only a few acres of agricultural land, the village is compact. The lineage lamas who control that valuable real estate wield great power, both in and outside the village. The long history of close ties, including intermarriage, between the villagers of Tarke Ghyang and the Rana regime continues today. Despite being one of the northernmost villages, Tarke Ghyang had the first school and the first electrification project in the region. In 1989, the villagers refused to be incorporated into Langtang National Park, even though the omission of Tarke Ghyang created a gap in the park boundaries. Long dependent on trade and absentee landholdings, Tarke Ghyang has few herding households when compared with Melemchi, even though both have contiguous access to high grazing land. In 1976, Clarke estimated only 7% of the Tarke Ghyang householders were involved in pastoralism, while the figure was 25% for Melemchi. Since fields are located elsewhere and farmed by tenants and little pastoralism exists, householders in Tarke Ghyang spend much time and effort in religious ritual, which contributes to their reputation as being among the highest status villages in the region. Unlike in Melemchi, women in Tarke Ghyang do not participate in pastoral or agricultural work, and, according to Clarke, prefer to marry within the village for this reason.

Tarke Ghyang provides a stark contrast to Melemchi, despite their proximity and the fact that they share the distinction of being the highest temple-villages in the region. The differences between the two villages result from differences in their physical layout and in their history. The village of Melemchi itself is much bigger than Tarke Ghyang, which makes high-altitude agriculture a feasible subsistence strategy there. Tarke Ghyang lacks suitable agricultural land and therefore depends on trade and distant landholdings that are worked by others. Melemchi people depend on food they grow themselves, while Tarke Ghyang families have traditionally eaten rice coming up from their landholdings below. The extensive availability of forested slopes adjacent to Melemchi has sustained agropastoralism far longer than has been possible in many of the southern and eastern Yolmo temple-villages. Without an agropastoral emphasis, Tarke Ghyang participated in the market economy earlier and to a much greater extent than Melemchi. Trade and wage labor has been important to Tarke Ghyang and has provided a cash income stream that came much later to Melemchi. And historically, Melemchi's position as a *guthi* and the experience of life under the control of the Chini Lama is a unique part of Melemchi's history that affected not only life within the village but also the position of the village within the region and its ability to articulate with the rest of the country.

The temple-villages of Yolmo exchange commodities and marriage partners. Most Yolmo residents marry within the region, and many marry within their own villages.

Livestock and their products are bought and sold within the region, with excess butter being transported to Kathmandu. Preferential cross-cousin marriage means that in many families, marriage partners go back and forth between two villages. For example, one Melemchi family gets daughters-in-law from Nim Dumbu village (where the mother was born) and sends its daughters there as brides. Both Tarke Ghyang and Kulu are common sources of marriage partners for Melemchi men, and Melemchi women have married into those villages as well. Melemchi residents claim that the beauty of their village, the richness of the natural resources, and the reputation of Melemchi village as a cohesive unit makes marriage with their sons an attractive possibility. Wives have come into Melemchi from nearly every village in Yolmo, and, except for some men who married in India and who haven't returned, there are no women from outside Yolmo attached to the village.

NOTES

[1] In all the accounts, the word "king" is used; in fact, it was probably the prime minister, Jang Bahadur Rana.

[2] A friend told us a story about the first Rana prime minister, Jang Bahadur Rana, that may be the source of the "1-rupee tax." Before he became prime minister in 1850, Jang Bahadur Rana had been banished to the Tarai, where he made a living catching, taming, and selling (in Kathmandu) wild elephants. One went rogue near the Patan Bridge in the Kathmandu Valley, and the king offered a *subidar's* coat (presumably with the attendant rank and position—the highest noncommissioned rank) to anyone who could tame it. Jang Bahadur watched the elephant and noted that it came to bathe in the Bagmati River, emerging to spray shops, knocking things down, and damaging every house within the vicinity except that of a tailor. The elephant stopped there and waited for the tailor to feed him. Jang Bahadur made a deal with the tailor and exchanged places and clothing with him. When the elephant stopped for food, Jang Bahadur jumped on his back and beat him on the head with a club and *khukri* until the elephant oozed from a particular spot on the head (which mahouts know is the only way to stop a rogue elephant).

The king gave him the *subidar* jacket, which had a coin in the pocket. Jang Bahadur handed the coin back to the king as a token of thanks. This became a Rana tradition, and since favors were always being handed out capriciously by the Ranas, everyone carried a 1-rupee coin to give in the event they were offered a favor. Without the coin, there was no favor (Upendra Shumshere Rana, personal communication).

[3] The first Chini Lama was Dai Fo Ching. The second Chini Lama, Buddha Badzura, was Chini Lama until his death in 1912. His son, Purna Badzura, born in 1889, was the third Chini Lama for 70 years, from 1912 until his death in 1982. Purna Badzura's eldest son, Pune Jwalla (Meme Babu), succeeded his father in 1982 but was ill and died after only 7 years. Meme Babu's eldest son, Andare Lama, assumed the position of Chini Lama until around 1994, when Meme Babu's youngest brother, Ganesh Thubten Lama, asserted his claim.

[4] *Pathi* is a local measure of volume corresponding to a standardized brass or copper vessel called a *pathi*. A smaller vessel for measurement is called a *mana;* there are 8 *mana* in 1 *pathi*. A *mana* measures about 34 cubic inches, so 1 *pathi* is about half a peck. As a dry measure of volume, it corresponds to 2.6 kg, or between 5 and 6 pounds of lentils, grain, flour, etc.

[5] *Dharni* is a local measure for liquid similar in size to a *pathi*.

[6] One rupee = 4.5¢ U.S.

[7] Clarke (1980b) uses the term *talpa*, which is used in Tarke Ghyang.

[8] In fact, no one has been able to recall any instance of a woman purchasing land in Melemchi, although they agree there is no rule against it.

[9] *Guthi* Tax Payment Day: July 16, 1993. Around 10 a.m., we headed down to the *gomba* and followed the women climbing up to the balcony in front of the *gomba* to the upstairs sanctuary—where Nyungne is held each fall. Women were clustered on the floor near the head of the stairs, on the opposite end of the balcony from the five *goba* who sat on benches against the railing. Against the wall of the *gomba* sat a few of the older men, including Gyella, Damai, and Pasang Pruba. Chiawa Karkiyap stood holding kettles of butter tea and *arak* alongside a big plastic sheet heaped with barley grain. As each woman appeared at the top of the steep stairway with a grain sack on her back, held by a head strap, she was greeted. Once it was her turn, she moved forward, opened her sack, and began to scoop out the grain into the copper *pathi* measure provided, leveling off the top, dumping it out onto the pile, and scooping again.

When she finished, she called out her name and the number of *pathi* given. Bolgyang Kami wrote down who paid, and how much, into the tax book.

A brief flurry of argument and interest was occasioned by Ibe Karmu, who brought old *changda* (barley grain) that was insect infested; finally after much argument her *changda* was put in a separate bowl and credited. In addition to her own payment, she paid for two of her sons who are in India but who own land. Karmu's husband, Mingmar, sat impassively along the wall while the adequacy of the *changda* was being debated, leaving the argument to Karmu and the rest of those present who had opinions on the matter. (Payment in kind leaves the taxpayer open to social scrutiny, while payment in cash [see below] is accepted without comment.)

Shangpa Karkiyap's wife brought 1 *pathi* for her brother, Ghale Tsowang, who was in India; Ghale Sherap Zangbu brought 7 *pathi:* 3 for himself, 3 for his son who was present, and 1 for a son who was in India. Babu Singhy brought 120 rupees ($5.50 U.S.)—30 rupees for each *pathi* owed. This is acceptable for those in India who haven't grown anything on their land. Old Ibe Kipe came to pay for her son; she held the position of *tal* for him after his father died, until he was married and came into his inheritance. Since he and his wife and children are in India, Ibe Kipe paid his 4 *pathi*. Two new men were added to the *tal* list: Ganesh and Sherap, both sons of *tal* and both in India. Their fathers each brought payments of 100 rupees ($4.50 U.S.) and a pot of beer *(shalgar* offering), which were placed as offerings in a dish of *changda* in front of the headmen. These young men have houses but still do not own land and so won't pay grain tax; however, this payment insures their position on the *tal* list.

Old Ibe Hlenjam complained good-naturedly that nowadays all she gets is a cup of tea and a cup of *arak,* whereas when the Chini Lama used to come up himself to take the tribute, he passed out cigarettes and other treats. People continued to come over the next 2 hours, stopping for some refreshment and a visit. Eventually, the five *goba* and other men present began to argue about whether the rules should be changed so that people with a house but no land should have to pay. They are taking up the place of a field, and more and more houses are being built. Others complained about the new high cost of becoming *tal*. When the *gomba* needed to be rebuilt, the Chini Lama sent word that it would cost 5,000 rupees ($227 U.S.) for a landowner to be added to the *tal* list; at least seven people paid these sums, but a number of others threatened to leave the village unless the fees were dropped. Finally the fee reverted to its former level of 100 rupees.

[10] In January 1971, when we were watching monkeys feed in an isolated wheat field away from the village, the field owner came upon the monkeys and began shooting at them with an antique muzzle-loader. John immediately jumped up and ran at him yelling and angry. The monkeys ran away, John and I went home, and the owner and his friends left. The owner was unknown to us but was a Melemchi resident. We were very concerned that we had ruined our relationship with the villagers through this encounter, and also concerned to have lost rapport with our monkey troop, which we had worked so hard to habituate to our presence. Our field assistant, Mingma Tenzing from Khumbu, tried to smooth over the situation with the villagers only to find that *they* were afraid we would go and tell the king that someone in Melemchi had a gun. They were also concerned that we would be unhappy, leave, and complain to the Chini Lama. With Mingma Tenzing's abundant skill and tact, everything was smoothed over, the incident was never repeated, and we were back in the monkey's good graces by the following day. We were shocked to learn that they thought we had access to the king, and to find that their first assumption was that the government would take reprisal against them, even though they were defending their own resources. This was the first inkling we had of the nature of their feudal relationship with the Chini Lama.

[11] Although the principle of youngest son inheritance is the rule for Yolmo residents, the lama lineages follow the Tibetan Buddhist principle of primogeniture in the transfer of power in the *gomba*. Therefore, Lama Pruba would sit below his brothers in the *gomba,* were they present.

[12] Clarke (1980c) describes a similar ritual called Dalha Pangto in Tarke Ghyang. It involves two figures, one representing a Buddhist and the other a non-Buddhist, and their knife fight symbolizes the ultimate triumph of Buddhism.

[13] There are five major *torma* constructed from barley flour, water, and a little butter for the Nara festival. After the ingredients are kneaded together, big balls of dough are threaded onto armatures made of wood and secured in place with bark twine. Once each large figure is properly sculpted, it is decorated with sculpted dough slabs and wooden paddles bearing beautiful decorations made from brightly colored butter, and finally drizzled with melted butter colored red from rhubarb stalks. Each major brightly colored *torma* represents a particular god; there are numerous small *torma* alongside on the altar, simple shapes decorated with medallions of uncolored butter and strings of butter piped onto them through a small hole pierced in a piece of bamboo that is filled with butter. A plunger pushes the butter out the hole in strings, in the same manner as a cookie press makes cookies. It takes up to 18 hours to complete all of the *torma,* which are made in a single day.

[14] The pasteboard hat is used in all funeral rituals, including the later rituals involving an effigy of the deceased. The copper pot is not a ritual item; it is used to hold and transport the body but reverts to its normal household uses after the funeral.

[15] Cicumnambulation is a religious devotion in which adherents walk around a sacred site clockwise.

[16] Lama Pruba's father and his four brothers were very wealthy and shared many fields. All practiced as lamas, but two were heavy gamblers and lost most of the family wealth. By 1972, all brothers including Lama Pruba's father had died, except for one man who lived outside of Yolmo.

[17] The following are the Yolmo clan names. Tamang names for the same clans are in parentheses (after Clark, 1980a): Ayogpa, Chiawa (Toka; Pakhrin), Chozangba (Mukhtin; Shendung-le), Dungba (Dong), Glan(e) (Ghale), Lhalungpa, Loba, Nachang Shakya Zangpo, Shyangpa (Thing), Sermo Lama, Tenyelingpa, Tomare, Tongsowa, and Yöba (Waiba). Note that in Melemchi three clans use the "Sherpa" name (Shangpa, Lhalungpa, and Chiawa), while Waiba use the "Tamang" name. This represents a recent shift. In 1971, Melemchi Yöba called themselves by that term; by 1986, the term *Waiba* was used more frequently.

[18] Clarke points out that in Yolmo a wife giver is superior to a wife taker, so in cases in which a lineage lama is in the position of wife taker, the father of the bride will avoid the celebration so he doesn't have to sit "above" a lineage lama. Tarke Ghyang, where Clarke worked, is much more hierarchically organized than Melemchi, but it is true that the bride's father often is not present at Melemchi weddings.

[19] Blessings at a wedding in 1989:

Urgen: "This is given by Waiba Kanza (groom's uncle). Blessings from Waiba Kanza. May you be very rich and have a long life. That is why he gives one *kata* to his son and one *kata* to the bride. After that, a present of 100 rupees."

Crowd: "O, la so!"

Urgen: This is from Zangbu. If you go to the river, you can build a bridge. If you go to the cliff, you can make steps in the rocks. He is very happy because Themba is getting married. He gives one *kata* to Themba and one *kata* to the bride, and a present of 100 rupees.

Crowd: "O, la so!"

With each speech, Urgen holds up the *kata* and money to show the crowd, then puts the *kata* on each one as he mentioned it, and concludes by placing the money in a plate of grain *(changda)* and burning incense sticks.

[20] Balmu described her father-in-law as extremely fat, with bulging muscles. His chest had 3–4 inches of "meat" on it and his hands were like "bread." He implemented his policies by force and inspired fear in everyone. He ate lightly and was able to consume large amounts of liquor without getting drunk. Another family member said that he was so fat that he had to dust his body with *tsampa* flour to keep it from chafing.

[21] In Tarke Ghyang, the same kind of relationship developed between village families and the extended kin of the Rana prime minister. There is only one reported case of a Melemchi woman being sent to the Ranas as a servant/mistress. She returned to Melemchi, where she later married a monk.

[22] Recently these two women have had a complete falling out. Each competed to provide a wife for the heir apparent Chini Lama from among their nieces. Once the choice was made, these two former allies became estranged. The stakes were actually quite high, after all. Each had given up any chance to have children as well as any legitimate claim on the Chini Lama estate themselves; finally, through her niece, each had a chance to gain something of what she had lost.

[23] In 1997, while this manuscript was being prepared, word reached us that in January Melemchi experienced three earthquakes within a couple of hours, severe enough to destroy several houses. As soon as the first quake was felt, everyone moved into their courtyards and set up *gode,* where they lived for the next week until they were sure the earth had subsided.

[24] There has been little ethnography done in the Yolmo region. *Body and Emotion: The Aesthetics of Illness and Healing in the Nepal Himalayas* by Robert Desjarlais (1992) is a study of culture and emotional distress among Yolmo people. It focuses on illness and the role of the healer or *bombo* in Gulphabangyang, a village at the southwestern edge of the region where Gurung, Tamang, and Yolmo Lama people live. The only other ethnographic work is that of British anthropologist Graham E. Clarke, who has conducted extensive work on the history of the origins of the temple-villages of Yolmo (Clarke, 1980a, 1980b, 1980c, 1983, 1985, 1991). His fieldwork was conducted primarily in the village of Tarke Ghyang, Melemchi's wealthy altitudinal counterpart. His description of the social structure of Tarke Ghyang village provides the only comparative material for this study. The following discussion draws heavily on his published work and unpublished doctoral dissertation.

[25] There are a number of villages in Yolmo. Those with *gomba* are the temple-villages in the strict sense; however, the entire upper valley shares a culture that is Yolmo culture, which includes participation in rituals situated in a *gomba,* regardless whether their particular village has one.

[26] Gortsahling, founded by Karma Tille Wangpo, is the oldest known Yolmo Sermo lama temple. His six brothers are responsible for founding six other temples: upper Bhotang, Chimi, Dechenthang, Lhakang, and Mani-Gyeldung in Yolmo and Shyabru in nearby Trisuli. From these, we can trace 12 more Yolmo temples founded by descendants of this lineage (Clarke, 1980a).

6 / Population of Melemchi (Demography)

During the year we spent in Melemchi studying the langur monkeys, it was difficult for us to figure out who else lived there. On our initial survey trek, Melemchi was virtually deserted—the fields in mid-September were dusty brown, many of the 30 or so houses appeared to be empty, and we rarely saw anyone. Having given up our impractical plan to live year-round in a tent in the forest, a semideserted village seemed the next best thing, so we hastened to Kathmandu to prepare to return. However, by the time we returned in October, there were more signs of life. The fields were being plowed and sown with wheat and changda. As residents, we made friends with a few families, who offered to supply us with firewood or milk. We got to know Kirkiyap and his wife, Balmu. Their three daughters hung around our house, trading off carrying their infant brother on their backs, while their son, Kami, hauled water for us and did errands for our assistant, Mingma. We got to know Themba, the "wood man," although we rarely saw him. He and his family lived on the far edge of the village; two of his sons brought our wood. By Losar (Tibetan New Year), in late January, we knew about 30 people by sight but not all by name. Everyone in Melemchi joined together for Losar, so after sitting with the same people for 7 days in different houses, we felt we knew everyone who was around. But much to our surprise, we learned that many of them were leaving for India as soon as Losar was over.

As spring became summer, we saw more and more people up from Tarke Tho for the day; eventually, they moved up to Melemchi for the summer. They would descend again in September. At the Nara festival in July, there were at least 150 people present in the village—some coming from the gode for a day or two, some who returned from India, and the summer population in residence. Even after one year there, we were still meeting people who were new to us but who belonged to Melemchi. And there are some we have never met in all the time we have been associated with the village. Who constitutes the population of Melemchi and how can it be measured? This became an important question once my research shifted focus from langur monkey socioecology to the relationship between the human population and the local environment.

POPULATION OF MELEMCHI

The population of a village is usually stated in a single sentence, with a single figure: For example, the population of Melemchi is 327 people. It seems straight forward

Portrait of everyone who attended our Losar party in 1972. Some people came in from the gode, *including Nogabu, our research assistant beginning in 1989, who is the small boy crouching on the right side of the photo.*

and simple. But in actuality, it can be difficult to find a simple answer to the question of how many people belong to a village. It is easy to count the number of houses. However, the number of houses does not match the number of households in Melemchi, nor does it indicate the number of people attached to the village, some of whom don't have a house. In Melemchi, it is common for villagers to live in gode and not own a house until late in life. Furthermore, many of the houses in the village are not occupied; they have either been built by parents for sons who live in India or by householders who return only sporadically from their gode or from India.

So, in order to define a population, you must count people, but the count also must be fixed in time. Populations change over time; people leave, marry in or out, get born or die, so the number of people constantly fluctuates. Many field studies are relatively short, so defining small populations is fairly easy: Just count everyone present. But in a field study that spans many years, such as this one, the fluctuation in number of people is continual. It is customary to specify a single year as the unit of measurement; for example, the Melemchi population in 1971 includes anyone who fits the criteria for membership at any time during 1971. To be accurate, the ethnographer should be present throughout that year so that short-term residents aren't missed. This is especially important in the case of Melemchi, because people are not always "at home." They may be in the gode, they may be away visiting or doing business, or they may be out of country in India. The population of the village also changes seasonally, as we learned; people go down to Tarke Tho in winter, and those in India tend to return home during winter months when work shuts down at high-altitude sites. If the ethnographer is there for only 2 months in a year, a population count can be quite inaccurate.

Since I am interested in whether the population is growing and, if so, how fast, I need more than one census year in order to evaluate change between them. Two populations were defined for Melemchi: the population in 1971 and the population in 1993. These two years represent the maximum possible separation between years for which there are good data available. We were present in Melemchi for the entire year in 1971, so this population count is complete. While the same was not the case in 1993, our brief visit was supplemented by demographic data collected throughout 1993 by a research assistant and corroborated in person in 1995.

Once the time frame is established, it is still necessary to set clear criteria for inclusion in the population. Given the peripatetic nature of Melemchi residents, this was especially difficult. For example, how long could a person be in India and still be considered a member? Was Dawa Sonam's son, Hlatul, who was serving in the Indian army and who only had been home on visits since he left in 1970, a member of the Melemchi population? What about Diki, who married a man from outside the village but who had divorced him and now works in India, returning to visit her mother every year or two? What about Mingmar Tongtong? In 1971, he lived in a gode with his wife and children, coming to Melemchi frequently but not owning property there. His father and brothers lived in Bolongsay, a village about five hours' walk away. By 1993, however, he and his father lived in Melemchi in a house he had built in 1978, surrounded by fields he owned, while his sheep gode was at high pastures being cared for by his son.1

For developing the criteria for who should be counted as a Melemchi resident, the essential issue is whether or not the person has any claim on resources in the village, rather than where they actually live. Any man who is tal (a member of the gomba) or the son or brother of tal can legitimately claim membership (and resources), as could their descendants, even if they live in India. Women born in the village or to tal are members until they marry; if they marry a man from outside Melemchi, they join his village and their children belong to his lineage. If they marry a man from Melemchi, they remain a village member. After a divorce, they have rights through their natal family, unless and until they remarry outside the village.

The following criteria were developed and applied in this study to determine the population of Melemchi:

To be counted for the Melemchi population for a particular year, a man must be

n Alive at some point during that year and tal, the son of a tal, or an actual resident in the village for some part of that year.

For a woman to be counted, she must be

n Alive at some point during that year and an unmarried daughter of tal or sons of tal, or the wife of tal or sons of tal, or the wife of a man residing in Melemchi during that year, or a woman who is divorced and not remarried and whose father is a Melemchi resident or tal.

By these criteria, the Melemchi population in 1971 numbered 349 individuals, while the population in 1993 numbered 483. This suggests that the population grew during this period of time, although it doesn't tell us anything about that growth. Is this rate of growth rapid? Is the population growing at a constant rate? Although this was not a carefully designed demographic study, it is possible to address the question of population growth during this period. And the simple answer is yes— Melemchi had an expanding population between 1971 and 1993.

Melemchi Population in 1971

In 1971, 349 individuals are counted as members of Melemchi village. Figure 6.1 presents a diagram of the population by age and sex, which indicates that in 1971 Melemchi had a growing population. This is shown by the typical pyramid shape, with many more individuals in the younger age cohorts than in the older ones. In fact, 47.3% of the population in 1971 is under the age of 20 years. This is close to the 50% figure characteristic of the rapidly expanding populations of the developing world (Macfarlane, 1976) or the overall figure of 52% for Nepal as a whole, provided by Banister and Thapa (1981). While there appears to be a reduced number of females age 25–39, this probably reflects a random fluctuation due to small sample size. Since it is only females and not males that show this, it is unlikely to reflect a population event occurring between 1912 and 1926. It could reflect increased mortality among women of childbearing age, but, given the small sample sizes, it is impossible to establish that for certain. The crude birthrate (CBR), which measures the number of births per 1,000-person population, is 37.2 per 1,000 in 1971 (see Table 6.1). The general fertility rate (GFR), which is the number of births in a census year divided by total women age 15–49 in the population in that year 3 1,000, is 171 per 1,000 women age 15–49. When compared with 1993's figures, both of these measures strengthen the case that the Melemchi population in 1971 was growing.

Melemchi Population in 1993

There are 483 people in the 1993 Melemchi census. The age-sex structure in 1993, as indicated in Figure 6.1, is not a pyramid shape. Overall, the shape suggests a population that is not growing at a stable, constant rate (i.e., sides are not in a smooth line). In the 1993 figure, the bottom or youngest cohort is not the largest; instead the largest bulge occurs around 1968–73, probably the last period of very high fertility in this population. Furthermore, the percent of the population under the age of 20 years has dropped to 34.6%, indicating that growth has slowed down considerably.

The 1993 population has a CBR of 14.49 per 1,000 and a GFR of 53 per 1,000 women age 15–49 (see Table 6.1). Both of these figures are substantially lower than in 1971: The 1971 CBR is 2.6 times larger than in 1993, while the 1971 GFR is 3.2 times larger. However, in both censuses, the population is growing, as evidenced by the higher birthrates than death rates and the fact that the population increased over 38% in the 22 years between 1971 and 1993.

FERTILITY

Population growth is determined by the relationship between births and deaths, as well as immigration and emigration from the population. Measures of fertility are fundamental to understanding birthrates in a population. Fertility is affected by a number of factors, and the study of the interaction of these in small noncontracepting

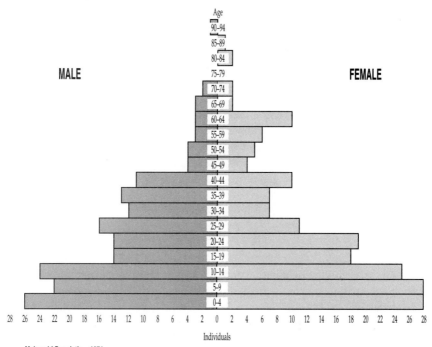

Melemchi Population: 1971

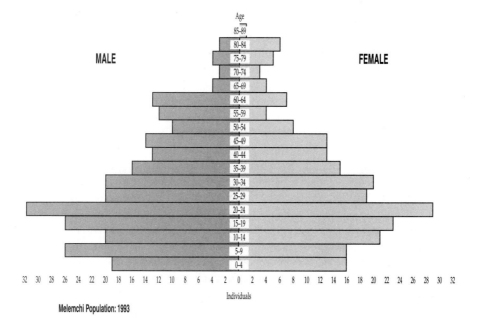

Melemchi Population: 1993

Figure 6.1 Age–sex structure of Melemchi village.

TABLE 6.1   A COMPARISON OF MELEMCHI POPULATION IN CENSUS YEARS:
1971 AND 1993

	1971	1993
Crude birthrate (CBR): (per 1,000)	37.2	14.49
General fertility rate (GFR): (per 1,000)	171 (age 15-49) 181 (age 15-44)	53 58.8
Crude death rate (CDR): (per 1,000)	3 per 1,000*	2*
Sex ratio in total population:	94.9 males/100 females	113.6 males/100 females

*Death rates are very low (based on only one death reported each year). See discussion of sample problems with mortality in this study.

populations is a growing field within anthropology, especially among those working on life history parameters in the field of human evolutionary ecology. Fertility must be examined over the life course, since the likelihood of conception changes during a woman's reproductive lifetime. Cultural, environmental, and physiological factors all affect the probability of conception. For Melemchi, cultural factors include age at marriage, the delay in cohabitation once married, the possibility of premarital sex, subsistence activities that keep men and women apart for long periods of time, diet, duration of lactation, and subsistence strategy choices that favor or penalize large family size. In addition, fertility in Melemchi may be affected by environmental stresses associated with moderate altitude, including hypoxia, iodine deficiency, and nutritional stress. Factors such as health status, sexually transmitted diseases, and use of contraception may also affect fertility in Melemchi.

This was not a demographic study by design, and not all of these factors were investigated. However, in the course of our interviewing individuals in the population, reproductive histories were collected, and these afford us some information about demographic aspects of Melemchi. Reproductive histories were collected for 162 women in Melemchi. Each was evaluated according to whether or not she had completed her reproductive life. Women over the age of 45 were considered to have completed their reproduction; women between the ages of 15 and 45 were considered not completed. Furthermore, each history was assigned a confidence rank. Excellent: I had interviewed the woman in depth and cross-checked the information. Good: High confidence through either interviews or repeated cross-checks with relatives of high reliability; however, abortions or stillbirths could be missed. Fair: may contain errors of omission—based only on reported data. The analysis of fertility is based on the 162 reproductive histories, which vary in completeness. Therefore, sample sizes vary for each measure; in each instance, I used all the data available.

Methodology

Reproductive histories were collected from women by me with the assistance of male interpreters; the husbands were almost always present. Both husbands and wives participated in the interviews, helping each other to remember birth order, birth years, stillborn children, and other details from their lives. Men and women in Melemchi share an open and relaxed relationship, in general; although recalling deceased children often brought tears and painful memories to both women and men, there was almost uniform willingness to cooperate with my questions and provide information. These interviews in 1971 were carried out with families we had come to know well over the year we lived there. We provided birth control information and supplies for those who wanted it, which included most families. Beginning in 1986, I undertook systematic interviews of every married woman in the village, plus interviews with family members about daughters living in India. These interviews were repeated and updated in 1989, 1993, and 1995.

The context of these interviews must be clear; I conducted the interviews with the assistance of a male field assistant (nonlocal in 1971 and 1986; local in 1989, 1993, and 1995) usually in the home of the interviewees. Occasionally there were visitors who came by and listened and participated. The interviews were formal only from my perspective; I took notes, followed a set of questions, and pursued points of contradiction. Interviewees were informed of the purpose of my work and agreed to answer the questions. However, from their perspective, it was a social visit. They fixed tea, arak, fried eggs, and, if the interview took long enough, boiled potatoes with marza (freshly pounded garlic, chili, and salt). We were friends, and, as such, we spent much time in friendly discussion of a variety of subjects. I rarely pursued areas people were reluctant to talk about; if I could find the information out indirectly, I did, but sometimes I never got the answer. Because I first met everyone when I lived there studying monkeys and not them, I was occasionally reluctant to presume on friendship that had been forged under different circumstances.

With only a few exceptions, women talked easily about their children, their birth experiences, and their own health. I finally gave up asking about age at menarche, the onset of menstruation. Here, my use of male assistants, especially nonlocals, did affect women's willingness to discuss personal matters; furthermore, a number of women seemed to have real difficulty remembering the specific age. Each woman interviewed was asked about the age, gender, and name of all children, living and dead; the same information about stillborn children; miscarriages; age at first marriage; her year of birth; and identity of parents.

Melemchi people use the Tibetan calendar for determining year of birth; this is the same as the Chinese calendar, with a 12-year cycle, each year represented by an animal. People know they are born in the year of the dog, and, by extrapolation, it is easy to figure out which calendar year this is. The use of the Tibetan calendar results in remarkably accurate information in most cases. However, it doesn't correspond exactly to the Western calendar year (the Tibetan year begins anywhere from mid-January through February), and it lacks the specificity of birth months within the year. People are only concerned with the year of their birth and, in some cases, the day. For some people, the day of the week on which they were born constrains their activity. For example, we were told by several people that they don't touch money, or they don't begin journeys, or they don't leave their house on a particular day of the week, based on the day of the week on which they were born. I assigned a Western year to each individual based on the Tibetan year of birth; this can result in ages that are off by 11 months, but at least the error is consistent. For births that occurred during the years of my study, I usually have the full date of birth, but for recalled dates, I have only the Tibetan birth year.

Melemchi residents have a phenomenal memory for this sort of information, not only with respect to their own families but also for others. Informants provided remarkable detail on birth years, names, and genders of other people's children over several generations, all of which proved correct. This skill with recalled information has proven valuable as well in constructing the genealogies of families dating back as far as six generations.

Fertility Data

Age at marriage and age at first birth are two measures used to understand the repro-ductive lifespan for women in a particular population. Early marriage and early con-ceptions increase the number of years at risk for conception, while delays in either reduce it. In Melemchi, the average age at first marriage among the 80 women for whom data are available is 20.2 years of age. The average age at first birth is 22 years old; however, there is a wide range (16 to 37). If we look at only women of completed fertility (those born prior to 1948), the average age at first birth is 22.5; for those younger women (not yet completed fertility) the average age at first birth is 21.5 years of age. It is possible that the trend away from capture marriage and toward love marriages contributes here; in a capture marriage, there is often some delay between the "marriage" and cohabitation (exposure to risk of pregnancy), which would delay conception, while in a love marriage this delay doesn't occur.

For those women who have completed their fertility, the average number of births is 7.2 children (with a range of 0 to 13 births per woman). In order to see if total number of births has been decreasing over time,we considered the women of com-pleted fertility by the decade of their birth. It appears that the younger women (born after 1940) had fewer children than their older counterparts. The completed family size (CFS) of those born in 1940 or after is only 5.45, while the CFS of women born in earlier decades ranges from 7.2 to 8.6. This reduced family size probably results from the use of birth control by women born after 1940.

Age-specific fertility rates (ASFR) describe a population in terms of the way fer-tility changes with age. ASFR tables provide a profile of the population, which can then be used for comparison, either with itself over time or with another population. Age-specific fertility rates are a measure of the actual number of births per woman-years at risk for a particular age category. Most tables use a 5-year age interval as the category: (15–19, 20–24, etc.). To calculate age-specific fertility rates, you must know the number of births that have occurred in each age interval (i.e., how many births have ever occurred to women in that population age 15–19 years, 20–24 years, etc.) and the woman-years at risk during each interval (or, how many women have been that age in the population?). A woman contributes one "woman-year at risk" for every year she was exposed to the risk of childbirth; for example, one 22-year-old woman would have contributed 5 years of risk to the 15–19 year interval and 2 years of risk to the 20–24 interval. The ASFR is calculated by dividing the number of births in an interval by the number of women-years at risk.

ASFR were obtained from the reproductive histories of a sample of 37 women who have completed their fertility. The sample was determined by using only those women whose year of birth was known for themselves and all of their children. (It is necessary to apply this strict criterion so that all births that occurred during a period of risk are included.) Since all 37 women had lived through the ages of 15 to 19, they each contributed 5 years of risk of conception to that age-category sample, or a total of 185 years at risk. Likewise, they had all been alive through the ages of 20–24, 25–29, and so on, and the total years at risk were the same (185 years) until the age of 45. At this point, their ages differ and so there are fewer years at risk (i.e., 158).

The age-specific fertility rates for **women with completed fertility** were as follows:

Age	Births	Year at Risk	ASFR
15–19	4	185	.022
20–24	48	185	.259
25–29	68	185	.368
30–34	46	185	.249
35–39	49	185	.265
40–44	24	185	.130
45–49	4	158	.025

Total children = 243
Total women = 37
Average births per woman = 6.57

Comparable data for 39 **women who had not yet completed fertility** were also obtained:

Age	Births	Years at Risk	ASFR
15–19	8	191	.042
20–24	37	176	.210
25–29	21	132	.159
30–34	10	81	.123
35–39	4	30	.133

Total children = 80
Total women = 39
Average births per woman = 2.05

When we compare the ASFR for older women (over 45 years) and younger women (between 15 and 45 years), we see a general similarity in the overall pattern: The rate is lowest in the youngest age cohort and immediately rises. This suggests that women in this population between the ages of 15 and 19 are less likely to become pregnant than when they are in their mid-20s, and their fertility increases rapidly in their 20s. Despite similarities in pattern, there are differences in the values between these two groups. Women under 45 years who have not completed their fertility have lower ASFR in the age groups 20–24, 25–29, 30–34, and 35–39 than women who have completed their fertility. This may be an artifact of small sample size, or it may result from this sample of under-45-years women, which includes eight women who had no children but contributed years of risk. (The sample of women over 45 years of age included only one woman who contributed years of risk but had no children. This probably results from the methods used to obtain reproductive histories of women of completed fertility. In 1971, I did not do systematic interviews; I happened to interview only women with children. I didn't interview unmarried women until the late 1980s, and, by that time, several who would have been included in the "older" and "completed fertility" group had died and, so, were never included. A third explanation for the differences in ASFR between the younger and older group of women is that the younger women have lower fertility. This likely results from the use of contraception, which was not generally available to this population prior to 1970 but has become widespread.

Another difference between these two populations is the much higher absolute ASFR for the 15–19 age group in the "not completed" or younger sample. This confirms the earlier observation that women are now having babies earlier.

Data on ASFR tell us something about fertility rates as they change with age and can be compared across populations, as well as within a population over time as we have here. There are also factors other than age that can affect fertility and risk of conception.

Marriage   In Melemchi, the delay between marriage and cohabitation results in reduced fertility for young women when they would otherwise be expected to be fecund. Thus, the recent increase in love marriages could be expected to increase ASFRs for the first two age cohorts: 15–19 and 20–24. The incidence of premarital sex is also important in terms of the exposure to risk of conception. I do not have good data on premarital sex. When I asked informants about the generally disapproving but lax attitudes toward premarital sex, pointing to the dearth of unwed mothers, I was told that the girls "must know how to take care of it." Certainly adolescent girls in 1989 were quite bold around young men, sharing sexual jokes and socializing easily, even disco dancing, albeit without partners, while in 1971 this wasn't observed. One night in 1993, a teenage girl did not come home until morning in the household in which we were staying; although her parents weren't happy about it, there were no serious repercussions, "as long as she doesn't get pregnant." We were also told of certain older women in the village who knew how to handle unwanted pregnancies.

Separation reduces the risk of pregnancy. Traditionally, Melemchi men spent time away from the *zomo gode* on supply runs (day trips), transporting butter for sale, purchasing new livestock, sheep trade in Tibet, and managing village agriculture. These absences were relatively short term—usually no more than several weeks at a time—and probably had relatively little impact on fertility. With wage labor in India, husbands and wives may be separated for much longer periods, even up to several years. Thus, as subsistence choices shift, the exposure to conception risk may be diminished.

Contraception   It is likely that contraception is in great part responsible for reducing population growth rates in Melemchi. Even in 1971, there was interest in birth control. During the year we lived in Melemchi, we were approached by six married couples who wanted information and assistance with contraception. One couple had six children and wanted a vasectomy but took birth control pills and condoms, since that was all we had. One more child was born to them after we left. Another couple also had six children; despite wanting a vasectomy for her husband, the wife was using birth control pills following the birth of their sixth child; 5 years later, the seventh and last child was born. Another pair, with three daughters, took birth control pills from us, but they went on to have three more daughters before their last child, a son, was born.

In 1971, there was also ambivalence and secrecy about birth control among Melemchi residents. People speculated about who in the village was using contraceptive pills. Several younger couples mentioned that their parents would be angry if they knew the couples were using birth control. Everyone knew about one man in the village who had a vasectomy, but another told us privately that he too had the surgery in Kathmandu; it had left him weak and in fact hadn't worked—he conceived a child 9 months after his surgery.

By 1993, most Melemchi residents had easy access to contraception on their frequent trips to and through Kathmandu, except for the very old or those in gode. Younger couples spoke of wanting only two or three children. Families in gode continued to produce large families. It is impossible to establish quantitatively, but it appears that large family size remains associated with gode life, while among families dependent on circular migration, family size varies from large to small, depending on circumstances. I suspect benefits to large families in gode counterbalance the costs. However, there is no way to test that. Sample sizes are too small and the variables involved all interact. One would need to consider only couples who have completed their reproductive lives. Furthermore, the fact that people alternate between gode and wage labor would necessitate separating these effects. Finally, access to contraceptive information and supplies throughout the reproductive lifespan differs with those two subsistence patterns, so one would need to be able to discriminate between large families that result from lack of alternatives and those that result from conscious choice.

I had hoped to document quantitatively my strong impression that Melemchi, even as recently as 1971, was experiencing high fertility and relatively low mortality. This is because large families were beneficial, not because they didn't know any better or have access to contraception. Large families are useful in gode, especially for mountain agropastoralists who need flexibility and diversification. The costs are slight, while the labor is the kind that benefits from the assistance of children, especially as they grow older. Anthropologists have been pointing out that fertility varies in the absence of contraception; natural fertility populations don't all have high fertility. It remains for researchers to explore the basis of high fertility, such as Melemchi's. Small sample sizes, the extraordinary mobility of Melemchi residents, and the absence of a research design specific for demographic work make it impossible to do anything more than hypothesize at this point, but the issue of family size and composition, in relation to individual economic choices, is extremely interesting in a situation such as Melemchi's.

Diet   Nutritional status has an important effect on fertility. Families in *gode,* in the village, and in India have substantial differences in their diets, which would affect both fertility and health. In the *gode,* people eat primarily dairy products and grain. In the village, grain and potatoes are supplemented with fresh vegetables and a more varied diet, given the opportunity to store food brought from Kathmandu. In India, all food must be purchased.

Individual families vary in their access to adequate nutrition, both in the village and in India. It is clear that there have always been poor families in Melemchi; in addition, families have gone through periods of disaster and shortage. Even in the early part of this century, hunger was known in Melemchi households. Several people told us that migration for wage labor had always been, for some people, an escape from hunger. Although Melemchi has not suffered the fate of so many middle-altitude villages where food production is adequate for only two-thirds of the year's need, dairy and agricultural production are limited by season. There are predictable lean periods, unpredictable environmental disasters, and long-term disparities in wealth. Neighbors attribute the poverty of some to laziness, having poor land, or just bad luck. In a couple of cases, gambling debts were implicated in a family's poverty.

In 1971, we knew of a few families that ate cornmeal mush much of the year, while others were eating potatoes and occasional meals with rice. These poor families seemed to be dependent on cash from India, cash that never came. Elderly people, too old for farming or gode life, also lived very sparingly, dependent on children for infusions of cash or produce. They were usually the ones who had time and need to gather wild foods, such as stinging nettles, fungi, and field greens. Several of our elderly neighbors came by periodically to sell us gathered produce or eggs from their chickens.[2] Bad years and big families caused hardships for some. By 1993, people were much more likely to be dependent on cash incomes, whatever their source. This left some especially vulnerable. Those who return from India too late to plant crops must subsist on savings until they can plant and harvest. And everyone is beginning to notice the effect of having so little local agriculture and herding. For example, there is an acute butter shortage; at Nara in 1993, the breads were fried in a mixture of butter and salad oil. The nutritional and health implications of the recent dependence on cash and migration remain to be documented.

SUMMARY: FERTILITY IN MELEMCHI

The data on fertility in Melemchi altogether suggest that fertility in this population has been and, to a lesser extent, remains relatively high. Younger women (those born after 1951) have their first babies earlier than their mothers did but have fewer babies overall. This is confirmed by the general fertility rates: Although the population continues to grow, the rate in 1993 is greatly reduced from the rate in 1971.[3]

Another way to gain perspective on the specific attributes of Melemchi's population is to compare it with similar populations. In Table 6.2, the population structure for the two census dates in Melemchi is compared with Nepal in general. Note that the age breakdown of Melemchi in 1971 is similar to the figures for Nepal in

TABLE 6.2   COMPARISON OF POPULATION STRUCTURE :
NEPAL AND MELEMCHI

Age Breakdown	Nepal, 1991	Melemchi, 1971	Melemchi, 1993
<15	42.3%	46.3%	28%
15–29	25.7	23.5	31
30–44	16.7	16.0	20.6
45–59	9.7	7.5	10.4
60–74	4.7	5.2	6.9
75+	.9	1.5	3.1

Nepal birthrate (1994) = 37.6 per 1000
Melemchi birthrate (1971) = 37.2 per 1000
Melemchi birthrate (1993) = 14.49 per 1000
Figures for Nepal from *Encyclopedia Britannica 1996 (on-line)*

1991. Both are rapidly expanding populations. Melemchi's age structure in 1993 differs dramatically from the nation as a whole, reflecting changes in fertility in Melemchi. The birthrate in Nepal in 1994 of 37.6/1,000 is similar to Melemchi's of 1971—37.2/1,000—and quite different from Melemchi's of 1993—14.49/1,000.

MORTALITY

Despite its inevitability, mortality has proven difficult to analyze in the Melemchi population. Out of 886 people listed in the database as part of the Melemchi population (members or relatives of members), the years of birth and death are known for only 70 individuals. This is in part because most people haven't died—only 28% or 252 people listed in the large database are in fact dead. Of those known to be dead, many deaths are not dated. And there are a few older individuals for whom we know the year of death, but they were never interviewed, so their birth year isn't known. The small sample size makes any quantitative analysis of mortality highly suspect.

In this sample of 70 individuals, there was some clumping of deaths for males between the ages of 15 and 29 (risk-taking behavior? exposure to accidents in unskilled wage labor jobs?) and for females between 25 and 44 (corresponding to the dangers of childbirth?), and roughly equal numbers of deaths were recorded for males and females 50 years and older.

Without a larger sample of ages at death, it is impossible to construct a life table or mortality schedule for Melemchi.

Causes of Death

Although quantitative death rates are unavailable for Melemchi, there is qualitative information on causes of death. Just as in any society, people in Melemchi die from accidents, illness, suicide, homicide, and childbirth. A certain number of babies die at or shortly after birth. People in Melemchi also die from causes without clear empirical bases, such as intentional poisoning or psychosomatic conditions such as "soul loss."[4] During the year in which we were full-time residents of Melemchi, we compiled a list of all ailments that were brought to us for consultation or treatment (see Table 6.3). It is included here not as a medical document but rather to indicate the range and frequency of problems that Melemchi residents considered treatable by Western medicine in 1971.[5]

Accidents

The most commonly reported accidents occurring in Melemchi involve fire, *khukri* knives, falls, and injuries by male livestock.

Fire Fire-related accidents most often involve infants and children, who fall into the hearth or are burned by liquids; despite this, in 1971 it was common practice for adults to banish noisy children at gatherings, telling them to "Go outside and build a fire!" In 1993, one woman died 3 weeks after she fell into the fire at home. She didn't seek medical help; she was 87 years old and had bad arthritis. Her family cared for her until she died.

Knives Every man in Melemchi, and most boys past the age of 12, carry *khukri* knives in scabbards tucked into their belt. *Khukri* are used to cut wood, clear brush, do fine woodworking, and even trim toenails. They are sharp and heavy, shaped somewhat like a cross between a machete and a scimitar; in fact, the Ghurka armies are famous for their *khukri*, which will behead a buffalo with a single blow. *Khukri* are used so widely for so many tasks that it is not surprising to find *khukri* involved in work-related accidents. One tragic death involved a 10-year-old boy who was accidentally punctured in the abdomen with a knife tucked into someone's waistband as several boys wrestled. Despite an expensive helicopter evacuation to Kathmandu, he died. *Khukri* are also the source of wounds from and to adult men, who use them in arguments and fights. There are several men in Melemchi who bear scars on their head or arms from fights involving knives.

Falls Slopes are steep and trees are tall; injuries and occasionally deaths from falls occur in this community where men climb mountainsides as well as trees in the course of their daily subsistence activities.

Animal Attacks Managing large bovids can result in accidental injuries to the men who handle them, usually broken or bruised ribs, which are disabling but not fatal. Attacks by Himalayan black bears have also occurred; one man from another village had his face ripped off by a bear. He went to India for plastic surgery after living for some time with a cloth covering his face.

Homicide and Suicide

Homicide and suicide are both rare, as might be imagined in a small community, especially one in which people can so easily move in and out. Interviews of living residents produced one recent instance of homicide in the village: Two young men

TABLE 6.3   SUMMARY OF MEDICAL COMPLAINTS: MELEMCHI 1971–72

The following medical complaints were brought to us during the 12 months we lived in Melemchi between 1971 and 1972. (No physicians were consulted.)

Wounds

1. *Khukri* accidents: 3 men cut off knuckles while chopping bamboo; 1 woman and 2 children cut off fingernails.

2. Burns: 2 infants (1 on foot; 1 on chin) from crawling in the fire.

3. Grain-pounding accidents: 1 man with lacerated and bruised finger.

4. Foot injuries: Many complaints of cracks in the soles of feet during winter; 1 man with puncture wound on foot from bamboo; 1 man cut side of foot on grass; 1 boy dropped a rock on his toe.

5. Dog bite: 1 child bitten on the thigh: broke skin and bruised the muscle.

6. Eyes: 1 man with wheat chaff in eye during harvest; many women asked for Chinese toothpaste, which they put into their eyes, which were irritated and weepy from smoke; the toothpaste produces copious watering, which relieves the pain.

7. Falls: 83-year-old woman fell down steps: bruised on face and body, broken wrist, twisted knee; 1 infant fell off porch and bruised shoulder; 1 man fell and scraped his face.

8. Bone abscesses: 3 men came with extensive suppurating wounds on their shinbones (tibia); in two cases, the underlying bone was gone. (All claimed these were recent injuries, since they knew we couldn't do anything about chronic problems; in fact, each case appeared to be a re-injuring or possibly a spontaneous opening of a site of previous infection.)

Illnesses

1. Gastrointestinal: included prolonged diarrhea (3 infants, 2 children, 4 adults); nausea and vomiting (5 adults); extreme dysentaries with fever, bloody stools (2 adults); and extreme gastrointestinal distress with distention, severe pain, diarrhea, inability to eat (2 women in their 60s and 1 boy recently returned from India).

2. Gynecological/obstetrical: woman (21 years) with severe menstrual cramping but no menstruation for 3 years; woman (30 years) with weakness following spontaneous abortion—her fourth child in 5 years; woman (49 years) with postpartum fever and pains—her water broke 3 days before delivery, and the placenta was expelled 3 days after delivery; woman (43 years) with swollen legs, loss of weight, and extreme fatigue following the birth and subsequent death after 20 days of her 10th child in 20 years—she came to us for medical assistance 3 years after the birth, still complaining of the symptoms.

3. Respiratory: numerous requests for cough medicine; 4 people thin, no appetite, and coughing blood (tuberculosis?).

4. Dermatological: 2 cases of body rash in summer; 5 cases of unidentified rashes, numerous complaints of infected sores on legs and feet during summer monsoon (1 child had sores on head and neck: parents said a previous child died from this affliction; another child had large scabs and sores on face and testicles.

5. Miscellaneous: 1 case of a bee sting allergy in a 13-year-old boy causing hives over entire body and delirium (survived); 4 complaints of chronic joint pains in arms and 1 in knees—all women over 45 years (arthritis?).

fought and one was killed in what seems to have been a crime of passion. The survivor ran away to India but then married a Melemchi girl with whom he lives in Bhutan. The one suicide that took place in the village was a man in his middle to late 50s who hanged himself inside his house. A second suicide was reported from India. A 23-year-old Melemchi boy hanged himself from a tree in 1990, despondent over the impending marriage of his younger brother. He felt he should be married first and was himself in love with the girl his brother was to marry. Following the suicide, the marriage was called off and the younger brother married a different girl.

Poisoning   Some deaths are inexplicable, in terms of known causes of illness. These are often attributed to poisoning. Especially in 1971–72, it was common to hear of family members who had been killed by poisoning. We were told in which village, or sometimes even by whom, a brother or sister was given poisoned food. This explanation for illness or death was rarely invoked by the mid-1980s. It is notable that, unlike their Hindu counterparts who view food as a potential source of pollution or purification, Melemchi people do not refuse food from the hands of particular groups and have little concern about eating leftover food. The only instance of concern about food pollution reported to us was villagers who were unhappy about **Ghale Karsong** fixing food with his hands at festival events, since he had visible signs of leprosy.[6] Yet Melemchi people in 1971 were quick to attribute mysterious deaths to intentional poisoning through food.

Illness

In 1971–72, residents of Melemchi only occasionally sought medical advice in Kathmandu; the time it took away from the village and work, the necessity for cash payment, and lack of familiarity with the Nepali language and the city meant most people with illnesses were dealt with in the village. The distance and the terrain were other impediments. Without roads and helicopters, people had to be carried on the backs of others, which was extremely uncomfortable for everyone involved. When Pasang **Pruba** fell ill, he was carried by two teams of two men each, who bore him—all 5 foot 5 inches, 135 pounds—up and down the steep slopes over a 3-day journey. On another occasion, when his nephew was fatally injured in the knife accident already described, the family paid to have a runner go to Kathmandu and call in a helicopter. This is one of two times that helicopters have come for Melemchi people in the 25 years we have known the village; the expense and the logistics make it an impractical response. People might consult a doctor if they are in Kathmandu on their return from India or on the rare occasions they go down to the city, but in general people use home remedies or stockpiled pharmaceuticals purchased in Kathmandu and consult the local practitioner, the *bombo*.

Bombo   *Bombo* are shamans, who divine the cause of illness and the appropriate cure through trancing rituals. *Bombo* are quite different from Tibetan Buddhist lamas, who also can perform divinations and Fprovide medicinal and other remedies. Although Melemchi people consult lamas if lamas happen to be in the village on retreat, their primary health practitioner is one of the local villagers who has been trained as a *bombo*. *Bombo* perform blood sacrifices (usually chickens, but also sheep or goats), which lamas do not do. *Bombo* in Melemchi do not consult books; lamas may often use books in their divinations. *Bombo* wear a harness of bells and go into trance with the help of rhythmic drumming on a special drum; they drum and chant, with occasional help from an assistant. Their *puja,* or rituals, are performed at an altar on the floor near the hearth or at special sites outside the house. The altars contain various items prepared especially for the *puja:* flowers, grain, eggs, purified water, and *torma* made to represent local deities and spirits. *Bombo puja* can go on all night. At one we witnessed for a woman who had chronic illness, the *bombo* sacrificed chicks, feeding the blood to the gods in the *torma,* danced, spoke in tongues as the gods entered his body, was possessed by various animal spirits, and beat people with branches dipped in boiling water that he had magically cooled. At intervals in-between, he rested and chatted with onlookers over cups of tea. The *puja* finally finished at around 8 a.m. It is difficult to say what the exact outcome of a *puja* is or should be. In this case, the woman who sponsored this *puja* maintained that **Karpu Bombo's** sessions made things better for her. Thus, she stayed in the village rather than in India, so she would have access to his services. Shortly after the *puja* just described, she left her husband who was in India and ran off to Kulu with Karpu Bombo.

In Melemchi, the *bombo* is a local resident who has received training in divination and rituals. At various times, there have been as many as four *bombo* among the men of Melemchi. Often, they are the son or nephew of a *bombo*. People seek assistance from the *bombo* for illness, in the broadest sense, among humans or even livestock. When things are not going well, the *bombo* is called to communicate with the spirit world and seek the cause of the problem. **Dorje** called the *bombo* when his herd was struck by disease; while in trance, the *bombo* was asked why John and our son, Noah, had been ill recently. We learned that John had not carried out an expedition to climb Yangri peak, and the local deity, Ama Choma Yangri, was angry. Furthermore, our house was not being properly purified. Noah's illness was diagnosed as soul loss, and the *bombo* came to our house for the next couple of days to perform the appropriate *puja.*

By the mid-1980s, people were more likely to seek medical help in Kathmandu owing to the increased frequency in travel there, greater access to cash, and increased fluency in Nepali language. However, for the sick villager locally, there was not much change from 1971. Even though two health posts sponsored by foreign non-governmental organizations[7] were opened within one long day's walk from Melemchi, they were usually unattended; villagers who made the trek found the clinic closed or the health-care worker away. In the 1990s, villagers did what they always had done: administer local care, call the *bombo,* and hope for the best. Over the years we were called to help several people who were dying. By the time we were consulted, they had languished for days or even weeks; their relatives were making the *arak* for their funeral, and no one had much hope, us included. In a couple of cases, we offered antibiotics or pain relief, and, in most cases, they recovered and slowly regained their strength. This is as much a testament to their own strong constitutions and the skill of the *bombo* as it is to any Western medicine we might administer.

Fortunately for Melemchi, the local environment promotes good health through good water sources, minimal crowding within the village, an altitude and climate that

Karpu Bombo, 1986. In some rituals, he dances and drums while in trance, wearing a harness of bells.

precludes tropical diseases such as malaria, and a diet of dairy products and grain. Low population density makes the absence of any sanitation system, other than household latrine areas on the second floor, less risky. The local system of throwing down layers of gathered leaf litter into the latrine, and then twice a year digging out the night soil and using it in the fields, seems to produce little more than shared roundworm infestations. There are seasonal health problems: In winter, cold, dry air encourages respiratory illnesses and keeps people inside houses that are poorly ventilated and smoky from the sole source of heat and fuel, the open-hearth fire. In summer monsoon, especially at the *gode,* there are skin infections and rashes from the perpetually muddy ground and exposure to animal viruses through openings in the skin left by leech bites. Ground leeches are not common in the village but abound at *gode* pasture sites, attracted by the animals but willing to feed on people and animals alike. The bites are painless; however, the anticoagulant that is injected with the bite to keep the blood flowing causes an itchy inflammation that invites infection.

As traffic increases between India and Melemchi, the health profile of the village will no doubt change. There is anecdotal evidence of diseases that are encountered in India: Measles, chicken pox, and tuberculosis have all been implicated in deaths of Melemchi people in India.

Nutritional deficiencies may also emerge, as people become dependent on cash for food, especially in the work camps. Numerous reports of alcohol-related problems, as well as deaths, indicate that the circular migrant lifestyle has costs to health that are new for this population. Wage-labor migration can increase exposure to sexually transmitted diseases (STD's), including AIDS; it is possible that the tendency in Melemchi for families to migrate together rather than just men alone could help diminish exposure. I am unaware of problems involving either AIDS or STDs in Melemchi at present.

ALTITUDE AND ENVIRONMENTAL STRESS ON FERTILITY

Goiter

Iodine deficiency is a potential problem in landlocked mountain communities, such as are found in Nepal, where iodine-poor soils resulted from the melting of the quaternary glaciers. When the glaciers melted, they washed away the iodine-rich soils, which were replaced by iodine-poor soils from crystalline rocks (Ward, Milledge, & West, 1989). Iodine is necessary for the synthesis of the thyroid hormone, thyroxine, and is usually ingested in food grown in iodized soils or water. When the body senses a lack of thyroxine, the anterior pituitary secretes thyroid-stimulating hormone (TSH) in an attempt to get the thyroid gland to produce thyroxine. Since that is impossible without the iodine present, more and more TSH is produced to no avail, and the condition called *goiter* can result. Goiters are enlarged thyroid glands caused by TSH-stimulated production of the colloid thyroglobin into the follicles of the thyroid gland. Glands full of colloid can be as large as 20 times normal size (Guyton & Hall, 1996). Goiter is common in the Himalayas and Tibet, although the actual distribution is quite spotty. One study of Sherpa in Solu-Khumbu found 92% with palpable goiter (invisible but detectable by feel), while 63% had a visible goiter (Ibertson et al., 1972, as cited in Ward, Milledge, & West, 1989). There is no medical survey of iodine deficiency in Melemchi or in the Yolmo region. The only individuals with noticeable goiter in Melemchi were two sisters. Both lived long lives (one died at 55 and the other at 75 years of age), and each had 12 children. They appeared normal in every other way, although one of them did experience at least two lengthy episodes of a mental disorder: once for 5 years following the birth of her 11th child and again for the 6 years prior to her death. In both instances, she lost the power to speak intelligibly and behaved erratically.[8]

Goiter is not the only symptom of iodine deficiency. Iodine deficiency disorders can result in abortions, stillbirths, and neurological cretinism (including mental deficiency and deaf-mutism) in the fetus, as well as impaired mental functions and retarded physical development in children and adolescents (Hetzel, 1989). Between the two sisters' 24 children, 5 of the children died at or shortly after birth. It is possible that some or all of these were related to their mothers' iodine deficiency. However, of the 19 who lived, none showed visibly enlarged thyroid glands or any other symptoms of iodine deficiency. The only other individuals in Melemchi with possible symptoms of iodine deficiency were two unrelated deaf-mutes, one man and one woman. Neither married, but the man lived alone until past the age of 70. Both were capable of independent living; beyond that, we were unable to assess neurological deficits. In Melemchi, deaf-mutes were said to result from offense given to a river god or spirit. In **Phu Gyalbu's** case, his mother had washed the bloody cloths after his birth in a stream in Gosaling; this fouled the water and enraged the stream's spirit, who rendered the baby deaf and mute. He was eldest of 13 children; none of the others showed obvious signs of iodine deficiency. He communicated with everyone using an animated sign language, telling stories about losing his toes to frostbite in a snowstorm on a high pass or foretelling an event or festival, describing everything from the food to the fights that were to come.

This small sample suggests that while there may be some environmental iodine deficiency in Melemchi, it is not widespread. It is more likely the result of individual biological variation. People vary in their physiology and genetic makeup, as well as behavior, and thus show differential response to environmental factors, even in an area of high iodine deficiency. Some foods such as cabbage and turnips contain antithyroid compounds, which can, in some people, block the production of thyroid hormone, resulting in a TSH-stimulated goiter. Other people have genetic abnormalities that inhibit production of thyroxine and hence show goiter, regardless of the environmental factors. Finally, it is possible that more than one factor may affect thyroid hormone production. For example, hypoxia, or low oxygen pressure at high altitudes, is known to inhibit TSH secretion, so it is possible that goiter will be more common at moderate altitudes than at high altitudes. At higher altitudes, hypoxia suppresses TSH production, so the thyroid gland won't produce goiter as readily. However, at moderate altitudes, where hypoxia is less strong, there is little suppression of TSH from hypoxia and the thyroid may continue to grow (Gosney, 1986a, as cited in Heath & Williams, 1989). A biomedical study is necessary to evaluate all these factors, but it appears, based on the frequency of obvious symptoms, that Melemchi has little evidence of iodine deficiency.

Altitude and Fertility

There is a body of literature that suggests that fertility is reduced in human populations living at high altitudes. A variety of explanations have been offered to account for this effect. One explanation is based on the physiological stress of hypoxia,[9] which occurs at high altitudes and results in reduced amounts of oxygen reaching the tissues. Physiological studies indicate that hypoxia affects certain aspects of fecundity (the biological capacity to conceive). Most of the documented effects are on the male: mild and reversible damage to the germinal epithelium and physical changes to the sperm at altitudes of 4,270 meters (Heath & Williams, 1989). Demographic studies in both the Andes and the Himalaya have suggested that high-altitude populations have reduced fertility, as measured by completed family size. There has been a tendency to attribute this to hypoxia, but in fact there are several other factors that may explain it better. Weitz et al. (1978) suggest that cultural factors such as delayed marriage and institutionalized celibacy (daughters who become Buddhist nuns, sons who become monks) are responsible for the reduced fertility seen in Himalayan populations; if even a small number of individuals are involved, it can reduce population fertility overall. A final suggestion to account for reduced fertility at high altitudes is that it has been confused with increased infant mortality. Low birth weights at high altitudes and the resultant increased infant mortality has been interpreted as reduced fertility, while, in fact, the babies are being born and hence fertility is unaffected (Dutt, 1980).

The publication of a critical article by Goldstein et al. in 1983, calling for methodological changes in the analysis of fertility data from different altitudes, signaled a hiatus in studies of this topic. Goldstein and his colleagues pointed out that several of the high-altitude studies included women who, for cultural reasons, were not at high risk for conception and thus depressed the fertility for that population. Women who had never married, married extremely late in life, or married early but were widowed and didn't remarry reduce the fertility rate in a population. They urged that studies compare fertility control for these factors. They argued that "based on the reexamination of the Andean and Himalayan data, it is concluded that the case for the presence of a hypoxic effect acting to reduce fertility and fecundity in long-term resident native populations in the Andes and the Himalayas is scientifically unproven, despite its widespread acceptance" (Goldstein et al., 1983, pp. 46–47).

The data from Melemchi on fertility can be compared with other published data from moderate- and high-altitude populations (see Table 6.4). The standard measures include age at menarche, age at first marriage, age at first childbirth, and completed family size (CFS). Melemchi's CFS of 7.2 is among the highest CFSs recorded, regardless of altitude. Average age at marriage is slightly later for Melemchi, but it may reflect, in part, previous unsuccessful capture marriages. Regardless, the age at first birth in Melemchi, which is 22, is comparable to that of most of the other populations.

The data from Melemchi, based on longitudinal data collected over 25 years, offers no corroboration to the idea that fertility is reduced at high altitudes. However, it must be acknowledged that at 2,600 meters, Melemchi is at the high end of "moderate altitude," not a "high-altitude population." An additional difficulty in applying these categories is that mountain people move up and down mountainsides over the year, so women in mobile populations are exposed to varying altitudes over their reproductive lives. Although Melemchi village is at 2,600 meters, women in Melemchi, in fact, move between the altitudes of 2,440 and 4,118 meters over the year. We also know that exercise makes a difference in hypoxic stress. For instance, the physiological effects of hypoxia are felt at rest above 3,050 meters, but, during physical exertion, they can be evoked as low as 2,440 meters (Frisancho, 1993).

TABLE 6.4   COMPARISONS OF FERTILITY AT VARIOUS ALTITUDES
IN HIMALAYAN POPULATIONS

A. Fertility in moderate-altitude populations (CFS = Completed family size):

	Menarche (age in years)	1st Marriage (age in years)	1st Child (age in years)	CFS
Bangham and Sacherer (1980) (2,200–2,600 m)	16.3	18.4	22.0	7.8
Laurenson et al. (1985) (2,590 m)	16.2	19.6	21.9	4.9*
Ross (1984)				
Thakuri (2,300 m)				7.4
Dhingaba (2,500 m)				7.0
Melemchi (2,590 m)	**no data**	**20.0**	**22.0**	**7.2**

B. Fertility in high-altitude populations:

	Group	Altitude	CFS
Goldstein (1981)	Limi (Tibetan)	3,900 m	7.4
Goldstein et al. (1983)	Kyilung (Buddhist)	3,500–4,000 m	6.4
	Kyilung (Muslim)	3,500–4,000 m	7.2
Gupta (1980)	Khumbu	3,400 m	4.5
Laurenson et al. (1985)	Khumbu	3,800 m	3.2*
Weitz et al. (1978)	Khumbu	3,400+m	4.8*
Goldstein et al. (1983)	Khumbu	3,400+m	6.3

*This CFS includes women who were not fully exposed to the risk of pregnancy, that is, not "fully married."

Since women in *gode* exert themselves in both agricultural and pastoral tasks over a wide altitudinal range, it becomes difficult to evaluate exposure to hypoxic stress. Furthermore, many women spend periods of time in India. Melemchi women living in India may live at much higher altitudes than Melemchi village. Their work in India varies as well; as young women, they might do heavy labor such as carrying heavy loads, but as mothers, they tend toward sedentary tasks, more compatible with child care. There are, then, two issues here. First, what is the hypoxic stress on Melemchi women over their reproductive lifespans? This is much different from assigning them an altitude of 2,600 meters on a comparative chart of fertility and altitude among Himalayan populations. No one has collected these data, although Catherine Panter-Brick and her colleagues working in Salme in neighboring Trisuli Valley have investigated women's energy intake, energy expenditure, and time allocation during pregnancy and lactation, as well as ovarian hormone excretion (Panter-Brick, 1993; Panter-Brick, Lotstein, & Ellison, 1993). However, given what we know about the lives of Melemchi women who have completed their reproductive careers, it seems hypoxic stress is only one of the stresses that might affect their fertility. The second issue remains, and that is whether there is any definitive evidence that high-altitude hypoxia affects fertility. Studies to date indicate that the effect, if any, is likely to be small in populations native to high altitudes, except at the greatest extremes of high altitude where additional environmental stresses will interact with hypoxia.

DISCUSSION: DEMOGRAPHY OF SMALL POPULATIONS

In contrast with most demographers who do regional or national analyses, anthropologists tend to work with small local populations, such as villages like Melemchi. This gives the anthropologist the benefit of working face-to-face with people, allowing an intimate understanding of the processes and patterns that underlie the demographic structure and characteristics of the population. Anthropological populations tend to be finite units that represent particular cultural systems, rather than nations or regions, which encompass many cultural systems. It is much easier to understand the way cultural and biological interactions produce a particular demographic profile in a smaller system and from there generalize to larger groups. Several aspects of the Melemchi data have implications for health policy. For example, the number of factors that affect fertility include cultural and behavioral aspects that would be overlooked if only quantitative fertility data were examined. Another example is the relationship between altitude and fertility, which is much more complex, as was just demonstrated, if one considers that women live at different altitudes doing different things through their reproductive lifespan, even though their village may be located at a particular altitude. Thus, these ethnographic village studies offer important guidance to those working in other fields, such as public health, health policy, or education policy.

While anthropological populations may frustrate us in terms of quantitative data, they are an excellent source of qualitative data (Swedlund & Armelagos, 1976). For example, despite the problems with documenting mortality rates in Melemchi, there is a great deal of information about how people die there. This emphasis on qualitative information can also assist in making anthropological data more accurate than those collected in large surveys. For example, in Melemchi, I collected age at first marriage in a number of interviews over several years before I realized that the question was ambiguous, in local terms. Because of the local pattern of grabbing marriages, which may not be consummated for a number of years, if ever, some women assumed I wanted to know their age in the marriage in which they stayed, while others told me the age at which they were grabbed. In a large population with questionnaires used for data collection, it is quite possible that the data collected on age of first marriage would conflate these two views. In my case, once I realized the problem, I was able to go back and ask again. This type of error could grossly affect calculations of fertility in a population, which, as we have seen, is crucial for an understanding of human reproductive ecology.

Demographers face the problems of documentation and reliability regardless of the size of the population they are studying (Carroll, 1975). Demographic studies need to be able to accurately document the characteristics of a population. This can be more difficult in a short study than in a long-term study, because change is an important aspect of demography. Longitudinal studies, such as the one of Melemchi, permit comparisons of the same group over time and provide time and opportunity for knowledge of the population to provide feedback that can inform the study itself. In the case of Melemchi, a long-term slowdown of growth in the population could be documented and compared to other changes in the society occurring at the same time. In contrast, a cross-sectional study provides a static glimpse of a population at one point in time and then compares it with other glimpses of other populations. In such cases, it is more difficult to understand the dynamic underlying the differences among populations, since there are so many variables to consider and little information to bring to bear. Reliability is also crucial in demographic work, regardless of the sample size. One must have confidence that the information collected and documented accurately reflects reality. This can be easier to establish in anthropological populations because the researcher can cross-check the information and address inconsistencies.

Some difficulties are distinctive to small populations. Techniques suitable to small populations and their resulting small sample sizes must be used. For example, it is easy to establish adequate age cohorts for studies of populations involving hundreds of thousands of people. But in small populations, there may be only a few individuals, or none at all, of a particular age. To overcome the problem of small or nonexistent samples, data must be grouped in such studies. This technique was used with Melemchi. Depending on the measure, I grouped individuals into 5-year age cohorts, or, in other cases, into two groups: women of completed fertility (ages 45 and over) and women not completed (ages 15–44). This created sample sizes big enough to be analyzed. Unfortunately, grouping still could not solve the problem for mortality rates, because the basic sample was simply too small.

All demographic studies must define the limits of the population. Large populations are likely to be geographically and politically bounded. Definitions of inclusion tend to be general and easy to apply, and errors cancel each other out. In small populations, where group boundaries are less clear and where every individual counts, researchers take pains to apply more rigid criteria for inclusion, which are often quite different from those used for large populations. Anthropologists tend to use factors such as kinship, residence, inheritance, and marriage to determine membership in the population, as I did with the Melemchi data (see page 115). Large demographic studies use different criteria (and frame different research questions) because they cannot collect such specific information. For example, the U.S. federal census treats everyone within a particular geographic area as a population, for purposes of analysis. If you are there on the day the census worker visits, you are part of that neighborhood. As a result, census data can address only some types of demographic questions.

Random variation and fluctuations are more visible in small samples and have a bigger impact on the analysis. Anthropological populations are susceptible to this; for example, because they contain relatively few people, there may be very few births or deaths in any particular year. Furthermore, these rates may vary dramatically and randomly from year to year. Any particular year therefore may not be representative of the general pattern and characteristics of the population. For example, in 1993 in Melemchi, there was a sex ratio of 113.6 males per 100 females. Considered alone, this raises the question of what risks females suffer in Melemchi that males do not. Without longitudinal data on other years or ethnographic information about the population, it is impossible to know whether this figure is significant or merely random variation. In fact, there are sex ratio data for one other year, 1971. In that year, there were 94.9 males per 100 females. Since there is no evidence for selective infanticide or preferential neglect of girls or cultural patterns that suggest increased adult female mortality, and the two available sex ratios suggest opposite trends, it is likely that the larger number of males to females in 1993 is random variation.

Another example of random demographic fluctuations in Melemchi can be seen in the 1993 death rates. With a small population such as Melemchi's (approximately 500 people), few vital events happen each year. In 1993 there was only 1 death; this suggests an extremely low crude death rate of 2 per 100 individuals. However, in 1990 there were 6 deaths, a very high death rate. Since nothing happened in the population that could explain the difference in numbers of deaths, this is assumed to be random variation from year to year.

There are other aspects of anthropological populations that pose difficulties for the demographer, in addition to their size. For instance, in nonliterate populations, people cannot always tell the researcher their age in years. Age is crucial not only for age-specific mortality and fertility rates but also for determining the age structure of the population. Each researcher has developed specific ways of accommodating this problem, depending on his or her situation. For example, among the Ache hunter-gatherers of Paraguay, Hill and Hurtado (1996) used event calendars and relative age lists to determine the ages of many of the people in their populations. Asking people whether they are older or younger than individuals of known ages, or whether they were present and, if so, how old they were at particular events, can be a laborious but successful way to determine ages. They also used photo comparisons; by assembling a sequence of photos of children of known age and then comparing a photo of the individual of unknown age, they could corroborate age estimations based on other criteria. In the case of Melemchi, I was fortunate to be able to take advantage of the Tibetan calendrical system for year of birth. Everyone knows his or her own year of birth and often those of others. However, I was not able to overcome another difficulty resulting from the absence of written birth records: determining ages of people I could not interview. In some cases where reliable family members or friends knew the birth year, I could determine the age of someone who wasn't present, but in some cases my informants were too old to accurately remember birth years, or no one who knew was available to ask. Parents always knew the birth order and usually the year of birth for their own children, but when parents weren't available, I was much less successful. Since so many Melemchi residents were unavailable when I was in the village, there are much smaller sample sizes for some measures than would be expected due to population size alone.

I underestimated the complexity of collecting demographic data for even such a limited population as a single Himalayan village. When I began my work in Melemchi on human ecological adaptation, it seemed an easy thing to include: Just ask every married woman about her reproductive history. People were willing to give me the information, I could cross-check it easily since I knew people well, the population was small enough so that everyone knew everyone else's situation, and, with preferred cross-cousin marriage and a high incidence of village endogamy, families were closely linked so that I encountered the same people over and over in my interviews. Instead, I discovered a village that grew like Topsy; the more people I interviewed, the more new people entered the database. Ultimately, I couldn't get all the information I needed on all the people I wanted to include; some died before I realized they were important to interview, some were in India when I was in the village, and a few didn't want to or were unable to give me accurate information. In parallel to our first year in Melemchi where a semideserted village became a complex matrix of many people moving in and out, my study of Melemchi demography expanded to include the Yolmo Valley and even India. It was a graphic illustration of the principles we learn early in our anthropological education: that no human population is isolated and that change is always occurring. Demography assumes an artificial situation in which populations are bounded and fixed in time, according to criteria that are an abstraction of real life. Anthropological demography, especially when applied to living populations, encounters a different set of factors: Populations are changing faster than the measurements can track them, and people are making decisions with demographic implications and outcomes based on multiple considerations that cannot easily be codified into rules and principles.

NOTES

[1] According to the criteria used, Hlatul is included in both the 1971 and 1993 census; although he has not become *tal* in Melemchi, he still is the son of *tal* and is eligible. Diki is also counted in both censuses; she married after 1971, so in 1971 she was still a resident; her divorce in the late 1980s left her a resident in 1993. Thus she is a member of the Melemchi population for both years. Mingmar Tongtong and his male relatives are not included in the 1971 census, since no one owned any property in Melemchi during that year. By 1993, his wife had died, but he and his father and children were all included in the 1993 census since by then he was *tal*. His brothers were not; one was dead and the other in India.

[2] Ibe Rike, our elderly neighbor, sold us 10 eggs one day; she knew we liked omelets for breakfast so she saved her eggs for us. Later in the afternoon, she rushed in and asked for the eggs back. Some tourist trekkers had arrived in the village, and she could sell her eggs to them for more money than she charged us. We, of course, cooperated and returned the eggs.

[3] With sample sizes as small as we have in Melemchi, there is always the possibility that inaccuracies in the data are magnified. For example, the younger women for whom I have only "fair" confidence in the accuracy of their data are excluded from the sample. These are the younger women living now in India for whom I lack personal interviews, depending exclusively on their families for information. They may have had additional babies of which their families are unaware, which would increase the overall population size in 1993 and more specifically raise the ASFRs for women in that sample. Still, the difference in number of births per women in the two samples (completed and not completed) are very large, and it is unlikely that adding in those women with "fair" confidence rankings would change the difference by much.

[4] For a complete description and discussion of the cultural and psychological dimensions of illness in Yolmo, see Desjarlais (1992).

[5] Because we were ourselves without access to medical care, we carried with us a medical kit prepared in consultation with Dr. James Roberts, who had been on the 1967 U.S. Everest Expedition. These few supplies included antibiotics, burn ointment, suppositories for violent vomiting, injectable morphine in the event of a fracture, topical antibiotics for eyes and skin, strong analgesics, bandages, and a book written to assist mountain climbers with emergency medical diagnosis and treatment of conditions likely under mountaineering circumstances, *Medicine for Mountaineering* (Wilkerson, 1967), now in its third edition. Our rationale was that we were at least 3 days from emergency medical treatment, so we had

what we might need during that period of either evacuation or waiting for treatment to be brought in. In Kathmandu, under the direction of a World Health Organization nurse who supervised health posts in Nepal, we purchased large quantities of aspirin, wound disinfectant, adhesive bandages, antacids, and vitamins to distribute for first aid in the village. We did not practice medicine in Melemchi; we offered first aid and encouraged people to seek assistance in Kathmandu. As for ourselves, we were fortunate to suffer only scabies, colds, and one eye injury while living in Melemchi that year.

[6] His father was greatly disfigured by leprosy, before he died in the mid-1950s. No one knows how the father got it, since he spent his whole life in a *zomo gode.* A second child, a daughter now in her late 30s, has recently shown evidence of the disease as well.

[7] Nongovernmental organizations work in a foreign country with support from sources other than their home governments. OXFAM is an example of a well-known NGO with projects in many countries; it is based in Britain and funding comes from private and public sources.

[8] The first episode began at a high-altitude labor camp 10 days after the birth of their 11th child, when her milk stopped. She was amnesic and unable to speak. Ten days later the child died, and the family returned to Melemchi. En route, they spent 1 month in Kathmandu seeing doctors who were unable to cure her with medicine. In Melemchi, she stopped speaking Yolmo language, became fluent in Hindi and Nepali, and spent most of her time in the forest, even climbing trees. The *bombo* was unable to help. Five years later, her husband was the *chiba chikla* for Nara and she helped him with the duties; when Nara was over, she was spontaneously cured with no memory of anything that had happened during her illness, including the birth of the baby.

[9] Strictly speaking, we are referring to high-altitude hypoxia; that is, reduced oxygen caused by low oxygen pressure in the atmosphere. As altitude increases, the partial pressure of oxygen in the atmosphere decreases. This results in reduction of the oxygen delivered to the body's tissues, especially the trachea and alveoli. Depending on whether the situation is acute (short term) or chronic (constant), the body responds in different ways. Hypoxia can result anytime the body is unable to obtain adequate oxygen; for example, carbon monoxide poisoning occurs when carbon monoxide displaces the oxygen in the atmosphere. Pneumonia, drowning, respiratory paralysis, and anemia can all interfere with the take-up of oxygen by body tissues.

7 / Change in Melemchi: 1971–93

Rex takes such nice photos—in color and the children look so nice! Not like those photos John took when you were first here. Our children looked so dirty in those photos. They didn't have nice clothes and their hair was not combed.

Interview with **Ibe Balmu,** age 60, 1989

Ibe Balmu shifted position to take the potatoes off the fire, moving her grandson, Tashi, off her lap as she spoke. Tashi is the 4-year-old son of Balmu's youngest daughter, Zangmu. Zangmu married her father's sister's son, and they were in India with their youngest baby, leaving Tashi with his two grandmothers in Melemchi. I remember those photos taken of Zangmu and her sisters in 1971: beautiful black-and- white portraits of wide-eyed girls with shorn heads (to avoid head lice), black Tibetan dresses patched so many times that they were three and four layers deep in some parts, and their noses running. No one had shoes then, and many boys wore only the Nepali tunic shirt—no pants until they were 12 or 13. By contrast in 1993,

Sisters Kando Hlamu, age 7, and Sumjho, 6, of Melemchi. Girls under 12 years of age wear short hair for ease of care. (1971)

Tashi wore an embroidered Indian hat, cotton pants, a long-sleeved shirt with buttons down the front, and red plastic rain boots.

Melemchi had been transformed over the time we knew it; while much was still familiar in 1993, the village looked different and in fact was different. In 1971, one person in the village owned a radio, but batteries were too expensive and available only in Kathmandu, so we could never listen to the daily Radio Nepal broadcasts. The man who owned the radio was also one of the few men who spoke Nepali; other people spoke only Yolmo language and rarely ventured outside Boudhanath when they went to the Kathmandu Valley because it was so hard to make themselves under-stood. Those people from Melemchi who traveled to India took the bus from Kath-mandu to Delhi, where they bought a plane ticket to their final destination in India. Ibe Balmu's daughter, who had left Melemchi in 1971 and who had traveled back and forth to work in Ladakh many times, discovered only in 1986 that it was possible to buy an air ticket straight through in Kathmandu. Melemchi houses were furnished with simple decor in 1971; the rows of empty tin cans with colored labels left on, eggshells, and pretty colored paper taken from our trash in 1971 were replaced in 1993 by full cans of imported food, rows of copper pots, and Chinese porcelain teacups. Where the walls had been bare in 1971, now they were covered in pages from magazines and newspapers, with a few posters of movie stars. Many houses, especially those with schoolchildren, had graffiti on the walls and window frames outside: hearts with arrows through them, "Maya loves P. D.," and "I love you" written both in English and Nepali (Devnagari) script.[1]

The transformation of Melemchi was fundamentally an economic one: The shift from dependence on agropastoralism to circular migration and a cash economy, which was well under way in 1971, accelerated during this period. Numbers of herds dropped, new herd types were adopted, and new kinds of jobs for circular migrants in new locations became available. All of this contributed to increased affluence and the possibility for new kinds of relationships to the village for residents, young and old. Several external factors contributed to the accelerated change experienced during this 25-year period: the death of the third Chini Lama in 1982, which left his sons battling over succession; the incorporation of Melemchi into the Langtang National Park in 1986; the opening of a government primary school in the village in 1984; and a decade of political unrest in the country culminating in 1990 with the overthrow of the monarchy. This chapter examines the nature of the economic changes in Melem-chi as well as some key events during this period and their effect on the village.

CHANGES IN MELEMCHI'S ECONOMY: 1971–93

Between 1971 and 1993, the Melemchi economy continued to shift away from agropastoralism and a subsistence economy and toward a dependence on circular migration and cash. Although the 1971 census included only a few householders who never lived in a *gode,* many did not have one at the time of the census. Those few who never had a *gode* were members of particular families who, for various reasons, didn't have herds (for example, the lineage lama clan, Hlalungba). Nearly everyone else alive in 1971 had been or was being raised in a *gode*. However, even then, many adults were no longer living with herds. A substantial number of Melemchi families had given up herding and were involved in periodic wage labor. Although they retained their houses and fields in Melemchi, and even built and bought new ones, it was clear in 1971 that most of their children would never herd *zomo*.

Decline in Agropastoralism

There has been a steady decline since 1971 in the numbers of men engaged in transhumant herding. In 1971, there were 24 *gode* associated with Melemchi, while there were 20 in 1986 and 18 in 1989. This difference is more pronounced if it is considered in terms of a percentage of households with *gode;* in 1971, 32% of the households had *gode,* while in 1989 only 22% did. By the end of 1989, four men sold their *zomo gode* to herders from Kulu, Nim Dumbu, and Bolgyang, and, in the next couple of years, 3 of the 4 sheep *gode* had been sold, all to Kulu people. By 1993, there were a total of 11 *gode* associated with Melemchi: 5 *zomo gode,* 4 cow/yak *gode,* 1 sheep *gode,* and 1 goat *gode.*

The abandonment of *zomo* herding for wage labor was a trend of many years. Ever since we first came to Melemchi in 1971, sons had been choosing to go to India in greater and greater numbers, most selling off their inherited livestock either immediately or within a few years, causing the numbers of herds to dwindle. The older men who had maintained herds over the years were shifting to the easier life of herding cows and yaks. Only a few young men wanted to herd *zomo*.

New Opportunities in Circular Migration

The Melemchi men who worked in India, Burma, Assam, and Sikkim in the 1960s and 1970s did primarily laborer work: They carried mud, broke rocks into gravel, and carried supplies for road-building projects throughout the Himalaya. They were acclimated to the altitude and climate and able to perform well under difficult conditions. The pay was meager, and often they came back with little. Women carried loads or more often cooked, distilled liquor, or maintained hotels for the workforce. Melemchi migrants explained that they went where there were jobs, not necessarily family or friends. When word would reach Melemchi that there was work in a particular place, people would set out to try their luck there.

Eventually, Melemchi people gained the Indian contacts and experience to obtain skilled work, which pays better with fewer risks. Some became road contractors who "buy" a piece of the road to be built from the government; they are responsible for completing that job, which may or may not be subcontracted. An alternative is carpentering; several Melemchi men have become skilled carpenters, which they can also do when they return to the village. The motivation for working in India has always been economic. People weren't escaping life in Melemchi; they were going to obtain cash income, or just to eat. Urgen, born in 1937, said that in his father's time there was also hunger in Melemchi, but there was no India to go to. Fortunately, his father had plenty of pastures, lots of milk, good fields, and two wives to maintain households both in the *gode* and the village, but others were less fortunate. For

Urgen, the lure of India was economic: As the youngest son, he would inherit his father's house and land, but he wanted capital and didn't want to herd like his older brothers. For Urgen's children, the pull away from Melemchi now is both economic and social. Today's young men and women see life outside the village as both lucrative and exciting, whether it be Kathmandu or India.

Urgen went to India for the first time in 1954 when he was 17 years old; the youngest of five brothers, he went with a brother and two others to Gangtok, Sikkim, where they lived in a rented room. Their job was carrying loads up to Yatung, near the Chinese border. They carried 100 kg loads of rice, *daal,* kerosene, truck parts, rags, and so forth for 150 Indian rupees per month (today that would be about 150 Nepalese rupees, or $6–7 U.S.). Each round-trip took 8 days. After 9 months, Urgen returned home with his brother, both having amassed only enough money to pay their return fares. They had gone to India because there wasn't enough to eat in Melemchi. Only 13 or 14 people were growing potatoes or wheat in the village then; with so many *zomo* herders, prices were low for butter and cheese, so there was little profit.

After the Gangtok trip, Urgen went back to India and spent 2 years working as a coolie on roads; then another trip for 1 year to Bhutan as a coolie. Finally he got a contractor job in Bomdila (in Arunachal Pradesh) for 2.5 years, building shelters of bamboo plastered inside and out with mud. His last job was working as a contractor for road building projects in Spiti (Himachal Pradesh). It lasted for 6 years, and his job was to coordinate and manage crews to work on roads. It paid good money (300 Nepalese rupees per month) and wasn't hard work at all. His wife died in India and at age 45 he married a divorced woman from Tarke Tho, 15 years his junior, and they have lived in his house in Melemchi with their young son ever since.

Nogabu went to Spiti with his uncle Urgen when he was only 11. Nogabu's father had sold their *gode* and moved to the village; impoverished, they needed income. Although strong, Nogabu was small and thin. He got a job, collecting and carrying wood, and lived with a cousin's family for whom he labored before and after work. Continually cheated out of his wages, he finally found work washing dishes and doing errands in a teashop run by a Sermathang family who were also of the Shangba clan. After a year, Nogabu returned home with another uncle; the 20 rupees he had been able to collect were spent on his food on the way. When he got home, his parents beat him for not bringing home any money. He found day work with Melemchi villagers, and, for the next few years, he earned 35 rupees per trip carrying loads between Melemchi and Kathmandu and Melemchi and other villages in the region. All his income went to his family. He went to India once more in his life; again, to the western Himalaya, where he worked on roads. Nogabu came back to Melemchi, never to go again, after his childhood friend from Melemchi was blown up in a blasting accident. The friend had asked Nogabu to work with him that day, but Nogabu stayed back to eat breakfast. Around noon, someone at the worksite accidentally flipped a lighted cigarette into a box of dynamite. Nogabu heard the explosion, saw the smoke, and watched two bodies fly into the air. He ran to the river, where he found his friend still alive with his body "like ground meat." By the time he returned with help, his friend had died. Nogabu never went back to work and soon returned to Melemchi.

New Opportunities Outside Nepal

Today, for young Melemchi residents, there are new opportunities beyond the places in India where their families have always gone. Nepalese citizens, including some from Melemchi, have found lucrative work in Taiwanese garment factories. In 1990, Taiwan granted amnesty to illegal workers who had flooded in during the late 1980s and legally permitted six industries to begin importing unskilled foreign labor (Pang, 1993). Prior to 1990, the only way workers could come into Taiwan was either illegally or as Chinese nationals. Since Nepal does not officially recognize Taiwan (Nepal is careful to remain on good terms with the People's Republic of China), there is no consulate in Kathmandu. This makes it difficult, but not impossible, for Nepalese citizens to obtain work permits or visas. A network assists those who wish to work in Taiwan, usually routing them through Hong Kong, but it has variable success and is expensive. However, the payoff is great. Salaries for work in a blue-jeans factory are reported to be as high as 75,000 rupees per month, although visas are only for 6 months. We heard of young people from Melemchi working 12-hour shifts, being locked into their dormitories, and being unable to mingle with Taiwanese society or spend any of their wages, but these stories were matched by tales of huge nest eggs amassed, to be spent on land and houses in the Kathmandu Valley. In 1995, several Melemchi couples were in South Korea; visas there cost a great deal but were good for 18 months, and the salaries in the factories were said to be high. All young couples we knew working in Asia had left their babies home with grandparents for the year or two they were away.

A less-lucrative and far more destructive type of circular migration is the traffic in women from the Himalayan hills to be prostitutes in cities such as Bombay. (The local term for these women is "Bambai girls.") They are recruited in their late teens, sometimes by guile, sometimes by force. In India, women from Nepal, especially those with more Mongoloid features, are highly sought for the sex trade (Pradhan, n.d.). The Sindupalchowk district, in which Melemchi village is located, has long been known as a source for traffic in women. During the Rana regime, women from this area were recruited as concubines and mistresses; since then, it is alleged that many families, especially in several low villages, have sent or sold daughters to Indian brothels (Pradhan, n.d.). The southern village of Melamchipul Bazaar is among the better known of these villages, which is especially troubling to the high Lama village of Melemchi, with which it is frequently confused. No Melemchi family acknowledges that any Melemchi women have been involved, noting that it was always forbidden by the Chini Lama. We were told of a village meeting called in Melemchi around 1984, at which it was agreed that any woman who did this kind of work in Bombay would not be allowed to return to the village.[2] To date, the only Bambai girls associated with Melemchi are a couple of Yolmo women who married Melemchi men in India after giving up that work.

Prostitution is reported to be lucrative, and the Yolmo region contains a number of women who have returned from India, some even to marry, with great fortunes. Others marry in India and, if they have money, return to visit. However, many are never heard from again. Young girls are susceptible, especially if they have never left their village before. They hear wondrous tales of life in Bombay and see the wealth that women bring back. Many lower villages experience months of hunger each year, and migration is an obvious way out: Men leave for wage labor and women for prostitution.[3] The stories of deceit, abandonment, abuse, and being sold and resold often don't return to the source villages, since girls may disappear forever, so many young girls remain susceptible. However, a few recently publicized cases have made everyone aware of a new development in the 1990s: Bambai girls who return with AIDS.[4]

Shift from *Zomo* Herding to *Zomo* Production *(Cow-Yak Gode)*

Even more notable than the decline in total numbers of *gode* between 1971 and 1993 is the shift in the type of *gode* maintained in Melemchi. In 1971, all but 1 of the 24 *gode* were *zomo gode* (the other was a sheep *gode)*, while in 1989 there were 8 *zomo*, 6 cow/yak (down from a high of 8), and 4 sheep/goat *gode*. It was also notable in 1989 that those who adopted the new cow/yak herd type were older (mean age is 53 years), owned houses in the village, had wives living in the village or no wife at all, and had older children assisting with the *gode*. The same was true for men with sheep/goat *gode*. In contrast, those with *zomo gode* were either young (23–26) or middle aged (39–44). Only one of the *zomo gode* owners had a house in the village.

Cow/yak *gode* produce *zomo* calves, not butter. Unlike *zomo gode* where the milk is taken and turned into dairy products, in a cow/yak *gode* a herd of cows is maintained and bred to the yak in order to produce *zomo* calves for sale.[5] Prior to the 1980s, Melemchi *zomo* herders bought their *zomo* from breeders who kept yak— either to the north in the Langtang Valley or as far east as Solu, 11–15 days' walk away. Since there are difficulties in managing a cow/yak herd (species incompatibility in climate, in seasonality of breeding, and in temperament, as well as the general unsuitability of cows for Melemchi's high pastures), it is curious that Melemchi men started this in the mid-1980s. Those who did it were all older. They explained that a *zomo gode* is much more difficult: The daily work of milking and butter making is hard; the high pastures are isolated and uncomfortable, while with cows you can stay closer to the village; and women aren't needed at the *gode* for dairying, so they can stay in the village more of the year. While there was an elderly couple in their 70s still out in their *zomo gode* with the help of a grandson, most Melemchi men we knew gave up their *zomo gode* in their 30s or 40s; a few hung on into their early 50s. This was the point in their lives when their own sons would be marrying and be needing a herd of their own, and they themselves would have been living the transhumant lifestyle for more than 20 to 30 years—long enough.

These older men wanted to give their herds to their sons and spend more time in or near the village, but also recognized that they needed a way to earn cash. Five of the six men had given up their *zomo gode* and tried wage labor in India for a while; all returned with cash to invest in a cow/yak *gode*. They acknowledged that unskilled work in India became more difficult for older men to find and to do, and they had no specialized skills. It was also clear that they liked being in and around Melemchi, not India. A cow/yak *gode* gave them a source of cash, provided a challenge, and maintained their pastures for their sons.

A few others who retired from their *zomo gode* lived in the village and bred one or two village milk cows with a yak, hoping to produce *zomo* calves for sale in the village. *Zomo* could bring as much as 4,000 or 5,000 rupees, a nice supplement for an elderly couple living in the village on their savings and rents. Some combined this with running a lodge in the village, another good source of income.

The experiments with cow/yak *gode* in the 1980s and 1990s in Melemchi were not universally successful. The initial investment in the yak was large (5,000 rupees or more), and management of a yak was quite different from *zomo* and bulls. Several yak died, unable to spend even winter months at the village altitude of 2,600 meters. Also, some yak are not compatible with cows; a yak must be purchased when young so as to become tamed by the owner and used to cows. Once old enough, the yak may not prove to be a good breeder. Conception rates are low: For example, one man bred 6 of his 19 cows and got only 3 calves. The cow/yak herder must make large initial investments, and, even if the cows conceive, he is 3 years from a sale, during which time the herd must be supported and the calf could die. In contrast, a *zomo* herder can keep his herd in milk and produce butter for sale through much of each year.

By 1993, as the numbers of *gode* dropped to 11, the pattern observed earlier remained: *Zomo gode* were maintained by younger men (ages 22, 33, 41, and 46) while cow/yak *gode* owners were older (56, 60, 64, and 65). The sheep and goat *gode* owners were also older, 57 and 63, respectively, and took care of their herds alone. What kind of a man is herding *zomo* today? Two of the young men with *zomo gode* are brothers who each inherited half of their father's herd in 1981 and have never been to India.[6] Another *zomo* herder spent 20 years working off and on in India; then he married and has been raising a young family in his *gode* for the past 10 years, often sharing pastures with his elderly in-laws who had their own herd until they both died in 1991. The fourth *zomo* herder had 7 years of experience in India beginning when he was 17; since then he has maintained his family's pastures and, with his wife, raised a family of 10 children, still with no house in the village at the age of 49. If there is a pattern here it is that these men prefer to have herds rather than work in India, at least while their families are young. All but one have parental support and participation. The cow/yak *gode* owners all maintain their herds with help from their youngest sons; each has told us they are keeping the herd for their sons, although it is not clear that any of the sons want to remain herders.

EXTERNAL INFLUENCES: 1971–93

Several things happened during this period that were a part of the changes in Melemchi just described. All had the effect of redefining relationships both among the villagers of Melemchi and between them and the national government. The death of the third Chini Lama, the incorporation of the village of Melemchi into the Langtang National Park, the introduction of the first government primary school in the village, and less obviously the political transformation of Nepal's government in 1990 all affected the ways in which the economic changes which were underway in Melemchi developed.

The Third Chini Lama (1889–1982)

In 1982, the third Chini Lama died; he had become Chini Lama in 1912 at the age of 23, and for 70 years he held the power over both the Boudhanath *stupa* and *guthi* in the Kathmandu Valley and Melemchi village. For nearly every Melemchi resident alive when he died, he had been the only Chini Lama they had known. He had at least four official wives, one of whom was from Melemchi, plus three Melemchi women who acknowledged being his mistress. His successor was his eldest son, Meme Babu. There were two other sons: Meme Babu's full brother, Meme Lama, and his half-brother, Thubten. Thubten was involved in local politics for many years and made no secret of his desire to be Chini Lama. The principle of primogeniture made it clear that the title would go to his older brother, Babu. However, when Babu died in 1989 after only 7 years as Chini Lama, Thubten challenged the right of Babu's eldest son, Andare, to succeed. Various stories circulated both in Boudhanath and Melemchi about the struggle for succession. Andare was said to have received the official royal sanction upon the death of his father, while Thubten arranged for the Boudhanath *guthi* committee to proclaim *him* successor. The quarrels took place both in private and in public, with Melemchi villagers caught in-between. Finally, Andare withdrew his claim, but in 1995 the matter remained unresolved. To some extent, the issue is moot; the Boudhanath *guthi* now operates as a committee, and taxes from Boudhanath are not paid to the Chini Lama.

For the residents of Melemchi, the death of the third Chini Lama signaled the end of an era. Although the office continues, none of his successors has been able to maintain the feudal control he held over people who had grown up under his rule. This is in part due to their own personal qualities: Thubten comes closest to the "iron fist" of his father but lacks his authority as a religious figure; Babu was ill for most of his term and had never been terribly interested in Melemchi; and Andare is young and forward looking and uncomfortable with the feudal role. It is also the result of the attempts of both the Chini Lama and the villagers to reconsider and reinvent their relationship in the Nepal of the late 20th century. It is obvious that those families who had access to the power and offices of the Chini Lama, through marriage, were much more comfortable with retaining the close relationship and feudal patterns than were others who were eager to assume self-rule. A few villagers returned to the village and became involved with village affairs, after long absences, once the Chini Lama's reign had loosened. Finally, during this period, the village began to experience the national government directly through the Langtang National Park, rather than through the intermediary of the Chini Lama family, and began to view themselves as part of the national citizenry.

Langtang National Park

Langtang National Park was established in 1976. It covers 171,000 square kilometers and includes the western slopes of the Trisuli River Valley, the high, dry inner valley of Langtang along the southern border of Tibet, and the humid mountain region south of Langtang along the upper slopes of Yolmo. There are 15 forest types and more than 1,000 species of flowering plants and ferns within the park (Shresta, 1985).

The southern border in Yolmo was the last to be negotiated—those villages not included in the park would not have access to resources there, so there were heavy incentives to participate, despite the costs of being under the rules and regulations of the park. Tarke Ghyang refused to be included, while Melemchi was incorporated by the end of 1986.

There are two administrative centers: one in Dunche on the Trisuli River side and one in Yolmo at the village of Sermathang. The park warden is stationed at park headquarters in Dunche; the Nepalese army, charged with enforcing the park rules, is stationed at several locations within the park, but none near Melemchi. There are park check posts along tourist trails to collect entrance fees and monitor human activity, although no checkpoints are near Melemchi. Trekking groups in the park are required to supply their own nonwood fuel, although this is difficult to enforce. Unlike Sagarmatha (Mount Everest) National Park, where there are severe wood shortages for local residents, lodges serving tourists in Langtang National Park are allowed to use firewood.

The Impact of Park Presence in Melemchi   By winter 1989 Melemchi residents were discussing real and anticipated problems with living in the park—their own and those of other villages. There were indications of the park itself within the village: government-approved signs for trekking lodges appeared on several houses, and we witnessed a village meeting held to collect wood and grass fees for the park. Already, the park was the subject of black humor: As we walked along a hillside behind the village where a huge stand of hemlock trees *(Tsuga dumosa)* had mysteriously died, one man said, "See, the park has been here only 1 year, and already the trees are dying."

Melemchi people reacted to the park with caution in winter 1989. To suddenly have an administrative agency of the government in their midst, in the form of the national park, as well as its enforcing arm, the Nepalese army, provoked concern. There were no major complaints about the way Melemchi people had been treated by park officials, in contrast to stories from elsewhere, but it was undeniable that there were real changes in the village as the result of the park.

The national park regulated the cutting of trees for firewood, timber, or fodder, imposing fees as well as insisting on regulating access. All fees were given back to the village for the *gomba* fund, at the suggestion of the national park, and in fact the villagers themselves collected the fees in many instances. Living trees are cut by residents for house construction and for prayer flagpoles, and the park prohibited the cutting of any living tree without written permission of the warden. The warden determines which trees may be cut and where they may be taken from, imposing a fee of 7 rupees for each cubic meter of house timber taken from within the park. The park also decreed that one new flagpole could be cut by each household every 3 years. Melemchi people had minimal objections to the flagpole regulations, even though they were accustomed to a new pole every year. It was considered a nuisance to go to the headquarters to negotiate timber cutting, but, in fact, park regulation of timber seemed to be having little effect on house construction. In 1989, three houses were being built, with another three plus the school building completed during the previous year.

The park imposed a fee of 25 rupees per year to cut and gather dead wood for fires. There was some sentiment in 1989 that this was a burden on poor families, since, unlike house construction, every family must have firewood, regardless of its wealth. However, it was apparent to us that for even the poorest families the fee was nominal. Yolmo people do not burn animal dung; they are accustomed to burning wood and there has always been a plentiful supply close by.

The park regulations about fodder cutting were understood by Melemchi people to mean they could cut leaves and branch tips from trees and shrubs anywhere in the park, but not the tops of the tree, whole branches, or the entire tree. Why the issue of fodder cutting was of such concern to *gode* owners was unclear, since, on the face of it, these regulations didn't limit herders in any real way. It may have been the specter of regulation of any kind to which the herders were objecting, viewing future regulations potentially threatening.

The large oak forest that forms the northern border of the village of Melemchi had always been off-limits for cutting live trees or taking fodder. Residents claim this rule predates the Chini Lama and has traditionally been enforced through the office of the *shing goba* (village wood or forest wardens). These are three village men whose duties are to designate the part of the forest off-limits to cutting, to give permission to individuals for cutting specific trees, and to enforce the rules through fines. Now in Melemchi the park warden or his representative has control over this forest, and in 1989 park officials gave permission to lop fodder there, as long as no one cut off the tops of the trees. They even pointed to the village forest as a source of timber for the new school building. The village was split on the matter; while some people welcomed the relaxation of strictures that had imposed costs on people, in terms of traveling distance for daily fodder or for timber, others were alarmed at the disregard for village tradition and concerned for their long-protected resource. In fact, the school building was built with timbers from adjacent forests, and the rule about preserving the village forest remains intact. However, this exemplifies the potential for damage that even well-meaning outsiders bring and reinforces villagers' sense of loss of control over their environment.

The park administration also reserved the right to regulate grazing within its boundaries. The only actual restriction in effect prior to the winter of 1989 was in an area of bamboo forest important to the maintenance of the red panda *(Ailurus fulgens)*. This area was so far from Melemchi that no Melemchi herders were affected; furthermore, it turned out to be more difficult to enforce than anticipated, so the effect was minimal. However, Melemchi herders were affected by the general banishment of *gode* from the area surrounding the lodges at Thare Pathi and on up to Gosainkunda Lakes. According to Melemchi people, the park said the herds created too much mud and mess around the lodges during the rainy season. This made it difficult for those Melemchi herders who also had lodges at Thare Pathi, since they anticipated being able to maintain both simultaneously.

The park assumed the right to operate services for tourists, including lodges, restaurants, tea shops, and shops. Prior to the formation of the national park, Melemchi residents took paying guests into their homes, offering them lodging and food. This was mainly done by those who could speak Nepali or even a little English, and whose houses were near the trekking paths. It had even become competitive; tourists were spotted 30 minutes out of the village and children were sent to run up and bring them to their own home. Now with the national park, a permit was needed to operate a business for the public within the park. Lodges that existed prior to the park had 6 months to secure a contract with the park. Both an application fee and an annual fee were required, which limited this business to those who had wealth. Lodge owners were given time limits for making improvements, such as installing a metal roof. The national park set the rates for food and beds, issuing an official rate card for each area. Food prices vary among areas, depending on the distance the supplies must be carried. The park also instructed lodge owners in standards for cleanliness, hygiene, and manners for dealing with tourists. Lodge owners were responsible for maintaining clean premises and controlling any trouble in their lodge.

While there were some compensations to the new system—for instance, the park prohibited open competition for guests, which had been the source of anger and tension within the village, and lodge owners appreciated the clarity and formality of the rate cards—Melemchi householders also felt vulnerable to a system they didn't control and weren't sure they understood. In 1989, lodge owners expressed the fear that any tourist complaint about them to the park office would result in their losing their license and their lodge investment. They told of making extra efforts to pick up all trash in the vicinity of the lodges, even though it wasn't theirs, lest the park officials accuse them; they worried about unstable tourists who could make trouble for them. Numerous examples of tourists who ate many meals and then didn't pay were cited; although they had always been vulnerable to this sort of problem, now, rather than just losing the money, they might lose their lodge. Therefore, they absorbed all losses without making a scene to avoid trouble with the park. Another area of uncertainty was how licenses would be renewed. Several were afraid that they would pay for the construction and the tin roof, only to have their licenses not renewed and receive either no or inadequate compensation. The lodge business was a good one. They can make as much money maintaining a lodge either in the village or at Thare Pathi throughout the two major trekking seasons (March–May and October–December) as they can doing many wage labor jobs in India. Therefore, the loss of autonomy over managing their business caused some concern.

Finally, the park imposed a number of rules concerning activities and behavior within the park. There were rules prohibiting hunting, fishing, or firing a gun without park permission. As Tibetan Buddhists, most Melemchi men aren't hunters but some have old rifles. As the wild boar population grew in the park under these prohibitions, boar became a widespread nuisance and a growing menace, especially to *gode* families. Finally, the warden permitted boar to be killed by any traditional means other than guns. Bow and arrow were mentioned specifically, which provoked mirth among Yolmo people, who have never been archers. The other fallout from the gun ban was the loss of the traditional blank gunshots that marked auspicious occasions, such as Tibetan New Year and weddings.

Responses to the National Park   It was clear during the winter and spring of 1989 that their recent incorporation into the national park had generated fear in Melemchi residents about loss of autonomy and control. They were accustomed to living under the control of the Chini Lama; they had a vague sense of the national government,

Pinzo, age 38, the Tibetan orphan adopted by Meme Gyau, in front of his new lodge, Tashi Dhelake Lodge (Tashi dhelake is a Tibetan greeting meaning literally "good merit" or "good luck.") Pinzo has lived in Melemchi most of his life and has a Tibetan wife and son.

most often referred to as "the king." Now, the national park warden and Nepalese government soldiers were establishing new rules and constraints. Rumors were rampant about terrible things that had happened in other villages within the park, most involving the army who enforced the regulations in the park. These rumors had two main themes: People were being wrongfully accused and punished, or people, especially in *gode,* were being harassed or plundered by soldiers. These were tales of helplessness in the face of an outside authority that could change the rules at will. People talked about "rule books" that they had never seen but that would be cited when residents were accused of transgressions. The concern with rules themselves manifested itself in jokes about ridiculous rules. Park rules concerning noise pollution—which outlawed radios, tape recorders, or musical instruments at any place within the park, other than at hotels, lodges, restaurants, religious places, or residences—were claimed to include no whistling in the park, and no shouting; people warned that if you shout in the park and the army is nearby, you will be arrested. Park rules against animal killing were jokingly reinterpreted to include the admonition that you will be charged a fine of 15 *paisa* (cents) for each leech or head louse killed in the national park!

People were also concerned about loss of property or decline in its value. The park did not actually take over anyone's land in Melemchi; Melemchi residents were quite relieved when the park headquarters for Yolmo was sited in Sermathang rather than Melemchi. In fact, park administrators were instrumental in explaining to residents how to have their land surveyed and registered in their own name, as well as explaining that they no longer had to pay taxes to the Chini Lama. However, people did fear that their control over their investment in lodges was precarious and, more important, that the park had made it difficult to herd *zomo*. In these early years of the park, *gode* owners felt that the potential for restrictions on cutting fodder and wood, as well as the possibility of restrictions on herd size and pasturing locations, would make it difficult to maintain a *gode*. Melemchi men own their *kharke* (pastures); they wondered where they would take their animals if denied access to their pastures. Their subsistence strategy is complex, balanced between frequent buying and selling of livestock coupled with periods of wage labor in India and village life. Living in the park introduced the possibility that they would experience arbitrary interference in their management of their options; perhaps the park would impose herd size or composition limits, or control prices. In winter 1989, two-thirds of the *gode* owners in Melemchi said they wanted to sell their herds because of the national park. They perceived that it would become more and more difficult to keep a herd, and they wanted to sell before there were no longer any buyers. Especially at low winter pastures where overgrazing and the local ecology made it necessary to supplement grazing with fodder, these herders felt vulnerable to regulations about what and where they could cut. Herder after herder, young and old, said they wanted to get out of the business.

In the years since 1989, various of the misunderstandings have been clarified by the villagers and park authorities. The rule against cutting in the village forest has been reinstated. The individual in the army who was causing problems with local residents has been transferred. The village has continued to extract itself from its relationship with the Chini Lama, shifting over to the system of fees administered under the authority of the park. There are fewer *zomo gode* today than there have been at any other time in the past 25 years, yet it is not clear the park is the cause. The national park has clearly had a major influence on life in the village, especially in the early years of the park's development. However, a long-term perspective has to view it as only one of many impinging factors.

Establishment of the Melemchi Primary School: 1984

Beginning in 1975, free primary education was established in Nepal, with the government providing teachers, facilities, and supplies; although it was compulsory, there was no way of ensuring that all children in Nepal actually had access. In fact, in 1984, figures indicate that only 52% of school-age children in Nepal were enrolled (Shrestha, 1993). It was during 1984 that, due to an oversupply of teachers in Tarke Ghyang, a 17-year-old Nepalese schoolteacher was finally assigned to teach in Melemchi village, and the first primary school was opened there. Primary education in Nepal includes the first five years of school; this is followed by another 5 years of secondary school prior to university. When the primary school opened in Melemchi, few children had any experience with formal education; even those children who had spent time in India were rarely educated there. Most often they too worked or stayed home to help their parents. The schoolmaster rented a vacant house for the first classroom. Starting with about 20 students, he struggled that first year under cramped conditions with inadequate light and no place for the children to study. A year later, he moved the school to the social room next to the *gomba;* there he had enough space for different classes to sit separately, there was a play area in front, and there was good natural light to work by.

In the Melemchi school, children are taught in Nepali, not their native Yolmo, to read and write Nepali. The national primary school curriculum begins with Nepali language and mathematics, with science, English, history, Sanskrit, and health and morals added in classes 4 and 5. The teacher in Melemchi had never attended college and he had had no instruction in pedagogy. His fellow teachers in Tarke Ghyang helped him with curriculum and materials. His early classes were all taught in Nepali, because that was the language he knew; by 1989, he was able to speak the Yolmo language well and used it in the classroom when needed. However, he has never become comfortable with the English curriculum.

Not all village families send their children to school; over the years, support for the school has vacillated, but in general families agree that it is beneficial to send both their boys and girls when they are in the village. The difficulty is that often children aren't in the village. During most of the year, it is impossible to commute from *gode,* so *gode* children are excluded from education unless arrangements are made for them to live in the village with relatives. Several families have done this for children with particular aptitude or interest in school. One herder told us he planned to sell his *gode,* in part because he wants his only son to be able to stay in school. He sees his son's future as better secured through education than through the inheritance of a herd. Some children don't go to school because they have had problems getting along with the schoolmaster. A few parents are not supportive of their children's participation; in these cases, the master tries to convince parents by inviting them to the school to see the children actually reading and writing, something that the parents are unable to do themselves. Some remain unconvinced and feel they need their children at home. The children of families who work in India go in and out of the Melemchi school as their residence changes.

The teacher is supported by the government,[7] but the parents pay for copy books and supplies. A few parents object to the expense and refuse to pay or to send their children. Expense is cited as a reason for stopping school after class 5, since secondary education is not free and students must leave the village to board; so far, there have been no village children who have gone past class 5, except for a few sent away to Kathmandu or India. The village built a new school building in 1989 using funds raised from trekkers' donations (these can be substantial; in just 3 days during March 1989, donations totaled 1,250 rupees) for labor and the tin roof. The building is a simple structure, furnished only with benches. The teacher moves from group to group, teaching five grades in all subjects. He rarely finishes by 3 p.m., when school is supposed to end; often he works with student groups until 5 p.m., and in the evening he tutors.

The school has been an agent of change in Melemchi. Several residents mentioned that the school curriculum socializes their children in the broadest sense, introducing them to new ideas about health, hygiene, and the world outside Melemchi. This reinforces the experience so many have when they live for periods in India. The schoolmaster explicitly teaches children to wash their hands, to comb their hair and brush their teeth every day, to bathe once a week, to keep their books and bag clean, and to cover their mouths when they cough. In physical education, along with Nepali dances and songs, he teaches sports, providing access to the only sports equipment (a volleyball) in the village. Village social gatherings have changed since the school was started. The school picnic is a new institution, supported by donations from households, just as religious events are, but in this case the picnic is spontaneously organized by the schoolchildren and the schoolmaster. The village gathers

Melemchi schoolchildren and schoolmaster. (1993)

at the school where a meal of rice, *daal,* and potato curry is cooked, just as at Nara; if enough money is collected, chickens will be bought for meat curry. Because of lessons in hygiene from school, in concert with the experience of urban living in India and exposure to tourists in the new lodges, the plates at these gatherings are now cleaned with ashes, bar soap, and water; in 1971 when we went to village celebrations, plates were licked clean and passed along to be filled for the next person. The school picnic is a time for adults to visit and children to play; in contrast to traditional religious and ritual events, Sherpa line-dancing and singing is rare.

By 1993, the older children in the village had taken the idea of the picnic and transformed it into a social gathering for teenagers, who seemed especially bored by life in the village. The schoolmaster cooperated by offering his house, in part because he shared their sense of their own marginality and in part because many were his friends and former students. We visited one picnic in 1993 that featured Hindi popular music tapes played on a boombox, disco dancing, and singing by boys and girls, plus a meal. Various adults and younger children dropped by over the course of the afternoon but stayed only a short while. The party ended with the boys playing caroms on a portable carom board and cards, while the girls watched.[8]

In 1989, the schoolmaster participated in a pilot program, sponsored by the Department of Education, to provide adult literacy classes in Melemchi. He went for a month's training and returned to offer the 6-month course. Each week, he taught literacy for 6 evenings, while on the 7th evening he taught life skills such as building and maintaining latrines, oral rehydration therapy, and personal hygiene. Both men and women took his classes, at least 40 residents in all. Eventually, there were not enough eligible people in the village, so the classes stopped. Despite everyone's good intentions, this has not resulted in a literate adult population in Melemchi. Each individual was only allowed to take the class series once, which is not long enough to actually learn how to read and write.

While the transformation of Melemchi since 1971 is more an economic than an educational one, the introduction of the school has been one of the contributing factors, both explicitly and implicitly. The national primary school curriculum has explicitly introduced ideas, behaviors, and skills that transform the way Melemchi residents interact with one another and with the world external to the village. As literate citizens, some now can read and write documents; as speakers and writers of the national language, they can participate in the national agenda. Implicitly, education, even in the limited form in which it exists in Melemchi, is contributing to the exodus of children from the *gode* and Yolmo itself, as it provides the skills and opportunities that make this possible.

Politics in Nepal: 1971–93

The Panchayat *System*   Nepal's political system from 1961 through 1990 was the "partyless *panchayat* system," a hierarchical system of representative councils or *panchayats* at the village or town level, district level, zonal level, and national level. This system was imposed by King Mahendra in 1961, and despite the appearance of participatory government, the monarchy retained absolute power, in addition to serving spiritually as the representative of the god Vishnu in this Hindu country. The

Lhari, age 21, and Pruba, 19, en route to Kathmandu. Lhari has spent much of his life in India; Pruba has been in an Indian boarding school. (1993)

Tarke Ghyang *panchayat* was formed in 1969 and included the Timbu, Kangyul, and Melemchi areas. The first *panchayat* representative or *adache* from Melemchi was **Dame Gopu,** who was appointed in 1972 by the representative from Tarke Ghyang. As Dame Gopu explained to us, he didn't have to do anything except show up for the meetings when they were called. The Tarke Ghyang representative decided everything. For example, when the bridge across the Melemchi River to Nagote washed away, the Tarke Ghyang representative decided when and where and how it would be fixed and sent a message to Dame Gopu to bring Melemchi men to work on it. **Kulu Sonam** was the Melemchi *adache* from 1982 through 1987. He, too, traveled to Tarke Ghyang for meetings when called, but his fluency in Nepali permitted him a more active role on behalf of Melemchi. He even traveled to Kathmandu to pursue *panchayat* business; for instance, he was a forceful voice for a school in Melemchi.

He sold his *zomo gode* when he was named *adache* so that he would be available in the village to assist in solving problems. He complained that it is a job with no pay that cost him both in time and in beer; when village men are called to participate in a *panchayat* project, such as trail clearing or bridge fixing, they argue about who should go and how it should be arranged, and Kulu Sonam must provide beer to cajole everyone into cooperating.

It was notable that no matter how nominal the position was, each Melemchi district representative took the job seriously. He arranged to be in the village for his entire term. He accepted the responsibility to arrange for village representation on district work details, which nearly always included arguments and problems of cooperation from his fellow villagers. He withstood criticism of his activities and endured the political maneuvering of the village's governing *goba* and the Chini Lama as they all contested for power over village affairs. Melemchi was always subservient to the Tarke Ghyang representative; yet each Melemchi man who held the position of *adache* viewed himself as a key village representative. It was a learning experience as well. Kulu Sonam told us about sitting in the *panchayat* offices in Kathmandu holding a Nepali newspaper and ostentatiously pretending to read it, having seen how much better officials treated his literate colleagues.

After the political upheavals in the national government in 1990, the victorious democracy movement abolished the *panchayat* system, and a multiparty system was instituted in Nepal. Local representation was still required, but now the village representative is elected in Melemchi and belongs to a political party—in the case of Melemchi's *adache* in 1993, it is the Congress party. He meets with the other eight elected representatives two to three times per month in Timbu, with their deliberations reported to the district headquarters in Chautara. They continue to handle requests to the government for electrification projects, bridge repairs, development projects, and so forth, and also adjudicate some local disputes.

The Democracy Movement   In 1990, following a number of years in which there was rising political tension, the Nepalese monarchy was overthrown in an often violent series of confrontations between citizens and government forces. After much bloodshed and intrigue, the king lifted the ban on political parties in April 1990, and Nepal became a constitutional monarchy with multiparty democracy. The king remains chief of state, but there is clear separation of powers, and religious and cultural freedom is given to non-Hindus. At the national level, politics continues to be a complicated and changing set of relationships among those supporting the old *panchayat* system, numerous communist factions, and the Nepali Congress party. At the local level, all of these plus local politics and history are at play. By 1993, the political party system was in full swing and the various symbols of the parties were in evidence as graffiti on walls, rocks, and even stone *pathi* along the paths to Melemchi. Sometime after 1990, the system for choosing village *goba* changed to a lottery system. We were aware of growing tension between our old friends in the village and some of the younger men, a few of whom had returned to the village after many years away in India. Eventually, several older *goba* said they wanted to quit; they were tired of all the arguing and politicking. Thubten Lama, the second son and by then self-appointed successor to the Chini Lama position, came up to Melemchi and tried to convince several of the older men to remain as *goba*. Despite Thubten's appeals, the village insisted on a lottery system to select the *goba;* each *tal* was assigned a number, the numbers were written on paper, put into balls of *tsampa,* and then drawn from a hat. The new *goba* are all younger men; those fathers who happened to be chosen deferred to their sons, and the village is ostensibly under new management. The impact of this is unclear. In fact, many of the *goba's* jobs are now administered under the national park (e.g., taxes and regulation of wood, forests, and grazing); all the *goba* do is collect the money and record it. However, there is considerable mistrust within the village where money is concerned, and those who can write and read have an advantage over the others. The other duties of the *goba*—supervising the religious cycle—fall outside the experience of many of the younger men who may have lived much of their lives in India. In summer 1993, the young men were arranging for the Tupa Tsezhu altars with mixed success; they had the *tso* (ritual rice balls) and the *torma* ready, but no one could find the key to get into the Tupu cave.

The anomalous situation of Melemchi as a *guthi* within Yolmo makes the impact of national policy difficult to measure. From 1971 through 1993, there was a gradual diminishment of the influence and power of the Chini Lama over Melemchi affairs. This stemmed in part from changes in Boudhanath, in part from economic and social changes in Melemchi, and in part from national changes in Nepal itself. Not everyone in Melemchi experienced these changes in the same way; age, experience, clan affiliation, and sphere of activity and influence all affected the way in which this transformation was felt. There has always been tension within the village over power and authority, and given the nature of the changes during 1971–93, this has only increased over time.

Land Reform   There is no evidence that national land reform policy, intended to address issues of landlessness, had any effect on the use of land in Melemchi. Until quite recently, land has been available in the village, and the Chini Lama, not the national government, controlled it. In Melemchi, then, it was not land reform laws but the national park that provided the catalyst for individual ownership of village land. The park administrators explained to Melemchi residents that they needed to register their land under their own names. Despite the absence of cooperation from the Chini Lama, government surveyors arrived between 1985 and 1988, literate children and villagers helped fill out the forms, and many residents made the long walk to the district center in Chautara to file for ownership documents.

Citizenship   For those who travel so freely over the Nepalese-Indian border, proof of citizenship is useful, although not required. The huge influx of Tibetan refugees, and more recently Indian laborers, has provided incentive for Nepalese citizens to document citizenship. Furthermore, the expansion of travel beyond India by citizens of Melemchi has resulted in many villagers walking to Chautara to file for citizenship papers and a Nepalese passport.

DISCUSSION: LIVING IN A NATIONAL PARK

The rights of indigenous people over land that they either use or own is central to the issue of the development of inhabited national parks. Furthermore, it is part of an even broader question that is emerging throughout the world: Who will control not only land and its uses but also the presentation and expression of culture (Johnston, 1990)? Urban parks and heritage parks in the developed world are addressing many of the same questions that are raised in the establishment of national parks and protected areas in developing countries: How can local residents be incorporated into protected areas? What behaviors will be regulated within the protected area, and who will regulate them? Whose culture or heritage will be maintained and supported within the protected area? And what and whose purposes do protected areas serve? These questions are being asked worldwide as indigenous residents fight to maintain control over lands they use. The threats come from development projects (e.g., dams and road-building projects), private entrepreneurs (e.g., gold miners in the Amazon basin), international corporations (e.g., logging companies in Southeast Asia), and government agencies, as well as from efforts to preserve the environment through national parks and wildlife reserves. The interests of local residents and conservationists do not always coincide (Clay, 1985) and the stakes can be very high.

In the establishment of a national park, local people are constrained in their uses and in some cases removed, in order to (1) conserve and protect natural resources, including landscapes; (2) develop lands as revenue resources for tourism; or (3) retain some proportion of undeveloped open space for the future. Attempts to establish national parks in Nepal primarily focused on the conservation and protection of the unique flora, fauna, and landforms of that country. There was also an awareness of localized deforestation and environmental degradation, and, in addition, there was a growing emphasis by the government on the benefits of tourism as a source of revenue, for which pristine landscapes and wildlife are essential. However, it is nearly impossible to have a park without people in Nepal. With high population densities, especially if you consider only accessible or arable land, at present "all accessible land surface is either inhabited or used by subsistence farmers" (Sherpa, 1988). Therefore all park development in Nepal has taken place in negotiation with local people.

National Parks in Nepal

The national park system in Nepal was established in 1972 with the National Parks and Wildlife Conservation Act of 1972 (2029).[9] National parks were defined as "an area set aside for conservation, management, and utilization of animals, birds, vegetation or landscape together with the natural environment" (HMG, 1972). There is no mention of residents, despite the fact that all but two of the national parks contain villages. The act goes on to specify that within the park people may not: "build or occupy any house, hut shelter, or other structure of whatever materials ... occupy, clear, cultivate or plant any part of land ... pasture or water any domesticated animal or bird ... cut, fell, remove, girdle, burn or otherwise damage any tree, plant, bush or any other forest produce..." without permission of an authorized officer of the national park (HMG, 1972).

It is helpful to view attitudes toward residents living within park boundaries in historical perspective. Stan Stevens (1986), among others, chronicles the development of the international model of the national park as a wilderness preserve, with access retained by the public *but not indigenous peoples.* This is known as the Yellowstone model—based on the American national park where Indians were removed so that it could remain unspoiled for the recreation of others. Stevens points out that bodies such as the International Union for the Conservation of Nature (IUCN), which not only promulgated the national parks concept and defines its legal status but also controls much of the funding for park development worldwide, championed this position. Thus in 1972, when the Nepalese National Parks and Wildlife Conservation Act was enacted, the IUCN guidelines put forth that same year said that "indigenous inhabitants were to be 'tolerated only because they constitute inescapable obligations, but every possible step (should be) taken to secure their progressive elimination.'" Even in 1984, the IUCN still maintained that parks are called national parks only when "'the highest competent authority of the country having jurisdiction over the area has taken steps to prevent or eliminate, as soon as possible, exploitation or occupation in the area.'"[10]

Although all Nepalese parks are regulated according to the provisions in the act of 1972 and the Himalayan National Park Rules of 1979 (HMG, 1979), each has specific rules responsive to local conditions. The park system is designed to give the warden tremendous discretion in implementing and negotiating specific rules. This is appropriate, for the particular problems and issues involved in the transformation of inhabited land into parks very much depend on local history and conditions. Sherpa (1985) points out that all parks in the country share certain problems: isolation; difficulties in staffing parks with broadly trained, professional personnel; the required presence of the army to enforce park regulations (occasionally outnumbering park personnel by a considerable margin [Sherpa, 1987]); the multiple uses made of park resources by local residents and neighboring communities; and the impoverishment of indigenous people, making any loss of access to needed resources a severe hardship in an already pressed population.

The initial National Parks and Wildlife Conservation Act of 1972 concentrated on delineating rules and regulations for hunting wildlife in Nepal. The Himalayan National Park Rules of 1979 added rules about the control of tourism. At present, it falls to the management plans for each park to delineate rules concerning the activities of residents. In general, there is an attempt to see the needs of residents as important in the overall planning for the parks. For example, the Draft Statement of Management Intent for the Langtang National Park (National Department of Parks and Wildlife, 1989) includes the following policy statements:

> Langtang National Park will be developed and managed primarily for the protection of the Central Himalayan fauna and flora systems as well as the Park's existing cultural features. (p. 1)
> The basic needs of those people residing within the park will be met within the framework of sound ecological resource management. (p. 9)

These statements are followed by a variety of objectives that include a park resource user's steering committee and facilitation by park management to meet residents' needs for energy, construction timber, fodder, and protection of crops from wild animals, to name a few.

Middle-hill farmers in the Himalaya are highly dependent on forest access; this is not an aesthetic or ethical consideration—it is life or death. Ives and Messerli (1989) point out that forests supply fodder for maintenance of the livestock that provide draught power and, more important, fertilizer for the shallow soils of the mountains. Forests also provide firewood, as well as land for future cropland. To a lesser extent, forests provide many small resources for hill populations—for example, thatch and timber for houses and leaf litter. It requires 1–4 hectares of forest to maintain 1 hectare of agricultural land in the hills (Ives & Messerli, 1989). The possibility of loss of access to this resource by the implementation of national parks and reserves understandably arouses fear and anger in the subsistence farmers who have no other alternatives if they are going to farm in that environment. We can see, in the case of Melemchi, that this extends to mountain pastoralism as well.

The Future of Melemchi in Langtang National Park

It may turn out to be highly beneficial for Melemchi residents to be a part of the park. According to the Draft Statement of Management Intent, Langtang National Park is committed to maintaining and improving the park residents' quality of life. Melemchi residents are in a position now, as the result of experiences over the past 15 years, to participate actively in the incorporation of the national park in Yolmo. Earlier, they would have been very vulnerable. Today, there is interest among some of the younger men in developing participation in tourist trekking, something few Yolmo people have done. Most who tried it don't want to start at the bottom—as a porter—but the park provides other types of tourist business, including lodge ownership. Literacy skills are being developed that will permit participation in park affairs, ranging from making out permits to managing lodge books to participation in residents' users groups. The park has stated its intention to maintain traditional lifeways. Traditional lifeways are under tremendous pressure elsewhere, especially due to the degradation in the environment necessary to sustain them. Life in the park may in fact permit Melemchi people to retain these, even as they die out elsewhere.

However, there are potential problems that may develop. At present, the demand for park resources from the local population is low, due to the availability of work and good wages in India. This could change for a number of reasons; if all those with a claim on village resources were to return, it would be difficult for the park to meet those needs. Another problem is the potential for the recent shift to adopt herd types that are less physically demanding on the families, such as sheep/goats or cows and yak, to put pressure on the middle-altitude environments near villages, exacerbating a difficult situation. *Zomo* herding disperses the animals and people— and thus the environmental impact—over a wider altitude band. Finally, the reported goal of increasing tourism in Nepal by the year 2000 may increase trekking in this region so close to Kathmandu beyond the ability of the environment to absorb it. To date, Yolmo has been spared the extraordinary numbers of trekkers going to the areas where the snow mountains are visible.

In the winter of 1989, the national parks office asked me for comments on the management strategy for Langtang National Park, and I was able to offer a few suggestions. First, I urged them to extend park support for the maintenance of transhumant herds of cow-yak hybrids. This subsistence pattern has tremendous tourist appeal, as well as potential for spreading the impact of the support for large numbers of people over a wide area. This traditional subsistence system is threatened by the park as well as by the changing priorities of the residents themselves. In order to succeed, it requires considerable autonomy and flexibility on the part of the herder to make adjustments of many kinds: when and where to move pasture, continual adjustments of herd composition, and when to sell livestock and products. This is what the residents of this village know how to do; it has brought them wealth in the past and depends on land and pastures that have been passed along over generations. The park must avoid restrictions on herders developed without a firm research basis. Furthermore, the park can make a positive contribution through supporting research that will bolster productivity of these herds and make management more desirable.

Second, the park could use the schools not only to provide conservation education for village children but also as a way to make these children feel they have a future in the park. Providing literacy skills, as well as courses that support traditional life patterns and develop areas of skill that will allow residents to make local initiatives, will ensure that future generations begin to see their future locally rather than in wage labor in foreign countries.

And finally, I urged the park to be sensitive to the political history of the region of Yolmo. Langtang National Park spans a tremendous ecological and cultural diversity; Yolmo is only one region, and within it each village has a particular political and economic position. If users groups and other forms of local participation are to be effective, they must include a broad spectrum of users of the park and must operate according to decision-making principles acceptable to residents. A local perspective, such as that afforded me by being a long-time resident of one village, makes it clear that a unitary system of park rules is not easily applicable in a heterogeneous region such as Yolmo.

The Langtang National Park development in Yolmo, coming late as it does, has the opportunity to be the source of enlightened solutions for future park development. Inhabited parks are an experiment that is taking place all over the world, including the United States, and there is much work to be done by social scientists to complement the head start achieved by ecologists and wildlife biologists.

NOTES

[1] As we trekked to Melemchi in 1993, we were shocked when we descended from Tarke Ghyang, crossed the Melemchi River on the bridge, and saw the boulders that guard the Melemchi side of the river. They were covered with graffiti in charcoal and paint—an unexpected correlate of literacy.

[2] The actual wording was "would not be allowed to touch a village water tap, nor enter the *gomba*."

[3] In the summer of 1992, Nogabu was asked to help a friend find his cousin, who had been abducted from Kulu. Her stepfather had come down to Kathmandu looking for her unsuccessfully for two days. The girls were14 and 15, lured into going with their male cousins, who promised to take them to India to live with them and their wives, who would feed and care for them. The girls were promised a life of lux-

ury and no work. Nogabu and his friend looked around Boudhanath, where Yolmo people usually live, and waited one whole night at Thangkot, the main gate leading out of Kathmandu, all with no luck. Finally, they decided to look for them in the little hotels surrounding the central bus station, where buses take on passengers leaving the Kathmandu Valley. The boys went to each hotel, pretending to have come from the hills to meet their two friends who were travelling with two girls. Pretending to have forgotton where they were to meet, they asked whether the friends were staying there. At the fourth hotel, they located the girls with one of the boys. Nogabu's friend stayed with them while Nogabu went for the police. The police waited for the second boy to return and took everyone to the police station where they confiscated money, rings, watches, and belts from the boys. Both the boys and girls were beaten by the police. The girls, who spoke no Nepali, were taken for one night to police headquarters, and then to the district headquarters. After two days, they were sent back to Kulu. The boys were sent to prison.

Nogabu's cousin said that one of the girls' older sisters had been taken to Bombay a few years earlier and killed when she arrived.

[4] A case that has been written about extensively in Nepali magazines as well as in English-language publications concerns Geeta, an HIV-positive sex worker from Melamchipul Bazaar who returned to the village and was shunned by her family and the other villagers. She had been sold into prostitution by her family, and for 11 years her father had traveled to India to collect her wages to support his family. When she returned, expecting to set up a shop like other returned prostitutes, she was shunned by everyone except one uncle. She was not permitted to use the village water tap, couldn't touch anyone, and was not allowed to leave her house or go to the bazaar. Although an aid agency gave her a carpet loom and six chickens to enable her to begin supporting herself, she wanted a tea shop like the other girls had gotten and refused to make carpets. Finally, after 6 months of intensive intervention by her sponsors and her uncle, she finally gained more economic and social freedom, eventually setting up a liquor stall for passing porters. Hers is not a unique story (Bhatt, n.d.).

[5] It is possible to make the cross in the other direction; that is, breed a female yak (nak) with a bull. These offspring are called dimdzo. Melemchi pastures are too low for nak.

[6] Their father died in 1972, but their mother remained in the gode. She had her husband's father's help and that of her oldest son, Tundu Wangdi, who was then 11 years old. When Tundu Wangdi married in 1981, she gave him half the herd and kept the other half for her second son, Kamsung, the youngest, who remained with her. Since Kamsung grabbed a wife in 1991, he and his wife have managed the gode, while his mother spends periods in the village. The brothers share pastures and move their herds together.

[7] In 1989, he worked 6 days per week with 1 day of sick leave per month and 7 days of emergency paid leave. He has 2 months' vacation in winter and 15 days at Dassai.

[8] That same summer another picnic was held down at the gomba. Some of the young men approached the schoolmaster and proposed to organize a picnic, since it was Saturday and there was no school. They would cook food and have music in the social room next to the gomba. They gathered around 11 a.m. and finally ate by 5 p.m.: rice, daal, potato chips fried in mustard oil and potato curry. The afternoon was spent standing around, telling jokes, listening to Hindi, Nepali, and Western pop songs blasted from the portable speakers of a tape recorder, playing the Nepali drum, and generally showing off for each other while preparing the food. The main group included several men age 18 to 24 years, a few of whom are married and already fathers. A number are good friends of the schoolmaster, who remains unmarried at age 26. Several girls stayed for the afternoon—one 18 years old, one 20, and one young widow in her mid-20s. A number of adults dropped by for a while; younger children played outside in front of the gomba. Finally, the meal was served to the strains of Queen and Madonna. As it began to get dark, the whole group began disco dancing, led off by Sarkie Sukaa and Pemba Dorje, two 8-year-old boys. Zamling, a 26-year-old father of two, wore a T-shirt reading, "My friend came to Nepal and all I got was this lousy tee shirt." Tashi had on a T-shirt reading, "Free Tibet." All the young men sported razor haircuts, and several wore black rags tied around their heads, knotted in the back.

[9] 2029 is the Nepalese calendar year corresponding to the Western calendar year 1972.

[10] The IUCN national park status (IUCN, 1984) is considered important both for obtaining funding and technical assistance (see, for example, the discussion of the disadvantages of designating the Annapurna protected area a conservation area, rather than a national park [Sherpa et al., 1986]).

8 / The Present and Future in Melemchi

MELEMCHI: ENVIRONMENT, CULTURE, AND HISTORY

Some aspects of Melemchi culture are shared with other middle-altitude herders and relate to the universal conditions of *zomo* herding, regardless who does it. Other aspects come from the cultural heritage shared by all Sherpa and Bhotia (Tibetan) people. Their religion, Tibetan Buddhism, results in common rituals, beliefs, and practices, while their shared cultural history produces similar languages, food, and elements of social structure. Finally, some aspects of Melemchi life are unique: the product of its specific geographic location and its particular history.

Middle-Altitude Herding

Herding hybrid bovids involves different labor requirements, patterns of transhumance, and management techniques than herding yak or cows, making middle-altitude herding systems broadly similar regardless of where or who the herders are. While there are some similarities between herding yak and herding hybrids (for example, multiple high pastures are required, equipment is similar and must be easily transportable, and preparation of dairy products is identical), hybrids bring their own special problems. They require access to pastures in zones where agriculture predominates, and their transhumance patterns must be compatible with agricultural regimens. There is a constant outflow of money to purchase new animals, since the herd cannot replenish itself. The herds include two species, *zomo* and bulls, which have different biological requirements. Whether we look at Tamang herders in Kalingchowk, Sherpa herders in Solu, or Yolmo herders in Melemchi, we see similar solutions to the problems of middle-altitude herding. Animal husbandry techniques are identical, herd compositions are similar, and the same type of agriculture is done. The labor involved in transhumant dairy herding requires, in most places, family labor. Men tend to be available, rather than off in the army or on long-distance trading expeditions. This has demographic implications: The possibility for conception remains high year-round and, without the need for a house at marriage, young men can marry early as soon as they have a herd.

Ethnic Influences

Melemchi people share with other Tibetan-derived groups a culture in which Tibetan Buddhism forms the core. Melemchi people share the Tibetan calendrical system, including Losar or New Year's, a number of important Buddhist rites and annual rituals, a language based on Tibetan, and many cultural elements with Bhotia communities throughout Nepal, India, Bhutan, and Sikkim. This is because of their common ethnic heritage. Ethnicity has also circumscribed their interactions with those outside their communities. In caste-conscious Nepal, ethnicity often limits occupational choices. For example, British army recruiters targeted men from particular ethnic groups—Gurung, Magar, Rai, and Limbu—for the Ghurka regiments. Since service in the army took men away for long periods, subsistence patterns based on herding disappeared. Women were unable to manage the herds and all the work alone, so income from herds was replaced by army pay. The economic impact was far reaching. Soldiers received a pension for life; today many Gurung and Magar middle-hill villages are sustained by pension checks, since population has long since outstripped local resources. There were, of course, also social and demographic consequences of the dependence on army service and pensions: increased male mortality, reduced exposure to conception, and an economy that is in trouble, now that the Ghurka regiments no longer exist and pensioners are dying. The Tamang, another middle-hill ethnic group, traditionally work as porters or coolies to supplement their subsistence economies in the lower middle hills. Men leave the villages for sometimes up to half the year to be available for portering work. Mountain guiding became the purview of the Sherpa of Khumbu; infusions of cash, first from mountaineering expeditions and later from tourist trekking, have transformed their region and their lives in the high mountain valleys. For many years, it was difficult for anyone other than a Sherpa to work in this area; now it has opened up but still eastern Sherpa predominate. Yolmo people aren't soldiers, porters, or tourist guides. They are not known outside the region as specialists in any particular occupation. Their response to the pressures of population growth in the hills was to travel outside Nepal for wage labor. Communities of Yolmo people sprang up in Darjeeling, Bamdila (Arunachal Pradesh), Spiti (Himachal Pradesh), and Ladakh, following the work and providing support systems.

Geography

Geographic location also played a determining role in the lifeways of Melemchi. Yolmo people never specialized in trade like those Tibetan-derived people with easy access to mountain passes into Tibet. There is no pass into Tibet directly from Yolmo; people there trade with people in the Langtang Valley to the north, who serve as intermediaries for livestock between Tibet and Nepal. The closest pass to Yolmo is the pass into Kyirung, where the founding populations came from. This pass is also the one used by Melemchi men in the first half of the century to go to Tibet to buy sheep for Dassai in Kathmandu. However, other groups in the Trisuli Valley dominated that trade route. Yolmo never developed into a big tourist area, despite glossy government brochures proclaiming it "bold, bashful, and beautiful." Because of a quirk of geomorphology, it is impossible to see big snow peaks from Yolmo, even though Langtang

Lirung lies just to the north. So most tourists trek instead in Khumbu to the east or Annapurna to the west, where the Great Himalayan peaks form a spectacular backdrop.

Within Yolmo, Melemchi's position as the northernmost village in Yolmo and its isolated location on the west side of the Melemchi River have helped determine its economic situation; in particular, the development and persistence of *zomo* herding. Elsewhere in Yolmo, villages turned away from farming and herding and toward investment in land outside to support their families. The lack of land and adjacent pasture helps to account for the early participation in circular migration for wage labor and the abandonment of herding by many in the villages of Tarke Ghyang and Sermathang. In contrast, Melemchi is adjacent to substantial tracts of forest that support livestock and middle-altitude agropastoralism. There are no other villages near Melemchi; as one local person put it, "Melemchi has no boundaries." This has made it possible for Melemchi people to expand and adapt their use of their local habitat as needed over the years.

History

History can explain some of the specific attributes of Yolmo culture and Melemchi village in particular, in contrast to other Sherpa or middle-altitude villages. The Tibetans who settled in Yolmo came from a different part of Tibet and at a different time than did the founders of the eastern Sherpa community, resulting in distinctive languages as well as cultural differences. The lamas who settled Yolmo were from nonmonastic orders and were free to marry. Instead of the celibate religious specialists who perform the rituals in Khumbu, in Yolmo, rituals are conducted by all the village men, lay priests in a sense. With monasteries, population pressure is partially alleviated, since sons and daughters can go into the monastery and families can gain both religious benefit and limit population growth and demand for land. In Yolmo, sons wanted shares of the land and the *gomba*. This resulted in fissioning of villages and a proliferation of temple-villages throughout the region. In a system dominated by monastic lamas, religion is more elaborate than in the Yolmo Valley, where everyone participates and provides the religious ceremonies.

Melemchi's special history as a *guthi,* paying tax to the Chini Lama and not the government, is a factor in insulating the village from certain national policies to which others in Nepal were subjected, such as, the Forest Nationalization Act of 1957. Furthermore, the specific policies and actions of the Chini Lama had a major effect on the social and cultural development of Melemchi. Historical factors revolving around the relationship of the Chini Lama and the national government permitted Melemchi to remain a *guthi* much longer than might have been otherwise, leaving people in Melemchi more isolated and inexperienced with self-rule than some other villages in Yolmo.

The similarities among mountain people around the world are remarkable, some even uncanny. But in reality, mountains are complex environments themselves, and social systems result from more than environmental factors. Efforts to understand mountain adaptations, both biological and cultural, have focused on altitude (or vertical zonation) as a universal component. But altitude alone only predicts hypoxic stress. In reality, altitude interacts with latitude and climatic features, among others, to produce a complex of environmental constraints which may be highly localized or particularistic. Thus, universal models for human behavior in mountain habitats worldwide will prove elusive.

It must also be said that the elements of successful cultural mountain adaptation—flexibility, diversification, and fluidity—aren't unique to mountain-living groups. These are qualities that are helpful for any group of people dependent on an environment that is unpredictable and over which they have little control. But people in mountain environments share similar constraints, and comparisons of solutions can be illuminating. Mountains, by virtue of their marginal productivity, provide few options to accommodate population growth. It does seem universal that success in these environments requires a diverse set of local subsistence activities spread over several zones plus access to external sources of cash. The trans-Himalayan salt trade (Khumbu), circular migration for wage labor (Melemchi), mining (Bolivia), or mercenary soldiering (Törbel, Switzerland) all have helped provide the safety net for mountain people.

There are limited numbers of options for subsistence and income for mountain people in the Himalaya, and so we see similarities in types of response. Each group has its own story. In his ethnohistory of the Gurung of the Western Himalaya, Messerschmidt tells of how they shifted from a mobile pattern of pastoral nomadism with cattle and sheep, swidden agriculture, and hunting to a life of settled agriculture, with a few people continuing to be away—either in transhumant sheep herding or service in the Ghurka army (Messerschmidt, 1976). Melemchi presents a different history. From transhumant *zomo* herding, settled highland agriculture, and limited trade in sheep with Tibet, Melemchi's residents are shifting to a primary dependence on migrant wage labor, settled agriculture, and some transhumant herding of *zomo* and now cows. We have witnessed a transition in a process of continual change. We still are far from understanding the decision-making process; in a culture where being flexible and fluid is a premium, it has been hard to understand how options are perceived and what constitutes the long- and short-term view.

CHANGE IN MELEMCHI: THE FUTURE

As Chapter 7 recounts, the village of Melemchi has undergone significant changes during the 25 years we have visited there. These changes occurred in response to changes in the local, national, and international spheres. And there continue to be new developments. In 1991, the lights went on in Melemchi. A small hydroelectric plant across the Melemchi River provided a few hours of power each night to houses for a fee. Bare lightbulbs hang on porches, electric candles glow on the altars, and several houses even have television sets, although the reception is terrible. Jerry-rigged electric cords, ungrounded plugs, and home electrical repairs terrify us, evoking memories of the terrible fire that burned down the Thengboche monastery in Khumbu just after it had been wired for electricity. But it is magical to stand in Tarke Ghyang and look across at the lights in Melemchi as the sun sets behind Yangri. Melemchi was the last of the three main temple-villages to get electricity, and in 1993 there

Melemchi in summer 1993. Note the tin roofs on many houses, the fallow fields, the stone-walled kitchen gardens with fruit trees, and the prayer flags in front of each house. Electric poles run through the middle of the village.

was still lingering confusion and anger over the fact that you had to pay 50 rupees monthly for electricity.

In 1995, construction began on a major water project, tapping the water from the Melemchi River just south of the village of Melemchi and taking it via a 27-kilometer tunnel through the mountains down into the Kathmandu Valley (Dixit, 1992). Plans call for a road halfway between Melemchipul Bazaar and Melemchi village, which will bring trucks, goods, and workers within a day of Melemchi village. This Greater Kathmandu Water Supply Project will no doubt accelerate change in the Yolmo Valley, but it is difficult to predict just how. Roads bring access to markets and communication for village people, but they also provide others access to mountain resources. Mountain people worldwide are vulnerable to outside exploitation of the few resources they depend on: hydropower, timber, minerals, water, and space. Exploitation by governments or international companies often operates on a scale that can greatly disturb the local environment. The impact on the Yolmo region of diverting water from the Melemchi River remains to be seen.

In 1997, the first Melemchi person arrived in New York City to join 35 other Yolmo men who share a couple of apartments while they work 12-hour shifts in Chinese and Indian restaurants. After 10 years of work in India, in both the eastern and western Himalaya, he bankrolled himself a plane ticket and enough money to live for a couple of months while he tried to arrange working papers. This is the latest new frontier for wage labor—first Taiwan, then South Korea, now the United States. No longer limited to high-altitude sites in Buddhist-dominated areas of the Himalaya,

Melemchi residents are joining the transnational workforce, seeking jobs that leave them vulnerable to exploitation as well as providing new opportunities.

We are seeing the first Melemchi men marrying Yolmo women who have given up their lives as "Bambai girls." And over the past 5 years, a Melemchi enclave is developing in the Kathmandu Valley around Boudhanath and nearby Jorpati. Many young people prefer to return from India to the Kathmandu Valley and set up households there, rather than return permanently to the village. They go up to the village periodically to visit and help out their parents. And their parents come down to stay with them, spending weeks or months at a time, seeking health care, making a religious pilgrimage to Boudhanath, or escaping the rigors or boredom of life in the village.

Melemchi people are uncomfortable when asked to predict the future, either short term or long term. Whether this stems from their commitment to flexibility and opportunistic strategies or from the fact of extraordinary and unpredictable change within their own lifetimes, I don't know. Most families still expect at least one son to return to the family land, although no one suggests their sons will herd. Beyond that, the future isn't clear. Melemchi remains a beautiful spot, rich in resources and increasingly integrated into the region and its development. Members of the generation now in its twenties know the Yolmo songs, the religious rituals, and

Collecting data in Boudhanath with Nogabu's family. Seated in Nogabu's living room: author Naomi Bishop, Chenga (wife), Nogabu with Mingma (son), Nanu (sister) wearing the modern summer Tibetan dress popular in Boudhanath, Urgan (paternal uncle), and Dorje (father) who came down from Melemchi to visit. (1995)

how to make a living in the middle altitudes, but at the same time they are singing Hindi pop songs and negotiating international travel. When asked why Melemchi people stayed with herding after Tarke Ghyang people shifted to buying rice fields, a Melemchi man in his thirties shrugged his shoulders and said, "I guess we just felt loyal to our animals." It is this quality that makes me hopeful about Melemchi's future.

Glossary of Yolmo Words

Most words are of Tibetan origin, while some are borrowed directly from Nepali. English meanings reflect Melemchi usage.

adache: village representative to the local *panchayat*

ani: father's sister or mother's brother's wife; also in conversation, refers to wife's brother's wife

arak: distilled liquor; usually made from fermented millet or corn (Nepali = *rakshi*)

ashang: mother's brother or father's sister's husband; also in conversation, refers to wife's brother

ayah: a servant who cares for children

balu: thick fermented mash usually made from corn; can be eaten or drunk if water is added

birta: a land grant from the king to an individual in appreciation of his or her services or as a form of patronage; *birta* grants gave right of taxation to the recipient (Nepali term)

bombo: shaman

brimo: female F1 hybrid; product of a bull father and a yak mother *(brimu)*

brimu: female yak

chang: fermented grain beer

changda: high-altitude barley grown in Melemchi

chiba: the village householder responsible for organizing the four annual festivals: Dabla Pangdi, Yum, Nara, and Dassai; also called *chiba chickla* ("one man does all")

chilap: piece of the Nara *torma* eaten by participants when the festival is concluded

chinse: special items which are placed on top of the corpse to provide for it in the afterlife

chiura: pounded rice snack

chiurpi: dried cheese

chorten: Buddhist monument, often containing sacred relics

chutta: water-driven grain mill

daal: lentils; cooked into a porridge which is eaten with rice

dagar: term for landowner whose fields measure half the size of *ghima* fields

damian: four-stringed Tibetan lute, plucked with a bamboo pick

dharni: a local measurement for liquid similar in size to a *pathi*

dungmu: small churn used to make salted butter tea *(pe cha)*

dzau: wheat kernels with bran

gewa: commemorative funerary rite held in honor of the deceased

ghilang: cross between a *pulang* (Tibetan dwarf bull) and a lowland cow *(Bos indicus)*

ghima: a householder who owns the largest field size; also a standard size by which landholdings are locally measured

giu: clarified butter

goba: village men who govern

gode: (pronounced GO-day) refers both to the temporary shelter constructed from bamboo mats over a framework of poles in which herding families live and to living as a herder (i.e., having a *gode* means you have a transhumant herd and live with them)

goth: Tamang term for *gode*

gomba: lamaist temple

gur: unrefined brown sugar sold in blocks

guthi: a tax-exempt and inheritable land grant given for maintenance of a religious institution

guthiyar: recipient of the *guthi;* usually the head of the religious institution

karken: designs of colored butter which are part of the Nara *torma*

kata: white scarf of blessing

kharke: pasture

khoibansa: banging the heads of the bride and groom together three times

khukri: curved knife worn in a scabbard

kyowa ringa: pasteboard five-sided crown worn by the deceased in funeral

lama: priest

lamna: white funeral banner

lango: lowland bull *(Bos indicus)*; same as *ronglang*

mani: religious funeral hymns

mar: butter

martza: paste of pounded chili, garlic, and salt eaten with boiled potatoes

milam: a blessing of butter daubed on the top of someone's head

naamlo: (Nep) tump line or rope used to carry loads; the strap goes around the forehead while the rope holds the basket or load onto the person's back

naatcha: blessing by lama in form of a paste applied to the forehead; paste is a mixture of milk, raw rice, egg, and red powder

nak: Tibetan term for female yak

nama langdwang: "going to ask for the bride"; visit to the bride's parents by the groom's parents or representative to ask for permission to grab the girl

narchyang: special ladle used to put the *chinse* into the funeral pyre

nebar: anniversary funerary rite; also the term for the effigy of the deceased

nho: brother or male parallel cousins (father's brother's son or mother's sister's son)

nhumo: sister or female parallel cousins (father's brother's daughter or mother's sister's daughter)

pai: fried wheat bread braided into a double-tiered figure eight; made and distributed only at Nara festival

paisa: coins or cents (100 *paisa* = 1 *rupee*)

palang: lowland or hilly female cow *(Bos indicus)*

panchayat: hierarchical system of representative governing councils established in Nepal in 1961, ranging from the local level to the National Panchayat

pamu: F2 hybrid; the offspring of a *zomo* (F1 hybrid) and a bull

partza: woven bamboo mats which form the *gode* shelter

pashi: ceremonial separation of a boy from his natal family. This may occur before or after marriage. Relatives attend, and the boy receives his herd and household effects. At this point, he can become a *tal* (or village householder) in his own right.

pathi: (Nep) a volumetric measurement using a vessel called a *pathi* which holds about half a peck (actually, 2.48 kg of paddy, 3.40 kg of wheat or maize, or 3.28 kg of millet, according to Regmi [1978]); (Yolmo) stone living structure at pasture; may have wooden roof shingles or be covered with bamboo mats *(partza)*

pe cha: salted butter tea in its drinkable form *(pe = Tibetan; cha = tea)*

pulang: Tibetan dwarf bull *(Bos taurus)*

pullu: a local liquid measurement corresponding roughly to 1.5 pints

puja: ritual

ronglang: hilly or lowland bull *(Bos indicus)*; same as *lango*

saba: male offspring of a cross between a *ghilang* and a cow

sang: copper pot used to hold the body of the deceased

shalgar: an offering or blessing in the form of a container of liquor with *chilap* (three daubs of butter spaced equally apart on the mouth of the container). People bring *shalgar* to any auspicious occasion, as well as funerals.

shamdzo: F1 male hybrid; the offspring of a yak father and a cow mother

shamu: female Tibetan dwarf cow *(Bos taurus)*

sonam: religious merit

takpa checken: "break the string" or divorce; the couple tie a string around their fingers and break it

tal: member of the *gomba;* a householder responsible for maintaining the *gomba* and its ritual cycle

tara: buttermilk or the liquid remaining after the butter has been collected

tarkaari: (Nep) stir-fried vegetable eaten with rice and *daal,* usually seasoned heavily with chili and salt

thanka: lamaist painting

toljung: ceremony following the wedding in which the parents of the groom bring gifts to the bride's parents

Tom: litter suspended between two poles which carries the body at the funeral

tolko: F3 hybrid male; product of a *pamu* and a *pulang*

tolmu: F3 hybrid female; product of a *pamu* and a *pulang*

torma: ritual dough statues made from *tsampa,* water, and butter which represent deities in Buddhist rituals; in *bombo puja, torma* may be temporarily occupied by spirits or deities

tsampa: toasted barley grain ground into flour

tsaudi chi (ni): smallest size of land-holding in the village, a field one-quarter *(tsaudi chi)* or one-half *(tsaudi ni)* of the largest size *(ghima)*

tso: teardrop-shaped rice ball offerings; each household brings them to Tupa Sezhu, funerals, and Yum

tuga: homespun Melemchi wool jacket

Tursa: crematorium; a column built of stones about 3 feet in diameter; fresh fir boughs line top and the body is laid on them; a fire is built underneath which is fueled by wood added from an opening at the bottom of the *Tursa*

urang zomo: F1 hybrid female; product of a yak and a cow *(Bos indicus);* also *ushu*

urang zopkio: F1 hybrid male; product of a yak and a cow *(Bos indicus);* also *ushu*

wang: a tiny ball of barley flour, sugar, and butter, blessed by the presiding lama at festivals or rituals, who gives them to participants to eat

yakpu: yak

zarshie: a cow resulting from a cross between local cattle and imported European cattle breeds

zebu: Indian cattle *(Bos indicus)* distinguished by the dorsal hump

zhero: 12-inch-square fried braided wheat bread; ritually important in Nara festival

zomo: generic term for female F1 hybrid; produced by crossing a yak or *nak* with a cow or bull

zopkio: generic term for male F1 hybrid; produced by crossing a yak or *nak* with a cow or bull

Films on Melemchi

Himalayan Herders (1997) 76 min. A film by John and Naomi Bishop. Distributed by Documentary Educational Resources, 101 Morse St., Watertown, MA 02172 (800-569-6621). For updates, study guides, and additional information on shorter versions for the classroom, the Internet address is www.cda.ucla.edu/faculty/bishop.

Himalayan Herders was shot during fieldwork in 1986 and 1989, with additional footage from 1971–72 and 1993. The following film highlights are matched to this text, listed in the order they appear in the film:

1. Putting up new prayer flag on Losar, the Tibetan New Year (Chapter 5).
2. Ritual and socializing at the annual Tupa Tsezhu celebration at Tupu Cave at the top of the village (Chapters 1 and 5).
3. Life in a *gode* at Nading pasture (8600') and Thare Pathi (12,000'). This includes milking and making butter (Chapter 2).
4. Managing village livestock, including fodder gathering (Chapter 3).
5. The agricultural cycle, including making distilled liquor (Chapter 3).
6. Villagers comment on working outside Melemchi for wage labor in India (Chapter 4).
7. Shamanic possession of the *bombo* spirit medium (Chapter 6).
8. Funeral (Chapter 5).
9. Nara festival, including making large *torma* (dough and butter sculptures) and ceremonial bread (*zhero*), reading Nara texts in *gomba,* and dancing (Chapter 5).
10. A private Yum ritual in which the books from the *gomba* are carried to one person's house to be read (Chapter 5).
11. The primary school in 1986; the dedication of the new school building in 1989 (Chapter 7).
12. Winter pasturing of *zomo* herds and cow-yak herds, including discussion by herders of the effects of the National Park on their lives and futures; also why some are changing from *zomo* to cow/yak herds (Chapter 7).
13. Villagers comment on changes in marriage customs; a mock capture wedding (Chapter 5).
14. Modernization in Melemchi (Chapter 5).

Original footage from 1986 and 1989 shoots is annotated and archived at the Smithsonian Institution Human Studies Film Archive (http://nmnhwww.si.edu/gopher-menus/HumanStudiesFilmArchives.html).

A record of Melemchi music recorded in 1972 is available from Smithsonian Folkways (FE 4320). Titled *Music of a Sherpa Village,* it contains much of the incidental music used in the film.

References

Adams, Vincanne. 1996. *Tigers of the Snow and Other Virtual Sherpas: An Ethnography of Himalayan Encounters.* Princeton, NJ: Princeton University Press.

Alirol, Phillippe. 1976. "Le milieu et l'elevage dans la Region du Ganesh Himal (Nepal)." Ethnozootechine 15: 119–125. Paris: Société d'Ethnozootechnie.

Alirol, Phillippe. 1979. *Transhuming Animal Husbandry Systems in Kalingchowk Region (Central Nepal).* Bern: Swiss Technical Assistance.

Alirol, Phillippe. 1981. "Habitat des pasteurs transhumant népalais." In G. Toffin, L. Barre, and C. Jest, eds. *L'Homme et la maison en Himalaya,* 187-199. Paris: CNRS.

Bailey, Adrian J. and Hane, Joshua G. 1995. "Population in Motion: Salvadorean Refugees and Circular Migration." *Bulletin of Latin American Research* 14 (2): 171–200.

Baker, Paul T. 1978. "The Adaptive Fitness of High-altitude Populations." In P.T. Baker, ed. *The Biology of High-Altitude People,* 317–350. Cambridge: Cambridge University Press.

Bangham, C.R.M. and Sacherer, J.M. 1980. "Fertility of Nepalese Sherpas at Moderate Altitudes: Comparison with High Altitude Data." *Annals of Human Biology* 7: 323-330.

Bhatt, Pushpa. n.d. "Melemchi: A Case Study in Community Mobilization." In ABC/Nepal, ed., *Red Light Traffic: The Trade in Nepali Girls,* 56-63. Kathmandu, Nepal: ABC/Nepal.

Bishop, John and Naomi. 1978. *An Ever-changing Place.* New York: Simon and Schuster.

Bishop, Naomi H. 1989. "From Zomo to Yak: Change in a Sherpa Village." *Human Ecology* 17 (2): 177-204.

Bishop, Naomi, H. 1993. "Circular Migration and Families: A Yolmo Sherpa Example." *South Asia Bulletin* 13 (1&2): 59–66.

Bonnemaire, Joseph. 1984. "Yak." In I.L. Mason, ed., *Evolution of Domesticated Animals,* 39-45. London: Longman Publishers.

Bonnemaire, Joseph, and Teissier, Jean Henri. 1976. "Quelques aspects de l'elevage en haute altitude dans l'Himalaya central: yaks, bovins, hybrides et métis dans la valle du Langtang (Nepal)." *Ethnozootechnie* 15: 91–119. Paris: Société d'Ethnozootechnie.

Brower, Barbara. 1991. *Sherpa of Khumbu: People, Livestock, and Landscape.* New Delhi: Oxford University Press.

Carroll, Vern. 1975. "The Demography of Communities. In Vern Carroll, ed., *Pacific Atoll Populations,* 3–19. Honolulu: University of Hawaii Press and East-West Population Institute.

Clarke, Graham E. 1980a. "A Helambu History." *Journal of the Nepal Research Centre* 4:1-38.

Clarke, Graham E. 1980b. "Lama and Tamang in Yolmo." In Michael Aris and Aung San Suu Kyi, eds., *Tibetan Studies in Honour of Hugh Richardson,* 79-86. Warminster, England: Aris and Phillips.

Clarke, Graham E. 1980c. *The Temple and Kinship Among a Buddhist People of the Himalaya.* Doctoral thesis, University of Oxford.

Clarke, Graham E. 1983. "The Great and Little Traditions in the Study of Yolmo, Nepal." In Ernst Steinkellner and Helmut Tauscher, eds., *Contributions on Tibetan Language, History and Culture* 1: 21–37. Vienna: Arbeitskreis für Tibetische und Buddhistische Studien, University of Vienna.

Clarke, Graham E. 1985. "Hierarchy, Status and Social History in Nepal." In R.H. Barnes, D. de Coppet, and R.J. Parkin, eds., *Contexts and Levels: Anthropological Essays on Hierarchy*, 193–209. Oxford: JASO Occasional Papers, No. 4.

Clarke, Graham E. 1991. "Nara *(na-rag)* in Yolmo: A Social History of Hell in Helambu." In M.T. Much, ed., *Festschrift für Geza Uray,* 43–62. Vienna: Arbeitskreis für Tibetische und Buddhistische Studien, Universität Wien.

Clay, Jason. 1985. "Parks and People." *Cultural Survival Quarterly* 9(2): 2–5.

Desjarlais, Robert R. 1992. *Body and Emotion: The Aesthetics of Illness and Healing in the Nepal Himalayas*. Philadelphia: University of Pennsylvania Press.

Dixit, Kanak Mani. 1992. "Melamchi Boondoggle." *Himal* 5(1): 9–10.

Dutt, James S. 1980. "Altitude and Fertility: The Confounding Effect of Childhood Mortality: A Bolivian Example." *Social Biology* 27 (2): 101–113.

Eckholm, Erik. 1975. "The Deterioration of Mountain Environments." *Science* 189: 764–770.

Elahi, K. Maudood, and Sultana, Sabiha. 1985. "Population Redistribution and Settlement Change in South Asia: A Historical Evaluation." In Kosinski, Leszek A., and Elahi, K. Maudood, eds., *Population Redistribution and Development in South Asia,* 15–35. Dordrecht, Holland: D. Reidel Publishing Co.

English, R. 1985. "Himalayan State Formation and the Impact of British Rule in the Nineteenth Century." *Mountain Research and Development* 5(1): 61-78.

Federle, F.G. 1984. "Towards a Human Ecology of Mountains." *Current Anthropology* 25(5): 688–691.

Fricke, Thomas E. 1986. *Himalayan Households: Tamang Demography and Domestic Processes*. Ann Arbor, MI: UMI Research Press.

Frisancho, A. Roberto. 1993. *Human Adaptation and Accommodation*. Ann Arbor, MI: The University of Michigan Press.

Goldstein, Melvyn C. 1974. "Tibetan-speaking Agro–pastoralists of Limi: A Cultural Ecological Overview of High Altitude Adaptation in the Northwest Himalaya." *Objets et Monde* 14(4): 259–268.

Goldstein, Melvyn 1981. "Tibetan Fertility and Population." *American Ethnologist* 8: 721–729.

Goldstein, M. C., Tsarong, P., and Beall, C.M. 1983. "High Altitude Hypoxia, Culture, and Human Fecundity/Fertility: A Comparative Study." *American Anthropologist* 85: 28–49.

Gripta, R. 1980. "Altitude and Demography Among the Sherpas." *Journal of Biosocial Sciences* 12: 103–114.

Guillet, David. 1983. "Toward a Cultural Ecology of Mountains: The Central Andes and the Himalayas Compared." *Current Anthropology* 24(5): 561–574.

Guyton, A.C., and Hall, J.E. 1996. *Textbook of Medical Physiology,* 9th ed. Philadelphia: W.B. Saunders Co.

Hamilton, L.S. 1987. "What Are the Impacts of Himalayan Deforestation on the Ganges-Brahmaputra Lowlands and Delta? Assumptions and Facts." *Mountain Research and Development* 7(3): 256–263.

Harris, David R. 1996. *The Origins and Spread of Agriculture and Pastoralism in Eurasia*. Washington, DC: Smithsonian Institution Press.

Heath, D., and Williams, D.R. 1989. *High Altitude Medicine and Pathology*. London: Butterworth's.

Hetzel, B.S. 1989. *The Story of Iodine Deficiency: An International Challenge in Nutrition*. New York: Oxford University Press.

Hill, Kim, and Hurtado, A. Magdalena. 1996. *Adache Life History*. New York: Aldine de Gruyter.

HMG (His Majesty's Government). 1972. *National Parks and Wildlife Conservation Act, 1972 (2029)*.

HMG (His Majesty's Government). 1979. *Himalayan National Park Rules, 1979*. Ministry of Forests, Vol. 29, No. 21, Bhadra 25, 2036 (September 10, 1979).

Hoffpauir, Robert. 1978. "Subsistence Strategy and Its Ecological Consequences in the Nepal Himalaya." *Anthropos* 73: 215–252.

Holmberg, David. 1989. *Order in Paradox: Myth, Ritual, and Exchange Among Nepal's Tamang*. Ithaca, N.Y.: Cornell University Press.

Ives, Jack D. 1987. "Repeat Photography of Debris Flows and Agricultural Terraces in the Middle Mountains, Nepal." *Mountain Research and Development 7(1)*: 82–86.

Ives, Jack D., and Messerli, Bruno. 1989. *The Himalayan Dilemma: Reconciling Development and Conservation*. London: Routledge.

Johnston, Barbara, ed. 1990. "Breaking Out of the Tourist Trap: Parts One and Two." *Cultural Survival Quarterly* 14(1–2).

Joshi, Durga Datt. 1982. *Yak and Chauri Husbandry in Nepal*. Kathmandu, Nepal: His Majesty's Government Press.

Kansaker, V.B.S. 1985. "Land Resettlement Policy as a Population Distribution Strategy in Nepal." In Kosinski, Leszek A., and Elahi, K. Maudood, eds., *Population Redistribution and Development in South Asia*. Dordrecht, Holland: D. Reidel Publishing Co.

Karan, Pradyumna P., and Ishii, Hiroshi. 1994. *Nepal: Development and Change in a Landlocked Himalayan Kingdom*. Monumenta Serindica No. 25. Tokyo: Institute for the Study of Languages and Cultures of Asia and Africa, Tokyo University of Foreign Studies.

Laurenson, I.F., Benton, M.A., Bishop, A.J., and Mascie-Taylor, C.G.N. 1985. "Fertility at Low and High Altitude in Central Nepal." *Social Biology* 32: 65–70.

Mahat, T.B.S., Griffin, D. M., and Shepherd, K. R. 1986. "Human Impact on Some Forests of the Middle Hills of Nepal II: Some Major Human Impacts before 1950 on the Forests of Sindu Palchok and Kabhre Palanchok." *Mountain Research and Development* 7(1): 53–70.

Meadow, Richard H. 1996. "The Origins and Spread of Agriculture and Pastoralism in Northwestern South Asia." In David, Harris, ed., *The Origins and Spread of Agriculture and Pastoralism in Eurasia,* 370–389. Washington, DC: Smithsonian Institution Press.

Messerschmidt, Donald A. 1976. "Ecological Change and Adaptation Among the Gurungs of the Nepal Himalaya." *Human Ecology* 4(2): 167–185.

Metz, John. 1989a. "Himalayan Political Economy: More Myths in the Closet?" *Mountain Research and Development,* 9(2): 175–186.

Metz, John. 1989b. "A Framework for Classifying Subsistence Production Types of Nepal." *Human Ecology* 17(2): 147–176.

Metz, John. 1994. "Forest Product Use at an Upper Elevation Village in Nepal." *Environmental Management* 18(3): 371–390.

Moore, Lorna Grindley, and Regensteiner, Judith G. 1983. "Adaptation to High Altitude." *Annual Review of Anthropology.* 12: 285–304.

NDPW. 1989. "Statement of Management Intent for the Langtang National Park" (draft version, April 1989). Kathmandu, Nepal: National Department of Parks and Wildlife, His Majesty's Government.

Netting, Robert McC. 1981. *Balancing on an Alp: Ecological Change and Continuity in a Swiss Mountain Community.* Cambridge: Cambridge University Press.

Netting, Robert McC. 1990. "Reconsidering the Alpine Village as Ecosystem." In Emilio F. Moran, ed., *The Ecosystem Approach in Anthropology,* 229–245. Ann Arbor: The University of Michigan Press.

Pang, Eng Fong. 1993. *Regionalisation and Labour Flows in Pacific Asia.* Paris: Development Centre of the Organisation for Economic Co-operation and Development. Washington, DC: OECD Publications and Information Centre (distributor).

Panter-Brick, Catherine. 1986. "The 'Goths' of Salme, Nepal: A Strategy for Animal Husbandry and Working Behavior." *Production Pastorale et Société,* No. 19: 30–41.

Panter-Brick, Catherine. 1993. "Seasonality of Energy Expenditure During Pregnancy and Lactation for Rural Nepali Women." *American Journal of Clinical Nutrition* 57: 620–628.

Panter-Brick, Catherine, Lotstein C., and Ellison, Peter. 1993. "Seasonality of Reproductive Function and Weight Loss in Rural Nepali Women." *Human Reproduction* 8(5): 684–690.

Pawson, Ivan G. 1976. "Growth and Development of High Altitude Populations: A Review of Ethiopian, Peruvian and Nepalese Studies." *Proceedings of the Royal Society of London,* Series B, 194: 83–98.

Pradhan, Gauri. n.d. "The Road to Bombay: Forgotten Women." In ABC/Nepal ed., *Red Light Traffic: The Trade in Nepali Girls,* 33–40. Kathmandu, Nepal: ABC/Nepal.

Regmi, Mahesh C. 1978. *Thatched Huts and Stucco Palaces: Peasants and Landlords in 19th Century Nepal.* New Delhi: Vikas Publishing House Pvt. Ltd.

Richardson, B. 1982. "The Origins and Continuity of Return Migration in the Leeward Caribbean." In R.S. Bryce-LaPorte, K. De Albuquerque, and W.F. Skinner, eds., *Return Migration and Remittances: Developing a Caribbean Perspective.* Occasional Papers No. 3, Research Institute on Immigration and Ethnic Studies. Washington, DC: Smithsonian Institution Press.

Ross, J.L. 1984. "Culture and Fertility in the Nepal Himalayas: A Test of a Hypothesis." *Human Ecology* 12: 163–181.

Schaller, George B. 1977. *Mountain Monarchs: Wild Sheep and Goats of the Himalaya.* Chicago: University of Chicago Press.

Sherpa, Lhakpa Norbu. 1985. *Management Issues in Nepal's National Parks.* Paper presented to the International Workshop on the Management of National Parks and Protected Areas of the Hindu Kush-Himalaya, Kathmandu, Nepal (May 6–11, 1985).

Sherpa, Lhakpa Norbu. 1987. *Social Function of Rara Lake National Park: A Case Study of Park and People Interaction and Lake Rara National Park, Nepal.* Unpublished manuscript.

Sherpa, Lhakpa Norbu. 1988. *Conserving and Managing Biological Resources in Sagarmatha (Mt. Everest) National Park, Nepal.* Working Paper No. 8. Honolulu: East-West Center.

Sherpa, Mingma Norbu, Coburn, Broughton, and Gurung, Chandra Prasad. 1986. *Annapurna Conservation Area, Nepal: Operational Plan.* Kathmandu, Nepal: King Mahendra Trust for Nature Conservation.

Shrestha, C.B. 1985. "Trends of the Redistribution of Population in Nepal." In Kosinski, Leszek A., and Elahi, K. Maudood, eds., *Population Redistribution and Development in South Asia*, 123–138. Dordrecht, Holland: D. Reidel Publishing Co.

Shrestha, Nanda R. 1990. *Landlessness and Migration in Nepal.* Boulder, Colorado: Westview Press.

Shrestha, Nanda R. 1993. "Nepal: The Society and Its Environment." In Andrea, Savada, ed., *Nepal and Bhutan: Country Studies,* 53–100. Washington, DC: Library of Congress.

Shrestha, Tirta B. 1985. "Botanical Wealth of Mountain Parks and Reserves in Nepal." In J. McNeely, et al., eds., *People and Protected Areas in the Hindu Kush-Himalaya,* 127–128. Kathmandu, Nepal: King Mahendra Trust for Nature Conservation and the International Centre for Integrated Mountain Development.

Stainton, J.D.A. 1972. *Forests of Nepal.* London: John Murray.

Sterling, C. 1976. "Nepal." *Atlantic Monthly* 238 (4): 14–25.

Stevens, Stanley F. 1986. *Inhabited National Parks: Indigenous Peoples in Protected Landscapes.* Centre for Resource and Environmental Studies. East Kimberley Impact Assessment Project, Working Paper 10. Canberra: Australia National University.

Stevens, Stanley F. 1993. *Claiming the High Ground.* Berkeley and Los Angeles: University of California Press.

Stross, Brian. 1974. "Tzeltal Marriage by Capture." *Anthropological Quarterly* 47: 328–346.

Swedlund, Alan, and Armelagos, George. 1976. *Demographic Anthropology.* Dubuque, Iowa: Wm. C. Brown.

Tucker, Richard P. 1987. "Dimensions of Deforestation in the Himalaya: The Historical Setting." *Mountain Research and Development* 7(3): 328–331.

Ward, M.P., Milledge J.S., and West, J.B. 1989. *High Altitude Medicine and Physiology.* Philadelphia: University of Pennsylvania Press.

Weitz, Charles, Pawson, Ivan G., Weitz, M. Velma, Lang, Selwyn R.D. and Lang, Ann. 1978. "Cultural Factors Affecting the Demographic Structure of a High Altitude Nepalese Population." *Social Biology* 25 (3): 179–195.

Wiley, Andrea. 1994. "Neonatal and Maternal Anthropometric Characteristics in a High-Altitude Himalayan Population." *American Journal of Human Biology* 6: 499–510.

Wiley, Andrea. 1997. "A Role for Biology in the Cultural Ecology of Ladakh." *Human Ecology:* 25(2): 273–295.

Zurick, David N. 1988. "Resource Needs and Land Stress in Rapti Zone, Nepal." *Professional Geographer* 40(4): 428–444.

Index